Artificial Intelligence for Audit, Forensic Accounting, and Valuation

Artificial Intelligence for Audit, Forensic Accounting, and Valuation

A Strategic Perspective

AL NAQVI

WILEY

Published by John Wiley & Sons, Inc., Hoboken, New Jersey.
Published simultaneously in Canada.

For general information on our other products and services or for technical support, please contact our Customer Care Department within the United States at (800) 762-2974, outside the United States at (317) 572-3993, or fax (317) 572-4002.

Wiley publishes in a variety of print and electronic formats and by print-on-demand. Some material included with standard print versions of this book may not be included in e-books or in print-on-demand. If this book refers to media such as a CD or DVD that is not included in the version you purchased, you may download this material at http://booksupport.wiley.com. For more information about Wiley products, visit www.wiley.com.

Library of Congress Cataloging-in-Publication Data

Names: Naqvi, Ali S., 1968- author.
Title: Artificial intelligence for audit, forensic accounting, and
   valuation : a strategic perspective / Ali S. Naqvi.
Description: First edition. | Hoboken : Wiley, 2020. | Includes index.
Identifiers: LCCN 2020021960 (print) | LCCN 2020021961 (ebook) | ISBN
   9781119601883 (cloth) | ISBN 9781119601913 (adobe pdf) | ISBN
   9781119601937 (epub)
Subjects: LCSH: Auditing–Data processing. | Forensic accounting. |
   Valuation. | Artificial intelligence.
Classification: LCC HF5667.12 .N37 2020 (print) | LCC HF5667.12 (ebook) |
   DDC 658.0285/63–dc23
LC record available at https://lccn.loc.gov/2020021960
LC ebook record available at https://lccn.loc.gov/2020021961

Cover Design: Wiley
Cover Image: Dragon © Nipitpon Singad/EyeEm/Getty Images

Printed in the United States of America.

SKY10019969_072320

Dedicated to
My father, D. H. Naqvi (1935–2018) – the very first
accountant/auditor in my life

Contents

Preface

AUDITORS AND ASSURANCE PROFESSIONALS: Do you know how to build a comprehensive plan to achieve intelligent automation of your audit function? More importantly, at personal and professional levels, are you ready for the greatest transformation in the human history?

An artificial intelligence revolution is sweeping through the world. Auditors and forensic accountants in firms of all sizes and types are trying to understand what it means for them. Many want to explore how to build plans for total intelligent automation to move their companies forward into the new AI economy. Many have recognized the imminent need for augmenting skills because of increasing automation. The recognition that the AI economy will be led by business professionals is finally sinking in. But auditors, accountants, finance professionals, and forensic accountants must develop a deeper and more pragmatic understanding of the AI revolution. They must do it fast before the opportunity passes them by. This book will be your guide to improve and implement intelligent automation in your firms – and to do it in a structured, efficient, and disciplined way.

Artificial intelligence and audit are not strangers to each other. For decades researchers and practitioners have been trying to marry the two. Audit, if automated, can improve the audit quality and reduce its cost. On one hand it will improve the audit efficiency for companies; on the other hand it will enhance the trust and confidence of investors and other stakeholders who rely upon audited financial statements.

While the research and reports on artificial intelligence–centric audit automation have been plenty, there has not been a structured model of end-to-end audit automation. Sporadic collection of papers on audit does not translate into a workable audit model. Neither does haphazard capability building. In some ways, it was never deemed important to build a comprehensive framework from the perspective of how to build an audit automation plan for a company. After all, up until very recent times, the technology was not advanced enough to even begin to think about a fully automated audit. It was no different than the application of artificial intelligence in a car or an airplane. Automating some functional parts of a car's or an airplane's operation is one thing, creating an autonomous car or an autonomous drone another. But just as advances in technology have now given us the comfort to envision putting autonomous vehicles on the road and autonomous drones in the sky, the time for autonomous and continuous audit has come.

However, automating audit does not mean eliminating human work. If anything, it means eliminating the mistakes and errors, whether intentional or not, of the human work. Thus, a structured model of intelligent automation of audit will incorporate the automation of both cognitive and physical human work and will focus on enhancing the human ability to function far beyond what normal human capacities allow humans to do. Lifting the human constraints is not simply a function of enhanced computational efficiency. It results from embedding intelligence in machines.

Embedding intelligence in machines is no ordinary change. It is one of the most extraordinary developments in the course of human history. Machines have always been subservient to human control. The new type of machine, with a mind of its own, is something humans have no experience with. This new development implies that we cannot approach intelligent automation in audit as a standalone phenomenon. We must consider the management, economic, technical, organizational, and governance aspects of introducing this magnificent technology. The book addresses all of those areas and provides a comprehensive first look at the entire discipline of intelligent automation in audit.

The book has been divided into four parts. Part One orients you to the fascinating world of audit automation. By addressing the following questions, it establishes the foundational knowledge for an AI business professional:

1. What is the AI revolution and how does it impact economy?
2. What is the role of an audit professional? How does AI change that role?
3. What is artificial intelligence technology?
4. What are the best practices and methodologies to build intelligent solutions?

In the first six chapters, this book walks you through the amazing forces that have come together to launch the AI revolution. Chapter 5 introduces machine learning and explains some of the algorithms. The book is written for business audience and therefore the idea is not to make you a machine learning expert but instead to equip you with the knowledge necessary for you to take ownership of business solutions in AI.

With the foundational knowledge covered in Part One, we then introduce the intelligent automation of audit model in Part Two. This is a structured model that gives companies the ability to envision and understand what a comprehensive automated audit solution looks like. We dedicate five chapters (7 to 11) to the automation of the audit process. Each of the five chapters addresses a process area of audit, including preplanning, inherent risk, controls risk, audit procedure, and post-audit management. The approach in this book is to focus on automation. Since the book is authored for a global audience, reference to accounting standards of any single country was intentionally avoided.

After covering the audit process automation, in Part Three the focus shifts to fraud detection, forensic accounting, and valuation. Part Three is designed to equip assurance firms to develop automation to offer forensic services. The automation strategy in those areas is defined by introducing a model known as Infinity Cycle and building automation around that model. In four chapters (12 to 15) we cover various aspects of traditional and modern forensic accounting to build a highly automated forensic automation firm.

This book is about practical solutions. In the first three parts we covered the technical and automation aspects of intelligent automation of audit. Those parts are incomplete if we fail to address the fact the intelligent automation is not just changing the technology, it requires changing our approach and understanding of the organization. The organization in the AI economy will look and feel different than the one in the digital economy. The AI solution development will also require a change in how projects are developed. An intelligent solution also requires different types of governance than a non-intelligent machine. Developing a pragmatic solution necessitates addressing organizational issues, project management, and governance. Part Four has three chapters (16 to 18) and they address those critical solution development issues.

How to get the most out of this book?

There are three ways to get the most out of this book. First, read it with the mindset that you are designing and envisioning the future of your firm and the audit/assurance function. This means to think in terms of the framework. Second, as a businessperson, unless you want to, you don't have to understand the technical details beyond what is presented in this book. To take ownership of projects, you need enough knowledge to have a reasonable conversation with your data science or AI team. This book enables you to do that. If you encounter a technical concept that you don't grasp, try to understand it with the analogies provided in the book. Third, apply the knowledge by building a working plan for your audit automation.

Given the state of the technology, intelligent automation of audit is imminent. Start early to get a strong lead. Stay ahead by doing it effectively. Your journey has just begun. Expect the world to be transformed in the next few years. Have a wonderful journey!

Acknowledgments

I AM GRATEFUL TO MY WIFE for her unconditional support for my intellectual pursuits. I want to thank my children for their understanding as I spent countless hours working on this and other books. Many thanks to my mother for providing motivation to learn and develop.

Special thanks to Sheck Cho at Wiley. Also, many thanks to Elisha (Wiley) and the entire Wiley team. I have worked with several publishers; however, I find Wiley to be the most professional.

My courses are offered via AICPA and I want to thank the AICPA team, including Penelope Johnson, Sandeep Rao, Nisha Gordhan, Jeffery Drew, Jeremy Clark, and Ami Beers. Amazing people and a truly inspiring team!

I want to acknowledge all the researchers and authors whose work I have cited in this book.

PART ONE

Foundations for AI and Audit

P ART ONE ORIENTS YOU TO THE artificial intelligence revolution and prepares you for Part Two and Part Three, which are focused on audit automation and forensic accounting automation. Approaching it from a historical, business, and technical perspective, it is composed of six chapters. The first two chapters explain the underlying drivers of the artificial intelligence (AI) emergence as a global phenomenon. Chapter 3 to Chapter 5 explain AI and machine learning in a gentle and business friendly manner. Specifically, Chapter 5 introduces various algorithms but does so in a manner that people with no formal training in AI or technical background will be able to follow. Chapter 6 focuses on business analysis tools that are used to develop requirements and use cases for artificial intelligence applications.

CHAPTER ONE

Introduction: Staying Ahead of the Emergent Risk

THE AI TECHNOLOGICAL REVOLUTION is sweeping through the globe. Audit is no exception. The world of audit is about to change. With not just *automation*, but *intelligent automation*, the future of traditional, mostly manual, audit is being redesigned. IAA, or intelligent audit automation, is the next generation of audit services that encapsulates new audit business models, new audit professionals, new types of tools and techniques, new standards, and new ways of looking at knowledge creation. Welcome to the bold and new world of intelligent automation.

As your guide on this journey, my goal will be to first introduce to you the era of intelligent automation. It is important for you to recognize that intelligent automation is not just a phase or a temporary detour or even the next step in the evolution of the digital technology. It is an era of its own. Together we will walk through this amazing entrance that will lead us into a completely new age for humankind. The era of nonhuman intelligent workforce. Once past that point, we will then pick up some tools of the trade so we can develop a perspective about the nuts and bolts needed to function in these revolutionary times. These nuts and bolts – essentially our toolkits – will help us proceed to the next level of audit automation. The toolkits are general, so even if you are not an auditor trying to learn about how to automate audit, they will come in handy. Equipped with the toolkits, we will enter the realm of total audit automation.

As I walk you through this amazingly new and exciting world, I recognize that you are a businessperson who wants to learn about Intelligent Audit Automation. That is why my goal will not be to turn you into a data science expert or a machine learning guru, but instead to turn you into a visionary practitioner who can lead, guide, develop, and manage organizational transformations that can take a firm from today's AIS (accounting information systems) – centric capabilities to a totally and comprehensively automated audit organization. My goal is to equip you with the knowledge that will allow you to lead a legacy audit firm or audit department and turn it into one of the world's most advanced and automated firms. I do recognize that you may feel awkward or uncomfortable with the words "total automation of the audit organization" – mostly because that statement somehow comes with a billboard that says: "Humans not needed." That is not the case. If anything, as you will see in this book, there will be tremendous need for humans – but it will be in a little different capacity than we are used to. Do not worry, as we will address those issues also.

What IAA will do is not to eliminate human work, but instead eliminate human weaknesses that make human work prone to mistakes, errors, biases, and misconduct. It will create a more perfect human work product.

Like you, I am also concerned about the audit profession. If we take an inventory of where we stand, it is highly troubling. With rising criticism, scandals, audit failures, and growing anxiety among both practitioners and clients, the profession's future seems uncertain. When combined with slow-moving nepotistic knowledge creation, declining audit quality, and lack of innovation, we are confronted with the loss of the profession's credibility. No wonder regulators and governments are losing their patience. All these unfavorable conditions have placed the profession in disarray.

As we think about upgrading and improving the profession, we know that it will require a two-pronged approach that will include improving audit quality while reducing the cost of audit. IAA is the natural answer to accomplish that goal. Whether we want to eliminate the problems and challenges of audit, or we want to automate the audit process, our gateway to the future of audit is artificial intelligence (AI). This book is all you will need to develop a comprehensive understanding and strategy of audit automation with AI.

KILLER ROBOTS AND AUDIT

Pick up any general article on artificial intelligence and it likely begins with some anxiety-inducing sentence like "The mention of the words artificial intelligence brings to mind images of killer robots and autonomous drones flying over our heads" – and the next sentence is usually designed to reduce our anxiety and is something like "Don't worry, even though AI is here, there is nothing killer about it."

Unlike other authors who, at this point, will tell you to relax, and declare that all those sci-fi scenarios are the works of Hollywood's imagination, I will tell you the opposite. I will inform you that it is true that both killer robots and autonomous drones are now part of our world. In fact, even though many people will state that the technology is "not there yet," I will say the reverse. Looking at how rapidly the technology has developed in AI, nothing seems impossible or too far-fetched at this point. This applies to killer robots, and it applies to the field of audit. We can hope that the human civilization will use AI responsibly and not for destructive purposes. One of those extremely responsible and valuable uses of AI is in audit.

Audit is the foundation over which the entire global economy rests. Breaches or cracks in the foundation can easily crash the global economy. Therefore, it is incumbent upon us to protect the global economy by improving the audit quality and doing so with the best technology available to us.

If you are a businessperson, a professional auditor, internal auditor, or member of a finance organization, you will naturally want to learn about artificial intelligence. When you start exploring, it is likely that you will not get your answers from the IT department, or from general books on IT technologies, or from the highly confusing articles on machine learning and AI. It feels like you need a PhD in mathematics to read even a simple article on machine learning. I teach executives like you, and I know the problems they encounter when trying to understand AI.

The overwhelming complexity, when combined with its novelty, makes the field unapproachable. And that is where many businesspeople lose interest or stop caring about the great opportunities that await those who dare to pursue. But in this book things will be different. I will guide you through the complexities of the AI field in a manner that any businessperson will be able to follow the most relevant and important areas of the field. I want to equip you with only those things that will impact your audit transformation and save you from details that are unnecessary for a businessperson to know. If you find that some parts of the artificial intelligence field interest you more than others, you can then pursue other avenues to learn more or get trained in those areas.

Despite its business orientation, this book is not a pie-in-the-sky, wishful, futuristic, motivational book about artificial intelligence. Those feel-good types of books fail to acknowledge on-the-ground constraints and realities of technology. They also don't serve the needs of the practitioners who want applied knowledge and who want to learn things they can apply right away in their business. I wanted to give you a toolkit that you can deploy the next day in your business.

You are also not seeking a textbook or a book that feels like a furniture assembly manual. Those narrated manuals of the deployed capabilities dwell in the land of suffocating and hopeless pragmatism, and they often inhibit innovation.

This book presents a comprehensive and systematic approach to audit automation with artificial intelligence. In many cases I use existing, applied, and documented knowledge, but in other cases I give a bold but practical vision of the possible.

A pragmatic *vision* is always challenging. It lays out the path, it shows the destination, and it clarifies the roadmap. But to achieve the destination one must move, struggle, and strive. This book will be your guide to practical intelligent automation in audit. It is highly unlikely that any company in the world will today have all that is included in this book. But it is highly likely that companies around the world will be experimenting with parts of what is covered in the book.

Most new technologies and innovations are adopted without considering their own future evolutionary paths, much less how they will evolve and transform business. In such scenarios, companies adopt technology as if their business models are independent of technology, and as if technology is merely an enabler of their business models. In today's world this thinking can be detrimental. It constrains vision and the ability to grasp the full potential of technology. For example, almost every retailer in America adopted technology and rode the "digital" hype wave, but many major retailers (Macy's, Nordstrom, Sears, and others) could not compete with Amazon. For Amazon, technology was not an enabler; it was the primary business model. For others it was an enabler to their business strategy and model but not the core strategy itself.

One can argue that the reason the traditional retailers are struggling is because their business models are brick-and-mortar based. The response to that misunderstanding is that one should look at Walmart. Walmart can be considered as a company from the old brick-and-mortar times, but the firm always built itself around technology. Technology was not just an enabler to the strategy; it was at the core of the Walmart's business strategy – and Walmart is competing effectively. Thus, "brick-and-mortar" has nothing to do with being properly automated or digital; it is the strategic orientation and mindset that distinguish companies from being modern or outdated. That is another reason why bringing in the world's top consulting firms will not help you to become automated. As we will learn in this book, it will greatly depend upon your own leadership, people, strategy, and vision that will determine if you will thrive or barely survive in the new era. The winners build their entire companies around AI.

Similarly, when we think about audit, we need to pay attention to building the entire audit function and service around technology. In that regard, we need to part with the twentieth-century mindset that technology enables audit and adopt the modern outlook of building the audit function around artificial intelligence. This book shows how to do that.

BUILDING THE AUDIT FUNCTION AROUND AI

The world of audit is complex, broad, regulated, highly procedural, and standards-driven. Given that each audit situation can be unique, and that the business world is always evolving, it is natural for auditors to consider technology as an enabler. Traditionally, the audit technology has focused on audit management automation and not on intelligent audit automation. When we change the goal from enablement to building a company around AI, we need to understand what it means for the audit service delivery mechanism and how that will change the business model of audit firms.

In general, we know that the modern business is a fast-changing system. As AI enters the business world and becomes more pervasive, it is bound to impact audit in multiple ways. Regardless of the industry, intelligent automation is not only automating processes; it is also enabling companies and government agencies to become more intelligent and innovative. For example, the pharmaceutical industry is not only automating its core business processes with artificial intelligence but also implementing AI to discover new molecules. This means that "automation + intelligence" becomes the new competitive advantage.

With intelligent automation as the new competitive advantage, the adoption of intelligent technologies becomes a natural *survive and thrive* mechanism and, hence, will lead to rapid adoption of the AI technologies across the board.

As the example of the retail industry in the previous section shows, just because we are automating doesn't mean we are realizing full business value or establishing competitive advantage. Our business models and designs need to reflect the winning models and strategies. That comes by gaining a more thorough and holistic understanding of our environment.

Additionally, the accelerated introduction of the AI technologies in the business universe will have major ramifications for audit:

- It will introduce new types of emergent risks for which audit firms are not prepared.
- It will force audit firms to rethink their service delivery systems.
- It will require audit firms to stay a step ahead of the emergent risk versus always playing catchup.

Audit firms will have to become proactive innovators such that they can *always stay ahead of the emergent risk.*

STAYING AHEAD OF THE EMERGENT RISK

As we enter the AI era, let us establish some ground rules for the audit profession. One of these reminders is borrowed from the field of cybernetic systems. It is known as The First Law of Cybernetics and is derived from William Ross Ashby's Law of Requisite Variety. The law in its crude form (mostly due to my interpretation and use here) implies that the degree of control of a system is directly proportional to the information available about the system.

In order to monitor a system, particularly if we are approaching audit as a comprehensive verification, control, and monitoring system, we need to have control and feedback systems that are more intelligent than the system they are trying to monitor. Ashby presents the idea of requisite variety (Ashby, 1958). In this case he uses the word "variety" to signify diversity of information. To control a system, we need information about the system that is equal to or greater than the information available in the system. Again, in an analogous, but useful, manner we will interpret this law for audit as demanding that the information and intelligence of the entity responsible for auditing an organization should be at least as much as the entity being audited.

This is one area where audit has struggled. Audit has always played catchup. Audit has always been in a reactive mode and not a proactive mode. Scandal after scandal, and failure after failure, audit has functioned as a follower and never a leader of best practices. Being proactive means that audit must stay ahead of the emergent risk.

To appreciate the concept of staying ahead of the emergent risk versus chasing it, we can make the preliminary assumption that the audit function will innovate with the general speed of innovation in business. Since audit is also a business, any innovation that happens in general in the business world will sooner or later be adopted by the audit profession. Audit innovation will not happen in a vacuum. Along with many other areas of business, the entire accounting function is also getting automated and that means the impact of business and accounting automation will require a parallel innovation path in audit. Let us give this type of adoption a name: General Adoption. General Adoption of technology happens when firms adopt technology at the average pace and rate at which the business world adopts technology.

As shown in Figure 1.1, if clients are adopting intelligent automation, audit firms will also adopt intelligent automation for their core processes and would focus on the automation of the existing workflows, processes, and methods.

But for a profession that brings accountability and transparency to other systems, it must have greater intelligence horsepower than the entities it is analyzing. After all, the introduction of intelligent automation in the business universe will not only increase business complexity, but also give rise to new types of risks. The audit literature seems to be obsessed with Enron and Enron-type disasters but ignores the more systemic and catastrophic shocks to the global economy.

Take the example of the Great Recession of 2007–2009. The rapid introduction of an interlinked global economy enabled the financial (and business) world to introduce complex financial products, and package and sell risk in creative ways. That created a complex system with high systemic risk, which

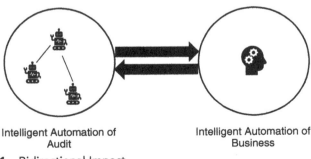

Intelligent Automation of
Audit

Intelligent Automation of
Business

FIGURE 1.1 Bidirectional Impact

exhibited domino-effect collapse characteristics and emergent dynamics. When an adverse event happened, the intensity and power unleashed was so enormous that the entire global economy collapsed. The shock was alarming, but not as much as the fact that the whole world – including the Federal Reserve bank – was in a state of complete obliviousness and denial. That catastrophic event was also a failure of audit at a consolidated level. Clearly, risk outpaced the ability of the audit firms to comprehend it. The Great Recession was a testament to the fact that the public audit profession must have greater intelligence horsepower than the entities it audits. Since the ability of the audit profession to stay ahead of the risk is paramount to its efficacy, to be truly effective audit firms need to have more advanced innovation and technology than their clients.

Since the AI revolution's impact are widespread and global, the audit response to the challenge posed by AI-related innovations needs to be proactive and comprehensive. Let us consider some examples of when AI has negatively impacted the economy or institutions:

- Gone are the days when humans made trading decisions, as the majority of trading these days is algorithmic trading. We have observed flash crashes in financial markets, where markets lose significant value within minutes. Some studies have attributed the increase in systemic risk and flash crashes to the rise of algorithmic trading and have shown the value of ex ante regulatory intervention as more beneficial (Paulin et al., 2019). Consider the question from an audit perspective: how to value assets when in the new world the market collapse can happen so suddenly?
- We observed the intervention of foreign bots in US elections in 2016. Similar approaches have been applied to destabilize products and services by companies. This implies that a type of engineered risk can take shape that can suddenly impact the value of a business. Should auditors account for that risk?
- The modern business is now composed of both human and digital workers. A system driven by the interaction between millions of digital and thousands of human workers can exhibit emergent forms of risks. For instance, some researchers attribute the Boeing 737 crash to AI (Pasztor and Tangel, 2019). Can a similar catastrophic failure risk arise in a business?

This brings us to the next level of intelligent automation that will be needed from audit firms. Let us give this a name and call it Superior Adoption.

Superior Adoption implies that given the nature of the business, some businesses must adopt technology at a higher pace and rate (and capability level) than other businesses (or adversaries). One example of this mindset is seen in national security adoption of technology. At all times, the national security technology capability, pace, and rate should be greater than the adversaries or catastrophic scenarios can unfold. This mission-critical approach implies that the system that is designed to monitor other systems must display a higher level of intelligence than those it is monitoring. Applying that to the audit profession, innovation will need to be far more robust and much stronger than it has been in the past.

As the rise of AI changes business, that change will demand increasingly greater change from the audit profession. This means that if the audit function wants to stay effective and relevant, its innovation needs to be constant, powerful, and impactful. Audit can no longer be the lagging profession that is playing catch-up to clients. It will have to adopt the proactive mission-critical mindset to innovation.

Despite the need to be at the forefront of modernization, we observe that innovation in audit has been sporadic, disconnected, and rudimentary. We observe that while large audit firms have made announcements that they are investing in audit automation, we have not seen any major strategies, designs, or implementations to show that. Except for press releases and cheap marketing videos, the real automation is rare and, when it does happen, it is focused on audit management automation and not audit automation. We observe the hype but nothing truly concrete behind the glamour.

In fact, if anything, we have observed a decline in audit quality, increasing audit failure rates, and more problems. The rate of innovation is once again exceeding the ability of the audit firms to adapt. It is only a matter of time before another major economic disaster happens.

 ## THE MUCH-NEEDED EVOLUTION OF THE AUDIT FIRM

Based upon the great transformation taking place in the economy, both the core structure of the audit firm and the business model will change. The new mission for the audit firm is to perform intelligent automation-led quality audits efficiently. Technically, it is possible to have a totally automated audit firm with zero employees. Obviously, from a pragmatic perspective, we don't expect that to happen anytime soon; however, structural changes in the audit service delivery model are inevitable. As the AI revolution moves forward, traditional audit firms will get a wide spectrum of opportunities to add greater value to their clients. Some of those opportunities are as follows:

- **Technology Provider:** Audittech firms will have the opportunity to develop, design, and install AI agents to help clients achieve better internal control and improve greater visibility to increase the understanding of inherent risks. These systems will be put in place for the internal use of the client firm and not for external use.
- **Audit as a Service:** Audit firms can now deploy AI agents that perform continuous audit and track new developments in a client's business. These agents will be visible to the audit firm.
- **Audit the Auditor:** Audit firms will acquire much better understanding of their audit teams and match the right people with clients.
- **Audit the Agents:** As agents become more pervasive, governance of audit agents will become an important issue. Audit firms will need the ability to audit the agents used by the clients.
- **Assess the Maturity:** Audit firms will be able to help clients determine their maturity in terms of being able to audit their intelligent and non-intelligent digital workforce.
- **Niche Players:** We will observe a sharp rise of audit-tech firms focused on niche areas of audit and these firms will sell their services to other audit firms.

 ## THE CLAUSTROPHOBIC MINI UNIVERSE OF AUDIT

Besides the audit firms, the audit universe includes professional societies (like AICPA), standards organizations (like FASB), regulators (e.g., PCAOB), academics, and tech firms.

The traditional relationship structure between the large audit firms, academics, and professional societies has been somewhat strange. The symbiotic nature of the relationship, which often focused upon maximizing each entity's profitability, constrained true innovation and development. It also reduced transparency and accountability. Thus, we observed a closed network, akin to a private club, of insiders that includes professional societies in tight configurations with large legacy audit firms, a small number of audit technology suppliers, and a concentrated group of scholars from a few universities. This nepotistic relationship map correlates with the ongoing decline in audit quality and innovation.

In the old model, professional societies functioned as the mouthpieces and extended marketing arms of large firms. The large audit firms had tremendous power over the entire industry and dissent was quickly reprimanded. In some ways, professional societies were indirectly run by large firms.

The emergence of the Public Company Accounting Oversight Board (PCAOB) challenged that symbiotic structure and has exposed many vulnerabilities in the system. In the new world, independence and transparency are being considered as important virtues.

Among other things, the AI revolution will also expose such nepotistic relationships and open the profession to be far more accommodating to external parties. We can also expect a large number of automation firms entering the profession, as we will observe a huge surge in audit-tech.

 ## THE PROBLEMS WITH TODAY'S APPROACH

While plentiful, the research in audit automation seems both directionless and sporadic. It is concentrated in the hands of a few researchers. While some attempts have been made to bring a broader perspective together, such efforts lack strategic orientation or a synthesized modular structure that forms an intelligent automation audit platform. Despite its concentration, the research has produced some powerful and revolutionary ideas – many of which are discussed in this book. There are 10 fundamental problems why a comprehensive and clear strategic approach to automated audit has not materialized:

1. The application of intelligent automation in audit, for the most part, has been done in response to specific use cases and not as a strategic enterprise adoption. When projects are implemented as specific use cases, they are often done in silos, launched on an experimentation basis, and designed without consideration for scalability and the evolution of technology.
2. Research, and appropriately so, developed in various small areas of audit. All of that research has moved the field forward; however, there is a need to bring the entire research together to formulate an enterprise-based intelligent automation audit concept.
3. The audit technology has evolved from multiple directions. Besides the standard IT systems, expert systems were used in audit. Later, process mining and RPA technologies were used. Simultaneously, the research also developed in machine learning. There is a need to tie together a technology vision that encapsulates the combined functioning of these technologies.

4. Intelligent automation is relatively new. Some of the new approaches in artificial intelligence, especially in the areas of machine learning, are recent. These approaches have not been fully integrated in the design and engineering of audit systems.

5. While due to the rise of AI, there has been significant investment in the finance technology sector, the broad fintech sector has focused more on market-centric technologies (e.g., investment and portfolio management) and not on audit.

6. The arrival of intelligent automation is the launch of a new era in computing. Even though this change is real, it creates a hype wave. When the hype wave takes effect, vendors tend to create significant confusion by repositioning their existing solutions to appear as part of the new revolution. Sometimes they achieve that by adding one or two simple features in their products, at other times not even that. This creates confusion, as it inhibits the real innovation in the market from being showcased.

7. Audit firms are making announcements about audit automation, displaying vision videos and conceptual plans – but having all that is one thing, and having a working product and a service another. No firm is offering a fully automated audit and even those that are claiming that they do automated audit seem to be at an early conceptual stage.

8. Data-centric technical platforms are not like digital technologies. They are not deterministic, and their design and engineering require a different approach. In certain cases, it is not easy to know if the system will achieve its goals or not. Unlike programming-based IT systems where you know that if the code is written the system will work, in machine learning there is no guarantee. This means we cannot have intelligent systems that are akin to the configurable IT systems (e.g., CRM, ERP) that we are used to. A lot depends on the data we have to help machines learn.

9. Unlike in regular software development and deployment where we can get away with a team of narrow skillsets, in intelligent automation we need people with many skills. A typical team may include people with business experience, data science, cognitive architecture, process mining, RPA, IT, cognitive science, governance, etc. Knowing how to assemble and deploy that team is critical.

10. Systemic and disciplined development for cognitive skills requires organizational and leadership commitment. The audit profession seems to be in the short-term mindset where leadership is more concerned about extinguishing fires than thinking about how to figure that fires don't happen in the first place.

ENABLING NEW THINKING IN AUDIT

Time has come to end the age of stymied innovation and launch a new era in audit. This is the era of end-to-end intelligent automation of the audit function. To understand how to make that happen, we will need to start by first understanding our own behaviors and mindsets about audit. For this discussion, we are approaching business as a system and audit as a feedback and control mechanism for business. There are five concepts we need to be aware of:

1. **Bounded Rationality:** We approach systems from a rational angle and try to understand specific actions and their consequences without the backdrop of human behavior. As Herbert Simon pointed out in his concept of bounded rationality, our decision-making capacity is limited by the information we have, our processing capacity, and time (Simon, 2000). We need to be aware of these three constraints in audits. How can machines help improve one or more of these three constraints?

2. **Behavior Matters:** Audit is more than just a numerical exercise or marking the checklist or filling out questionnaires. Well-trained auditors understand the importance of behavior analysis. For example, professional skepticism is a behavioral attribute. When combined with numerical audit, behavioral audit can do wonders in helping improve the audit quality. Recognizing and understanding behavioral patterns is key to a successful audit. In what areas can machines help us develop better behavioral analysis capabilities?

3. **Nonlinear Relationships:** We often approach audit with the mindset that we are looking at a linear system with a causal chain of interdependencies. For instance, we may think of a business as a chain of capabilities and processes. The modern reality is that business has become far more complex and is based upon a network of relationships. This nonlinear system has inherent complexities that cannot be ignored in audit. Viewing it from a Newtonian cause-and-effect manner can be counterproductive. We must approach it as complex adaptive system and learn how to adapt to the system's changes. Can machines help us understand the changes and the required adaptations?

4. **Our Sense of Control:** We tend to view the world of the auditee as composed of negative feedback loops. In negative feedback loops, the feedback received by the system is expected to reduce the fluctuations in the output. It promotes the system to move toward equilibrium. We operate

with a belief that the system is self-adjusting, and the feedback loop (e.g., financial statements) we deploy in companies will help the system become more stable. The opposite to that is the positive feedback loop, where feedback leads to greater instability. In many cases, the way we provide feedback tends to act as a positive feedback loop and instead of making the system more stable, it brings greater instability. For instance, providing indirect or casual feedback to a client about the suspicion of fraud may encourage the auditee to do even more coverup. Can machines help us deploy negative feedback loops such that the system (auditee's business) stays stable?

5. **Our Sense of Time:** An audit needs to perform at the speed of decision-making in enterprises. Slow and unactionable information is useless in today's world. Business needs dynamic and instantaneous intelligence to thwart and manage risks. This means we need to track the mapping between the business goals and the environment and be aware of the changes taking in both. Can machines help us perform at the speed of decisions?

As we start viewing our world and responsibilities differently, we can recognize the role played by machines in helping us improve the quality of audit.

REINVENTING THE LEGACY FIRM

The American Institute of Artificial Intelligence (AIAI) has developed the most comprehensive standards for intelligent automation in audit. In this book, I will cover the standards and design/engineering concepts offered by AIAI.

To understand the AIAI intelligent automation model, it is important to first comprehend the essential properties of the Intelligent Audit Automation (IAA).

- **Interconnected Automation:** Interconnected automation implies that IAA is not a collection of independent and disconnected parts of automation. Instead, IAA is a collection of interdependent and connected agents that work in unison to achieve the audit goals.
- **End-to-End Audit Automation:** This property implies that when the parts are put together, they address all areas of audit and nothing is left unautomated. The system is designed to be a fully automated system without any human intervention in the process and its footprint is exhaustive in the sense that it automates the entire audit process.

- **Scalable:** Scalability in this regard is more than simply the ability to scale at an enterprise level; it also implies that the technology can be grown or evolved without significant changes, rework, or replacement. As such, scalability possesses two goals: (a) the ability to scale at the enterprise level; and (b) to do so without major investment, rework, and throwaway.
- **Grow with Technology:** This property is different than the previous property as it refers to the ability to add known and upcoming forms of technology to the existing technology base without major rework or value loss. In other words, the base technology design is done in a manner that it can easily adapt to the new innovations in technology.
- **Grow with Data:** This property refers to: (a) the ability to process both structured (e.g., transactional data) and unstructured (e.g., voice, video, etc.) data; and (b) the ability to change and grow the intelligent agents as the underlying data changes. The change in the underlying problem/solution could be that new data is discovered, which may provide further explanation to the existing solution via introducing new variables. For example, new features are discovered that can have a meaningful impact on the solution. New data can also imply that the underlying distributions – based upon which the entire system was developed – have changed. As underlying data changes, the ability to grow the intelligent system without rebuilding the whole thing is a core property for design and engineering of intelligent systems.
- **Multidimensional Modular:** The system is designed to be modular and multidimensional. Modular is based upon the plug-n-play concept. It is an acknowledgment that if technology or data changes to a point where major rework is needed, it can be confined to changing the parts versus changing the whole.
- **Continuous:** From an audit perspective, the intelligent system must support continuous audit. Continuous audit is defined as follows: a continuous audit is a methodology that enables independent auditors to provide written assurance on a subject matter, for which an entity's management is responsible, using a series of auditor's reports issued virtually simultaneously with, or a short period of time after, the occurrence of events underlying the subject matter (CICA/AICPA, 1999). Continuous audit, according to the AIAI, is defined as follows: Continuous Audit is a system of machines and humans that constantly and effectively monitor the health of a business entity and enable preemptive intervention to preserve and protect its value.

- **Cost Efficient:** Deploying intelligent audit capabilities must result in reducing the overall cost of the audit.
- **Total Transactional Coverage:** Instead of selecting samples, IAA is designed to scan the entire transaction population.
- **Predictive:** IAA not only identifies patterns, but also predicts patterns. It enables preemptive intervention.
- **Simulative:** IAA includes the capability to simulate and create scenarios and learn from them. It can be self-critical and learn its weaknesses from playing the role of self-critic.
- **Flexible:** It also means that the system is designed to accommodate different types of work streams. Some work streams are simple and deterministic. Others deal with greater uncertainty. Thus, the system assigns the resources (think of it as matching) with the complexity of intelligence required and thereby eliminating mismatch between resources needed and the solution. In other words, IAA will not require a sophisticated machine-learning-based solution for a job that can be handled by a simple Robotic Process Automation (RPA).
- **Adaptable:** IAA should be built with the mindset that the business processes change in today's dynamic business situation and therefore the audit automation should be adaptable. This means it must be architecturally flexible.
- **Governable:** IAA must have governance frameworks to ensure that its design and performance meet the governance best practices and ethical frameworks. Simply put, IAA must be ethical. IAA should also be safe to use. Safety implies both mental and physical safety of human users. The complexity of IAA should be manageable and not rise to the point where the entire system becomes unstable.

 THE UNIVERSE OF ACCOUNTING

As we approach IAA, it cannot be done in a vacuum. It must be approached from the perspective of being a discipline that is embedded within what we at the AIAI call the wheel of modern finance.

As shown in Figure 1.2, the universe of accounting automation is defined by the nine practice areas and four capability levels (shown as rings). Each of the practice areas describes a separate functional area. Just as the rings on a tree stump tell you the age of a tree, the capability rings inform you about the relative capability levels of a firm in its total state of intelligent

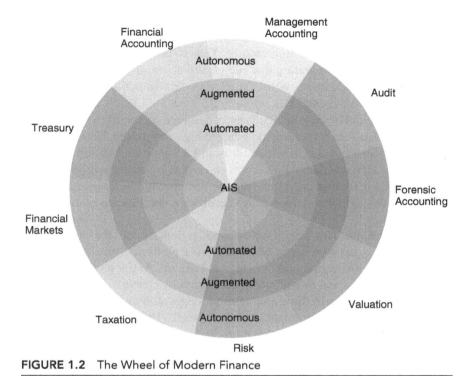

FIGURE 1.2 The Wheel of Modern Finance

finance automation. The capability levels are based upon the systematic and disciplined approach to move from the internal rings to the external bands, that is, from Transactional Automation (AIS, BA, BI), to Automation (RPA, Expert), Augmented (Machine Learning), and Autonomous (Intelligent Agents, Reinforcement Learning, Ensemble, Multiagent Systems). As intelligent automation matures, these four layers of automation will coexist in modern enterprises. This book will mostly focus on the Audit practice area. Let's look at the rings:

- **AIS:** Accounting Information Systems are systems that are used to record transactions, generate reports, and perform analysis. These systems include the typical accounting and related modules in ERP systems, the business analytics, and business intelligence systems. Most large and medium-sized companies have AIS in place. They are shown at the center because it is expected that firms will have those systems and because they are necessary to build the outer, more advanced, layers.

- **Automated:** The Automation layer is the first ring added on top of the existing AIS. This layer focuses on automating tasks that require low-level resolution of uncertainty. This is task automation where a certain work-task requiring low complexity of cognitive thinking is automated. This could be work-tasks such as matching, updating data, simple searching, or uploading files.
- **Augmented:** The Augmented layer is designed on top of the automated layer where the tasks require moderate to high complexity. These tasks can be automated but they don't result in full automation of a process. This is task automation where a certain work-task requiring complex cognitive thinking is automated. For example, automating the assessment of the culture of a firm based upon how executives communicate is augmented intelligence.
- **Autonomous:** The autonomous layer is built upon the augmented layer where the systems can independently perform entire functions or processes, with no guidance or help from humans. At this level, automated work-tasks function as a whole in an interconnected and interdependent manner and perform the entire work process autonomously. An example would be the full automation of cash audit. PricewaterhouseCoopers (PwC) has recently claimed that it now possesses the capability to perform the cash audit. The firm announced that "PwC's Cash.ai uses AI to automatically read, understand and test client documents, including reported cash balances, bank reconciliations, bank confirmation letters, foreign exchange and financial condition of the bank – in essence, the complete audit of cash" (PwC, 2019). This is an example of autonomous audit.

 THE GAME PLAN

As we move through the book, I will introduce the IAA framework developed by the American Institute of Artificial Intelligence. This framework (shown in Figure 1.3) contains the following:

- Five parts of integrated audit automation
- One part of Assurance, Forensic Accounting, and Valuation Automation
- Sales and Client Management Automation
- HR, Organizational Planning and Development, and Project Management Automation
- All the capabilities that are designed to be continuous, intelligent, and automated

FIGURE 1.3 Intelligent Audit Automation Framework of AIAI

The book has four parts. Part One introduces business readers to the field of artificial intelligence (AI). Part Two focuses on audit features and systematically builds five areas of automated pre-audit evaluation, automated risk assessment, automated audit procedures, automated audit reporting, and automated post-audit management. Part Three focuses on automated assurance, forensic accounting, and valuation. Part Four focuses on sales and client management, organizational planning and development, and project management. It should be pointed out that organizational planning, human resources, and project management for the AI economy will be different from the regular economy.

Key Points

- Intelligent Audit Automation (IAA) is a competitive necessity for companies and audit service providers.
- IAA offers many growth- and innovation-based business opportunities for legacy firms. Legacy firms must reorganize to build their firms around AI.
- Legacy audit firms need to transition to the IAA model.
- Transitioning to IAA means automating the entire audit and making audit continuous.

 REFERENCES

Ashby, W. R. (1958) Requisite variety and its implications for the control of complex systems. *Cybernetica* 1 (2): 83–99. Available from: http://pcp.vub .ac.be/Books/AshbyReqVar.pdf.

CICA/AICPA (1999) *Continuous auditing.* Research report.

Pasztor, A. and Tangel, A. (2019) Investigators believe Boeing 737 MAX stall-prevention feature activated in Ethiopian crash. The Wall Street Journal, 29 March [online]. Available from: https://www.wsj.com/articles/investigators-believe-737-max-stall-prevention-feature-activated-in-ethiopian-crash-11553836204.

Paulin, J., Calinescu, A., and Wooldridge, M. (2019) Understanding flash crash contagion and systemic risk: A micro–macro agent-based approach. *Journal of Economic Dynamics and Control, 100: 200–229.* Available from: https://doi.org/10.1016/j.jedc.2018.12.008.

PwC (2019) Harnessing AI to pioneer new approaches to the audit [online]. Available from: https://www.pwc.com/gx/en/about/stories-from-across-the-world/harnessing-ai-to-pioneer-new-approaches-to-the-audit.html (Accessed 11 April 2019).

Simon, H. A. (2000) Bounded rationality in social science: Today and tomorrow. *Mind & Society.* 125–139.

CHAPTER TWO

Fourth Industrial Revolution and Its Impact on Audit

GOOD PROFESSIONALS EXPEDITIOUSLY ADAPT as the world around them changes. Excellent professionals thrive by changing the world around them. This book is for both intrapreneurs and entrepreneurs. The common elements between the two cases are, of course, that the business world is changing around us and it is incumbent upon professionals to adapt and excel in this environment. Contrary to what one might expect from professionals, the ability to adapt and excel seems to be in short supply.

It took accounting professionals dozens of years to adopt computerization. The stories of accounting automation, particularly ERP implementations, still serve as exhilarating business dinner conversations, where tales of fear, failure, and fatigue are delicately intertwined to recall the fun times of tech transformation projects. Like camping stories, they present a perfect balance of the jitters and joys of advancing to the new era of computerization. Just when we thought digitization would be the last revolution we have to endure in our professional lives, a new revolution is brewing. Just when we began adjusting to the comfortable feeling of normalized uniformity, a major and overwhelming change is knocking on our door. The sound of that knocking is growing louder by the day. So much so that major governments and institutions across the world are recognizing that something extraordinary has happened. Welcome to the AI revolution!

This revolution will once again challenge us to the extreme and will do so in more ways that we can imagine. The power of the AI (artificial intelligence) revolution has already altered the accounting profession. Now it is time for the professionals to acknowledge, apply, and adjust to that transformation. This book is the first one to prepare accounting, audit, forensic, and management accounting professionals to understand and learn about the AI revolution. More than simply introducing you to the exciting dynamics of the AI revolution, this book will serve as your guide to help you upskill and reskill to meet the demands of the modern times.

FOURTH INDUSTRIAL REVOLUTION

Many practitioners may still remember the days when green paper ledgers were the preferred medium for accounting. Even in the 1980s many businesses lacked computerized accounting. The information technology revolution transformed the accounting profession in such a profound way that by the turn of the century, knowing how to operate computers, developing spreadsheets, and familiarity with accounting software became essential skills for accountants. Advance a few more years and business analytics and business intelligence software commanded mainstream attention. Accountants and financial managers had to learn how to produce sophisticated reports from BA (Business Analytics) and BI (Business Intelligence) tools, analyze data, and develop insights to support the ever-growing needs of various stakeholders for the accounting information. And now we have entered the new and powerful revolutionary times of AI. The question is how this technology will shape the financial management profession and what it means for finance professionals.

The general lesson from past developments is that when technology changes, accountants and auditors, like other professionals, must adapt and acquire new skills. However, adopting and acquiring new skills because of a technological revolution (Figure 2.1) has some unique features:

First, while your goals may stay the same (e.g., to produce a financial statement), your work tasks become different. For example, when using a computerized system, you may not need to do a manual bank reconciliation or a three-way-match because the computer does it for you.

Second, your work task is accomplished differently. For instance, instead of manually entering the data, the computer can take in a digital file and automatically update the database.

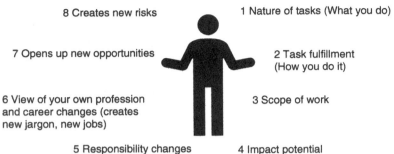

8 Creates new risks

7 Opens up new opportunities

6 View of your own profession and career changes (creates new jargon, new jobs)

5 Responsibility changes

1 Nature of tasks (What you do)

2 Task fulfillment (How you do it)

3 Scope of work

4 Impact potential

FIGURE 2.1 The New Professional for the AI Era

Third, generally your scope changes, that is, being able to do more. For instance, moving from manual to computerized accounting allows you to generate sophisticated reports, graphs, charts, and other such artifacts that you were not able to do before.

Fourth, it allows you to create a greater impact. With more rapidly produced and reliable information, you can now create an impact in multiple ways. Accounting computerization allowed you to provide sophisticated forecasting and projections for a wider group of stakeholders (internal customers, investors, creditors, government, etc.).

Fifth, your responsibility shifts. You are not only responsible for the accuracy of the numbers but also of the information systems that generate the numbers. For example, auditors needed to expand audit to include computer systems.

Sixth, your view of your own profession and expectations from yourself change. You no longer view yourself as a traditional profession – for example, prior technological revolution (Enterprise Resource Planning ERP, the Internet, mobile, cloud) transformed purchasing agents into e-procurement professionals, accounting professionals into ERP professionals, and marketing professionals into e-commerce professionals. You transition into someone new.

Seventh, it opens new opportunities for growth. When the Internet era began, those who learned quickly were able to create powerful careers.

Finally, it injects new avenues of risk. When the Internet came into being, those who failed to adapt perished.

Notice that I used the word "computerization" to signify the developments of the past half a century or so, rather than "automation." The choice was intentional as it is important to make a distinction between automation and computerization.

Computerization is the ability to record, process, and store digital information. Automation implies the use of machines to perform human work.

While computerization does automate some tasks, for example, the production of a financial statement once we have prepared trial balances and made our adjusting entries, such automation was limited to consolidating the data. The machine hasn't acquired the ability to comprehend accounting. It doesn't know how to do the journal entries. It doesn't understand how to make the adjusting entries. All it is doing is to create reports for us and display information in smart ways by processing it in a clever way. Thus, the wave of computerization (also known as digitization) did not automate the core human work that requires both cognitive abilities and physical work. It only enabled us to process information better. What we called automation was really not automation. It was simply the ability to consolidate and present information based upon predetermined rules and formats.

Based upon our definition of automation, automation necessarily requires some type of learning. A machine must learn how to perform a task that humans perform. The task could be as simple as entering data on a screen or as complex as designing a building that will be the next architectural marvel. The AI revolution is about automating human work.

Fast forward to modern times and the advent of AI is reshaping our professional and personal lives. Due to its impact on human civilization, this massive change is now termed the Fourth Industrial Revolution (Schwab, 2016). From interactive devices and personal agents (for example Siri on our iPhone) to autonomous cars and planes, our world is being rapidly changed by autonomous automation. AI is one of the hottest technology trends. Pick any newspaper, magazine, or news website and it is highly likely that you will find some coverage of this amazing technology.

While we may tend to view the AI revolution as an extension of the digital revolution, it is not. The AI revolution, while being structured on the foundations of computerization and digital movements, has its individual and unique characteristics that separate it not only from the digital movement, but also from all previous industrial revolutions.

HOW IS THE COGNITIVE REVOLUTION DIFFERENT FROM PREVIOUS REVOLUTIONS?

In 2015 Professor Klaus Schwab, founder and executive chairman of the World Economic Forum, introduced the term "Fourth Industrial Revolution." Schwab's use of that term had several manifestations (Schwab, 2016).

The term signifies successive states of revolutionary dynamics. It also implies that each revolutionary state extends and improves the performance of the previous state(s). Finally, the scale of change, which can also be viewed as the magnitude of performance improvement, unleashes a powerful force, which is strong enough to be classified as a revolution. The performance element can be a set of production, well-being, employment, living conditions, and other such factors that determine the progress of human civilization.

The invention of the steam engine in the 1700s propelled humankind on its first industrial revolution. This one invention enabled the transition from the agrarian society to a manufacturing society. The invention of the internal combustion engine in the early 1900s launched the second revolution. Rapid industrialization and mass production followed as electricity and oil fueled the engines of economic growth. The third revolution was less about mechanical engines and more about electronics and information technology. Technology was used not only as means to automate manufacturing but also to improve the entire value chain from exchanging data and information. As the third revolution morphed into a globally connected economy and enabled the potential to link every human in the world with every other human, economic progress took a new turn.

Today we stand at the cusp of a new revolution. This revolution is not the continuation of the third revolution. It is not an extension of the Internet. It is also not the prolongation of computerization.

Perhaps that is why one of the leading figures in machine learning, Andrew Ng, said, "Just as electricity transformed almost everything 100 years ago, today I actually have a hard time thinking of an industry that I don't think AI will transform in the next several years" (Lynch, 2017). Ng's assessment lays the foundation to an alternative approach of viewing revolutions.

In fact, Dr. Perez makes a distinction between industrial revolutions and technological revolutions and argues that technological revolutions are far more frequent and are different than industrial revolutions. Thus the advent of AI neatly fits the definition of technological revolution offered by Dr. Perez (Perez, 2002) as "a powerful and highly visible cluster of new and dynamic technologies, products and industries, capable of bringing about an upheaval in the whole fabric of the economy and of propelling a long-term upsurge of development" and that "each of those sets of technological breakthroughs spreads far beyond the confines of the industries and sectors where they originally developed" (Perez, 2002).

Fitting the definition of technological revolution offered by Dr. Perez, and the term "Fourth Industrial Revolution" by Professor Schwab, the new era of

Wide set of inputs

Learn, Adapt, Optimize, Accumulate Experience

Potentially Unobservable Processing and Unknown Pathways

Wide set of outputs

Industrial Revolution IV

FIGURE 2.2   A Different Type of Machine

intelligent automation has dawned upon us. We now stand at the cusp of a breakthrough that will fundamentally alter the way we live and work.

Moving from the paper-based society to a digital society transformed human civilization. The transformation achieved by digitization impacted all sectors and all industries. But despite being a technological revolution, there are some remarkable differences between this and the previous technological revolutions.

Specifically, in all the previous revolutions we considered machines to be subservient to human commands and controls. Machines, in the traditional sense, received limited numbers of known inputs and produced known outputs. Furthermore, if anything went wrong with the machine, the problem was solved by looking "under the hood" and fixing the problem. This was true with ancient textile machines and it is still true with modern computer programs. If a car breaks down, you can fix it by changing a part. If a computer program breaks down, you can debug it by fixing the lines of code.

But intelligent automation is different (Figure 2.2). In some ways it has a mind of its own. It can receive a set of inputs and it can give a wide set of outputs. Most importantly, in many cases we do not know how the machine did what it did. For example, in deep learning systems, the current technology does not allow us to fully understand how that technology made a decision.

In this new world of machines as digital workers, we now have a workplace where both humans and machines work together to accomplish and formulate business strategies and goals. This is something that humankind is experiencing for the first time.

YOU AND THE NEW ERA

You are no longer just an accountant or an auditor. In this new era of intelligent automation your role has changed. Now you are also an operator, designer, manager, leader, and visionary of intelligent automation. The intelligent automation will produce digital workers, and you, the human, are the professional leader and manager of these systems. I understand that it sounds strange and funny – but you will have to take this point seriously and understand what this means for your business and career.

Let us discuss a simple example. You use an agent (for example, Siri) in your phone to ask a question, schedule a meeting, make a call, or get directions. The agent knows you in the sense that it only responds to your voice. This means it only works for you. It is your digital worker. When you talk to the agent, from your activities the agent is learning about you and your preferences, schedules, and work habits. It is acquiring knowledge about you so it can serve you better. In a way, you are the boss and the agent is your loyal employee.

Now take this example and project it to your work situation. You can be surrounded with hundreds of these automated digital workers. One could be doing audit planning while another could be performing substantive procedures for another client. Your role now becomes that of a guide and a leader to teach, direct, manage, design, and architect these digital workers. You are no longer just an auditor; you are an AI audit professional. This is an important distinction. It is also key to unleashing your career and your future.

The prospect of creating new products and services, developing new ways of doing things, creating new workplaces, designing new processes, and developing new knowledge in the intelligent audit automation (IAA) domain are both exciting and lucrative.

This book prepares you to be a Intelligent Automation Audit Professional (IAAP) and leader. As you read rest of the book, keep in mind that you are reading it as the IAAP.

 ## OPPORTUNITIES AND PERILS OF THE FOURTH INDUSTRIAL REVOLUTION

The new industrial revolution will enable you to transform lives and help improve the human civilization. As I mentioned before, audit is the foundation on which the global economy rests. Audit failures destroy lives, companies, and even countries. With intelligent automation, you have the opportunity to close the loopholes, fill the cracks, and improve the audit quality. By doing that you can protect and safeguard the financial future of billions of people who rely upon the confidence that comes from audit.

To create the powerful value for the society, you will have the opportunity to develop, design, and implement new IAA in your firms and workplaces. You can be the entrepreneur who builds a company that produces these tools or provides these services. You can be the manager or leader who moves his or her audit firm forward. You can be the person who implements IAA in financial markets. The opportunities are limitless. The good news is that we are in the early stages of the revolution and the market is wide open.

But the opportunity also comes with many downsides. Like in every IT mini-revolution, there will be tremendous hype. The goldrush scenarios will develop. Suppliers who do not have intelligent automation capabilities will claim they have the functionality. Consulting firms will give you half-baked plans. Many will try to fool you into believing they have perfected the IAA when they may not have any capability to do that. Audit firms will show impressive vision videos of capabilities but will not have anything material to show in the form of an actual product. Embellished stories of successful entrepreneurs will flood the media. AI will even be used to break the law or for illegal activities in audit (we will cover some actual examples of that later in the book). Due to the confusion created by new technologies and the void created by the lack of a body of knowledge, these unfortunate developments will create more risk to the global economy and human civilization.

However, early warning and preparation can help alleviate the miseries of unexpected risks. This book will serve as the first comprehensive guide and body of knowledge for IAA and will prepare you to meet the future of audit.

SOURCES OF COMPETITIVE ADVANTAGE IN THE FOURTH REVOLUTION

A little more than a decade or so ago, if you went to shop for a cellphone or a car, you would not think about asking the salesperson questions such as "Does this cellphone have an agent that I can talk to?" or "Does this car park itself?" But now these questions are considered normal. What happened here? You can see that we are not just asking for normal digital or mechanical capabilities. We expect our phones and cars to be smart, intelligent, and autonomous. All that points to the fact that the core competitive advantage of a firm now gets defined by how intelligent and autonomous its products/services and operations are.

There are two sources of competitive advantage in the fourth revolution: "automation" and "intelligence."

- **Intelligence:** Intelligence implies the ability of an entity to constantly evaluate and understand its environment and develop an effective strategy to pursue its goals. This advantage is created by embedding intelligence in both products and services – as well as by developing the entire operational and management platform of a company. An intelligent company strives to increase its strategic, operational, and product/service-based intelligence. Collectively such intelligence results in creating higher customer value and allows the firm to win more clients, develop lasting relationships with them, and earn their trust. This attribute increases the competitive potential of an entity and impacts its ability to survive in the new business environment. Intelligence is manifested when an entity gains greater advantage in terms of pursuing its goals.
- **Automation:** Automation refers to all work automation – and not just mechanical automation. Automation can be intelligent or unintelligent. For example, a conveyer belt automates the transfer of goods from one point to another. It is automated but not intelligent. To make it intelligent, we can embed some intelligent features in the conveyer belt. For example, the conveyor belt will only run if apples or apple products are placed on it and not if they are oranges or anything else. The converter belt will run faster with apples but slower if apple juice is placed on it.

As shown in Figure 2.3, human work is both cognitive and physical. During the first three industrial revolutions we automated physical work using mechanical and electrical technologies. Now we are automating the cognitive work. Note that while all (synthetic) intelligence automates, not all automation is intelligent.

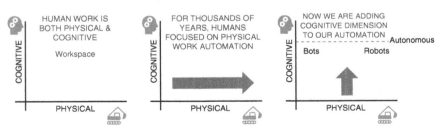

FIGURE 2.3 The Workspace Automation

AUDIT MAGNIFICATION

Even though the traditional audit is by design explicitly focused on the financial statements and the assertions made therein, the reality of business is more than what is reflected in the financial statements and the disclosures. Even with that extremely limited focus, audit has been ineffective to improve the quality of audit and to increase its effectiveness.

In their legendary analysis, DeFond and Zhang argue that "auditors' responsibilities extend well beyond the simple detection of 'black and white' GAAP violations, to providing assurance of financial reporting quality" (DeFond and Zhang, 2014). DeFond and Zhang clarify that while audit quality is a "continuous construct that assures financial reporting quality," it relies upon the financial reporting system of a firm, and that the financial system maps to the firm's underlying economics. In response to DeFond and Zhang's analysis, Donovan et al. proposed that the competitive advantages of auditors and the institutional factors of the audit process be incorporated in the definition of audit quality (Donovan et al., 2014).

Therefore, to establish the competitive advantage and to truly create value for clients, legacy audit firms need to be viewed as more than simply check-the-box firms. Audit quality in legacy audit firms, however, continues to be a problem. Even though auditors complain about the Public Company Accounting Oversight Board (PCAOB) and question the value of PCAOB inspections (Johnson et al., 2014), a PCAOB report claims that PCAOB inspections improve the quality of internal controls in audits (Defond and Lennox, 2017).

Looking at it from an outside-in perspective, we can state the unfortunate truth that audit is failing to deliver value, to earn and maintain public trust, and to improve audit quality even within the extremely limited and narrow scope of the responsibility undertaken by the profession. If we expand the responsibility to include factors such as business risk, operational performance, and strategy analysis, the profession seems to be unprepared to handle all that.

Since AI now allows us to go beyond the traditional and narrow scope of auditing, there are many compelling reasons to develop a new audit magnification framework. Here are some areas that can be improved with intelligent automation:

- **Fraud vs. Value Destruction:** Value destruction due to flawed operational or financial decision-making destroys more value than fraud and yet it rarely comes under scrutiny (Graham et al., 2006). Flawed decision-making can come from many areas. For example, companies may intentionally neglect to deploy resources in areas where they could receive better insights, thus practicing intentional ignorance. Management may destroy value by engaging in projects that serve the managers' own interests but at the cost of the shareholders.

- **Use Law as an Advantage:** In today's world, many firms believe that by surrounding themselves with the protective shield of attorneys they can operate on the edge of the law. The AI revolution will make it very hard to do that. Since the intelligent automation is, by definition, evidence based (i.e., based upon the data), the old-style nepotistic relationships will be easily discoverable.
- **Shareholder Value versus Social Value:** While shareholder value has been the driving force of value creation for a long time, modern society has recognized the value of including social responsibility as a driver of value. This means to understand the impact that a firm's activities make on society, environment, and the economy. This concept, well understood both in sustainability circles as well as corporate social responsibility forums, requires a fresh approach to incorporate nontraditional frameworks. Known as integrated reporting, in South Africa, where such reports are not required, companies voluntarily provide such information (du Toit, 2017). Legacy audits don't focus on this; however, in the new audit approach as discussed in this book, social value creation and financial audit will go hand in hand.
- **Preemptive Intervention:** The ability to preemptively intervene and fix business problems is not recognized as a value in audits. Auditors tend to focus on the historical financial statements while ignoring the future of the firm. The new audit will establish the temporal balance, giving auditors the ability to study the current position and analyze the future.
- **AI-Related Problems:** AI is bound to create its own problems. Countries, institutions, companies, and lives can be destroyed with the power of AI. Governance and ethics are important considerations for intelligent automation. From an auditor's perspective this introduces an entirely new set of risks.

AUTOMATION = 3 AS (AUDIT, ACTIVISM, ASSURANCE)

As such, IAA will enable us to consolidate the three broad areas of Audit, Activism, and Assurance. Activism in this context implies the use of forensic accounting to make or defend claims against a firm, as well as to introduce the concept of shareholder and stakeholder value creation assessment and preemptive intervention.

With the 3 As, the same framework or platform that is used for audit can also be used for value management and overall governance of a firm.

Key Points

- The AI revolution is not an extension of the digital revolution. It is an era of its own.
- The Fourth Industrial Revolution is upon us and intelligent automation is at its core.
- The new era offers incredible career enhancing opportunities to auditors and finance experts.
- A new type of professional IAAP (IAA Professional) will be needed for this new era.
- Competitive advantage comes from intelligence and automation.
- Audit magnification is expanding the scope of traditional audit to include other coverage areas.
- Audit magnification can be enabled by the same automated platform where it can serve audit, assurance, and activism needs.

REFERENCES

DeFond, M. L. and Lennox, C. S. (2017) Do PCAOB inspections improve the quality of internal control audits? *Journal of Accounting Research*, 55 (3): 591–627.

DeFond, M. and Zhang, J. (2014) A review of archival auditing research. *Journal of Accounting and Economics*, 58 (2–3): 275–326. [online]. Available from: http://dx.doi.org/10.1016/j.jacceco.2014.09.002.

Donovan, J., Frankel, R., Lee, J., Martin, X., and Seo, H. (2014) Issues raised by studying DeFond and Zhang: What should audit researchers do? *Journal of Accounting and Economics*, 58 (2–3): 327–338. Available from: http://dx.doi.org/10.1016/j.jacceco.2014.09.001.

du Toit, E. (2017) The readability of integrated reports. *Meditari Accountancy Research*, 25 (4): 629–653.

Graham, J. R., Harvey, C. R., and Rajgopal, S. (2006) Value destruction and financial reporting decisions. *Financial Analysts Journal*, 62 (6): 27–39.

Johnson, L. M., Keune, M. B., and Winchel, J. (2014) Auditor perceptions of the PCAOB oversight process. *Univ. Tennessee Work. Paper.* [online]. Available from: http://citeseerx.ist.psu.edu/viewdoc/download?doi=10.1.1.436.9940&rep=rep1&type=pdf.

Lynch, S. (2017) Andrew Ng: Why AI is the new electricity. *Stanford News* [online]. Available from: https://news.stanford.edu/thedish/2017/03/14/andrew-ng-why-ai-is-the-new-electricity/.

Perez, C. (2002) *Technological Revolutions and Financial Capital: The dynamics of bubbles and golden ages*. Northampton, MA: Edward Elgar.

Schwab, K. (2016) *The Fourth Industrial Revolution*. World Economic Forum (ed.). Geneva: Switzerland.

CHAPTER THREE

What Is Artificial Intelligence?

A S THE YEAR 2017 CAME to a close, the Big Four audit firms in the UK found themselves in hot water. Those whose assurance was supposed to be the pillar of trust upon which the financial markets' credibility and investor confidence reside were questioned and fined by the regulator. Something wasn't right. The audit quality was slipping. The process was failing. It appeared that audit firms were becoming better at winning business, but unable to deliver against the high standards set for the profession.

The concerns rose across a wide spectrum of stakeholders and the rendering of fines did not terminate the mounting trepidation. The actions of the regulators were followed by Parliament getting involved. A bill was proposed to break up the Big Four monopolies. In early 2019, the Business, Energy, and Industrial Strategy Committee of the UK Parliament held a session to question the representatives of "challenger" accountancy firms, including Grant Thornton, BDO, and Mazars (Parliament, 2019). The session was followed by questioning the Big Four – PwC, EY, Deloitte, and KPMG. The Committee raised concerns about the problems with the audit quality as well as lack of competition in the audit market. Pointing to the fact that 97% of the FTSE 350 market share is held by the Big Four audit firms, smaller firms pleaded that they needed to invest in technology and people in order to qualify for large clients (Competition and Markets Authority (CMA), 2019).

The growing rage from various elements of society demanded sincere introspection from the leading audit firms. They understood that the quality of audit needed to be improved, the reliability enhanced. As the Big Four reflected on what they could do, one of the major focus areas that emerged was the use of artificial intelligence (AI) to improve the audit effectiveness and efficiency.

While the example of the Big Four shows the adoption of AI to automate some parts of the audit process, consider the opportunity to strategically link these audit tasks in a series of interconnected and interdependent chunks to automate the entire audit process. Perhaps this is the reason why Osborn and Frey predicted, in their landmark paper, the likelihood of total audit automation as 94% (Frey and Osborne, 2017). Whether you are with the Big Four or not, clearly AI is the future of the audit and accounting profession.

The problems with audit quality, almost in every case, are human related and not procedural. In other words, the issues existed not because the audit methods failed or were not sufficient to perform a quality audit, but because of human error in judgment. AI does not eliminate human work as much as it eliminates human work errors, mistakes, and intentional misconduct.

A BRIEF HISTORY OF AI

The recent rise and the astounding novelty of AI belie the fact that the field has been around since the middle of the twentieth century. If you have seen the movie *The Imitation Game*, you will know that the movie is based upon a real story that depicts Alan Turing, the scientist who helped break the Nazi codes used in the Enigma machine and hence played a powerful role in helping the Allied forces win World War II against Nazi Germany. The same person also wrote an article published in 1950, titled "Computing Machinery and Intelligence," which began by asking the question, "Can machines think?" Alan Turning's article prompted others to think about the possibilities and nearly five years later three scientists sent out an invitation to several other scientists to hold a 6- to 8-week-long brainstorming session at Dartmouth in 1956. The proposal received wide acceptance and at the conclusion of that meeting, the field of AI was formally created.

The decades that followed turned out to be a rollercoaster for the field and the AI industry, as euphoric optimism was followed by states of hopeless despair. Periods known as the winters of AI happened in the 1960s, 1970s, and 1980s, when investment dried up and projects were folded. Overpromising and underdelivering led to credibility loss, and what was once considered possible turned into a despondent dream. Even though the failure was obvious, and the menacing overcast of negativity and pessimism could have shattered the research sanguinity, the AI research community continued to flounder through the wreckage left by the AI winters. Spirited and resilient in their pursuits, AI researchers produced some of the groundbreaking research in the 1970s and 1980s that would later create the foundation for a revolution to take shape.

 ## LAUNCHPAD FACTORS

While the research breakthroughs were central to advancing the field, many of the critical elements needed for the launchpad were provided by the Internet and mobile phone revolutions. Specifically, five areas of capabilities sealed the powerful rise and the fate of the AI revolution:

1. **Data, Data, and More Data:** Smart phones and the Internet became the sources of immense amounts of data. From pictures to videos and documents to voice, we began piling up representations of our physical, cognitive, and time realities, capturing them in digital formats and loading them into the ocean of Internet. The digital content swelled, and so did our ability to tap into that data to gain new insights, develop new perspectives, discover new knowledge, and make better decisions. Algorithms that had been around since the 1960s, 1970s, and 1980s, and that were famished for data, suddenly found a new life. Like an animal species discovering a new and immense source of nourishment, the algorithms were deployed to voraciously gulp down the vast data sets. The age of AI had arrived. Among millions of other potential applications, images were used for recognition, videos for CGI, voice for security, IoT data for improving machine performance, and transactional data for making business decisions. A cycle was created where data generation increased the ability to find new patterns, to classify based upon predetermined criteria, and even to learn from the age-old reward-and-punishment model. All of that was made possible because of the data.
2. **Data Storage and Management:** The ability to produce data is one thing; being able to store it in a cost-effective way and organize it for fast retrieval is another. The work done by software and hardware engineers, as well as data managers, enabled us to store all the data being produced by us and our machines. The storage cost declined with technologies such as cloud, and the data management profession, and the data management body of knowledge, added to our ability to organize quality data and to make data more usable. Algorithms that have the propensity to devour

data entered a world where data was plentiful and data's variety, volume, and veracity were manageable.

3. **Processing Power:** The increase in processing power can be viewed in two ways: the graphic processing unit (GPU)-based power and the architectural power. The GPU power enhancement improved the ability of a machine to process data and the big data architectural improvement enabled multiple machines to work together in collaboration with each other to process major volumes of data. The combined effect of the two empowered the algorithms to achieve learning efficiency. How long it takes to process something is a major performance attribute of computational efficiency. Besides the nature and volume of data and the type of algorithm selected to solve a particular problem, what drives this performance attribute is processing power. Problems that used to take days or even weeks to solve, can now be solved in minutes and seconds. Great strides were made in improving processing power and that had a direct impact on greater use of machine learning.

4. **Global Network:** Unlike other fields, research sharing in the AI community comes with its own style and subtleties. This unique style is interesting enough to be described as "swag" by younger generations. First, the style element of that swag is that research sharing is done aggressively. The generous research sharing, at least up until the governments got involved, created an aura of global collaboration. Second, the time between authoring a research paper and its publication was kept to a minimum. This means that unlike social sciences where researchers have to wait, for what often seems like eternity, to get published, the research in AI is published quickly. Third, the large number of conferences allow ample opportunity for researchers to present research. With the Internet creating a globally networked community, the AI field experienced a sharp surge in research. Discovery accelerated and AI products and services found a new life.

5. **Algorithms and Approaches:** Even though the AI field experienced several winters, the optimism among the AI research community never faded. Committed as ever, they worked diligently to create new discoveries and solve problems. It may have been winter outside, but inside the research centers it was always spring. Many new approaches and algorithms were developed and presented. In many cases, algorithms that lay dormant because of a lack of processing power or data suddenly got a new life. The AI world was ready to leave behind its final winter.

Collectively, the work product of the last 50-plus years found its zenith when all the above forces lined up to support a spectacular resurgence in AI.

This time around, however, the only difference was that there was no going back. Just around 2011 or so, the winters were finally over and a permanent spring started.

DATA SCIENCE, MACHINE LEARNING, AI, AND EVERYTHING ELSE

The plethora of terminology that exists to describe the AI field can be overwhelming for those who are not exposed to it. It would be beneficial for the reader to get an understanding of these areas. First, let us clarify some of the misconceptions:

- **AI is IT:** As business professionals discover the remarkable potential of AI, they tend to reach out to their IT teams to seek help. Your general IT function may not have the capability to understand or serve your needs in AI. IT is not AI, and AI is not IT.
- **AI is machine learning:** The AI field is broader than just machine learning. Machine learning is one area in the broad AI field.
- **RPA is AI:** Robotic process automation (RPA) is sometimes confused with AI. While one can argue that a simple functional RPA bot can be viewed as a simple agent that performs as it is instructed to do, literally any software can be described that way. Hence, it is important to view RPA as a either a very rudimentary AI or not AI at all.
- **Data management is data science:** Some people also make the mistake of confusing data management with data science. Data management deals with organizing data while data science refers to using the data to build intelligent products and services.
- **Machine learning is the new AI and the old methods are not relevant anymore:** Significant recent developments in the AI field (for example, deep learning) may lead some to believe that the older models and approaches are not relevant anymore. This is not true. The new approaches are complementary to the older approaches. In fact, the older approaches are more suitable for certain types of problem classes. More recent developments when combined with the older methods give more robust and comprehensive solutions. For example, in many cases financial services providers need instantaneous decision-making on credit approvals and while neural networks (modern approach) can do the job, given the current state of the technology it is not possible to explain the reasoning behind the decision made by the neural network. For regulatory reasons, however, such decisions need to be explained. For example, a

judge in a court of law may want to know how a credit decision was made. For these types of situations, the search methods from classical AI would be far more useful. The key point is that machine learning is not the only AI branch that will be needed for audit transformation. We will need to include other types of AI also.

- **Machine learning is not AI:** Machine learning is based upon one branch of AI that is derived from statistical learning methods. The AI field is composed of many branches. In his book *The Master Algorithm*, Domingos calls them the tribes of AI (Domingos, 2015). In some cases, the tribalism is so prevalent that some hardcore adherents may describe machine learning as independent of AI. From their perspective AI is the rules-based approach enabled by search mechanisms while machine learning is statistical learning and hence is independent of the AI field. As explained before, machine learning is a branch of AI. Machine learning is not one method. There are several methods, ways of doing things, processes, problem areas, and approaches to machine learning. Many of those are described in the next two chapters.

From the perspective of this book, I prefer to view the AI field as composed of two main areas: the rule-based approach and the statistical learning approach. The first approach gave us the expert systems and RPA. The second approach (i.e., statistical learning) is what is driving the machine learning revolution. The Defense Advanced Research Projects Agency (DARPA) breaks down the two types into what DARPA calls the first and the second waves of AI (Launchbur, 2017).

 ## DEFINITION OF AI

There are many definitions of AI. Several definitions cluster around building machines that can perform tasks that are typically performed by humans. For instance, IEEE defines artificial intelligence as:

> The combination of cognitive automation, machine learning, reasoning, hypothesis generation and analysis, natural language processing, and intentional algorithm mutation producing insights and analytics at or above human capability. (IEEE Corporate Advisory Group (CAG), 2017)

While I like most of those definitions, I define artificial intelligence as:

The technology with the ability to achieve goals in uncertain environments.

This definition establishes that we are conceptualizing an artifact that possesses artificial intelligence. This artifact dwells in or interacts with an environment. That environment can have many states. A single state environment has absolutely no change and will not require any intelligence to act upon. It will always be in the same state no matter what happens. It is not very interesting from our perspective.

A simple switch (on and off) has two states and can be viewed as an environment where, depending upon some condition, an AI entity can turn the switch on or off. This is an extremely limited use of intelligence – but at least now we have an environment that has some uncertainty (i.e., on or off).

As an environment becomes more complex, greater intelligence is needed to navigate through that. However, what do we mean by navigate through the uncertain environment? Why would an entity do that? The answer is that intelligent entity will not just wander through an uncertain situation purposelessly. It will always have a goal – even if the goal is to discover and explore (which may feel like purposeless wandering, but is not).

For example, performing a simple internal controls assessment based upon data provided is a process that has a large uncertainty. Even in a simple situation, there could be many possibilities. If you made a tree of how many on–off switches you would need for a complex problem like performing an internal controls audit, it can easily be composed of thousands or even millions of switches. To get to the right answers, your artifact will have to tread through that tree and make decisions along the way. But it will do that in accordance with some performance criteria and a goal. It will know when it has achieved its goal (i.e., completed its assessment).

An intelligent entity pursues and achieves goals in uncertain situations. Ideally, the intelligent entity will learn and constantly improve. It will accumulate experience and learn from mistakes. It will become better with each try.

In summary, artificial intelligence, or AI, is the technology (implying it is synthetic, engineered, and not natural or biological) that can pursue goals in uncertain environments.

TURING TEST

The Turing Test can be viewed as a measure of intelligence in an AI artifact. Another way to think about the Turing Test is to ask the question whether a computer can think like a human or not. It is named after Alan Turing (Turing, 1950). It can be viewed as a simple test where a human (Person B) and a computer (AI) interact with another person (Person A). The two humans and the computer are all located in separate rooms. The interaction is happening via computer terminals. Person A is talking to the computer (AI) and also to a human (Figure 3.1). Person A asks the questions and Person B and the computer (AI) answer the questions. During a sustained conversation, if Person A cannot tell the difference whether she is conversing with a computer or a human, the Turing Test is passed; else it failed.

Despite the advances in technology, it is safe to say that the Turing Test has not been fully passed. In certain cases, Turing can be passed if the environment is limited such that Person A can only ask specific or very limited questions. Even with the smartest computer, within a couple of minutes you will be able to tell if you are talking to a computer or a human. Humans have this great capacity to understand and tell stories, to understand and respond to humor, to talk about various subjects, to converse naturally, to use language creatively, and to understand the context in conversations. AI is still far away from having that.

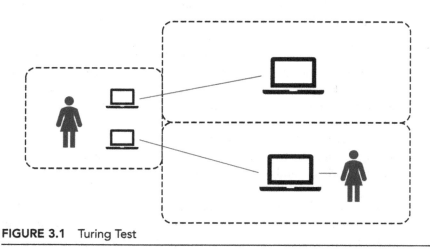

FIGURE 3.1 Turing Test

NARROW VERSUS GENERAL AI

Narrow AI

Narrow AI (also known as weak AI) is a system that can automate tasks that are typically performed by humans but do so in a specific narrow knowledge domain. The task could be descriptive, predictive, or prescriptive and the performance of the machine can be equal to or better than that of the human.

Artificial General Intelligence

Artificial general intelligence (AGI) is artificial intelligence that can perform human expert tasks in multiple domains. Their performance can be equal to or better than a human. AGI interacts with humans in a manner that humans cannot tell the difference whether they are acting with a machine or a human. In other words, they pass the Turing Test.

VIEW OF THE ENTERPRISE

For more than five decades, computers have played a powerful role in transforming our business and personal lives. The rise of computers in the business world can be described in four layers of recording transactions, analyzing or counting, optimizing, and predicting. These capabilities enabled us to design and develop descriptive, prescriptive, and predictive systems.

As shown in Figure 3.2, the left side displays the existing tech stack of a legacy firm. A legacy firm will generally have systems that transact, analyze, optimize, and predict. As shown in the middle, now we are adding learning capabilities. When we add the learning component, we get a three-layered architecture shown on the right (known as the CAT structure for Cognitive, Analytical, and Transactional). Our transactional systems reside in the bottom layer. Our analytical systems (e.g., Business Analytics) reside in the middle layer. And our Cognitive systems (e.g., RPA, Machine Learning) reside as the top layer.

In some ways we can assume that by adding the new learning layer, we are automating the four tasks of transacting, analyzing, optimizing, and predicting – and enhancing the machine's ability to autonomously perform the

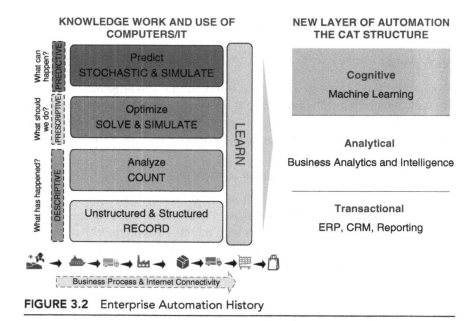

FIGURE 3.2 Enterprise Automation History

work of descriptive, prescriptive, and predictive analytics and with relevance and accuracy that is equal to or greater than a human's.

 TOOLKIT FOR INTELLIGENT AUDIT AUTOMATION

As we envision and design the cognitive architecture, we recognize that we will need to use many different types of intelligent technologies. In addition to the IT infrastructure composed of regular software, analytics, business intelligence, data repositories, ETL, and other regularly used IT tools, IAA requires four specific technologies:

1. **Robotic Process Automation:** RPA is designed to replace repeatable human work where automation is done in an outside-in manner (van der Aalst et al., 2018). RPA is a software that (1) uses structured input (2) to process the input through rules (3) in order to generate some specific output. It is essentially a digital bot that is configured to automate simple, repeatable, low options tasks. RPA is also designed in a manner whereby it minimizes coding and is easy to use. While RPA vendors will claim that anyone can use it and that people with no knowledge or background

can easily automate functions from their desktops, RPA is a bit more complicated. RPA is now being used for audit automation (Zhang, 2019).

2. **Expert Systems:** Built mostly with if–then rules, expert systems are systems that emulate human expert decision-making. Expert knowledge is expressed as rules and decision-making is enabled by reasoning. Expert systems have been extensively used in audit. Significant literature exists on their use for audit purposes. However, recent analysis shows that their use has declined, and it appears that some of the more prominent expert systems are no longer being used (Gray et al., 2014).

3. **Process Mining:** Process mining refers to having automated ability to scan and extract knowledge from event logs. Such knowledge is used to identify and monitor processes. Our existing systems collect tons of meta-data about transactions and that meta-data can be used to understand the origins, steps, and ends of various processes. The discovered processes can be compared against some standards to determine compliance. They are also used to identify exceptions or anomalies. Process mining is now extensively used in audit (van der Aalst et al., 2010; Jans et al., 2013) and when combined with other systems can produce powerful results toward integrated IAA.

4. **Machine Learning:** Machine learning is a statistical learning method that uses data and algorithms to teach machines to perform tasks that are typically performed by humans. Machine learning is used in automating processes as well as automating both physical and cognitive work. We will cover machine learning in detail in the next two chapters.

Learning machines can be thought of as types of systems: (1) machines that are taught a specific function, and once they learn the task, they can continue to perform that task; and (2) machines that continue to learn and improve through experience. In both cases, some type of a performance measure is established, and the machine performs or improves in reference to the performance measure. It also implies that the machine is trying to perform a task in accordance with a goal.

The "doing" part of the task means that there is some input that comes from the machine's environment. The machine processes the input and then gives out something as output. The experience part is related to learning, that is, the machine's ability to learn.

A learning machine therefore can be viewed as intelligent. This machine operates in an environment and its environment can be simple or complex. The machine must have a way to receive the input. It should also have a way to use a learning method so it can learn.

Key Points

- AI is being viewed as a solution to several recent problems in audits.
- AI is not a new field. It has been around since the 1940s.
- AI has experienced several winters.
- Five factors have influenced the recent surge in AI: data, processing power, global research networks, algorithms, and data management.
- AI, data science, data management, and machine learning are different concepts. It is important to clarify them.
- The modern enterprise can now be viewed as three-layered architecture of cognitive, analytics, and transactional systems.
- The toolkit for IAA includes RPA, process mining, expert systems, and machine learning.

 ## REFERENCES

van der Aalst, W. M. P., Bichler, M. and Heinzl, A. (2018) Robotic process automation. *Business and Information Systems Engineering*, 60 (4): 269–272. Available from: https://doi.org/10.1007/s12599-018-0542-4.

van der Aalst, W. M. P., van Hee, K. M., van eer Werf, J. M., and Verdonk, M. (2010) Auditing 2.0: Using process mining to support tomorrow's auditor. *IEEE Computer*, 43 (3): 90–93.

Competition and Markets Authority CMA (2019) *Statutory audit services market study*. [online]. Available from: https://assets.publishing.service.gov.uk/media/5d03667d40f0b609ad3158c3/audit_final_report_02.pdf. (April). [online].

Domingos, P. (2015) *The master algorithm: How the quest for the ultimate learning machine will remake our world*. New York: Basic Books.

Frey, C. B. and Osborne, M. A. 2017. The future of employment: How susceptible are jobs to computerisation? *Technological forecasting and social change*, 114 (C): 254–280.

Gray, G. L., Chiu, V., Liu, Q., and Li, P. (2014) The expert systems life cycle in AIS research: What does it mean for future AIS research? *International Journal of Accounting Information Systems*, 15 (4): 423–451. Available from: http://dx.doi.org/10.1016/j.accinf.2014.06.001.

IEEE Corporate Advisory Group (CAG) (2017) IEEE Guide for Terms and Concepts in Intelligent Process Automation. *The Institute of Electrical and Electronics Engineers Standards Association*, 1–16.

Jans, M., Alles, M., and Vasarhelyi, M. (2013) The case for process mining in auditing: Sources of value added and areas of application. *International Journal of Accounting Information Systems*, 14 (1): 1–20. Available from: http://dx .doi.org/10.1016/j.accinf.2012.06.015.

Launchbur, J. (2017) *A DARPA Perspective on Artificial Intelligence* [online]. Available from: https://www.youtube.com/watch?v=-O01G3tSYpU (Accessed 11 March 2019).

Parliament, U. (2019) *Big 4 accountancy firms questioned on future of audit inquiry* [online]. Available from: https://www.parliament.uk/business/ committees/committees-a-z/commons-select/business-energy-industrial-strategy/news-parliament-2017/big-4-accountancy-firms-questioned-on-future-of-audit-inquiry-evidence-17-19-/.

Turing, A. M. (1950) Computing machinery and intelligence, *Mind*, 49: 433–460.

Zhang, Abigail C. (2019) Intelligent process automation in audit. *SSRN Electronic Journal* [online].

CHAPTER FOUR

Rise of Machine Learning

A CCOUNTANTS UNDERSTAND AND SPEAK the language of business. Becoming an accountant is not a trivial undertaking. Through their training and education, they acquire the ability to abstract all the activities of a business to a higher dimension and then provide a measure of the business's performance at any given time. That ability to abstract and translate business activities into accounting frameworks requires years of sophisticated training. One has to understand the business context, observe the activity, determine if it is accounting worthy, abstract the key features of the transaction, cull out the recordable elements, and then record the transaction in the right buckets. The cognitive tasks of doing these steps are complex. Yet, experts are forecasting that most, if not all, of the accounting process will be automated. Many projects are underway to do just that. The optimism about the ability to achieve that automation is driven by the recent developments in machine learning. As previously stated, machine learning is a branch of artificial intelligence.

 POWER OF PATTERNS

Point to a toy car and ask a child what is it that you are pointing to and it is likely that the child will respond "a car." The child never sat in the toy car. She never went in that car for a drive. But she calls it a car anyway. In her mind the toy car carries some properties of a real car and therefore it is a car.

Nature's strategy for achieving complexity from simplicity is evident in both the physical and cognitive constructs of our world. Human learning is no different. While the apparatus used for learning in humans is composed of 2.5 pounds of matter that we call brain, this organ can create colossally impressive work products, emotions, strategies, and survival mechanisms.

At the root of all cognitive learning and functions are some basic mechanisms at work. For example, the ability to identify things, that is, to know the difference between a chair and a table, a car and a truck, a human and an ape. This ability to identify things goes beyond being able to name things. For instance, when we scan a bar code, the computer returns the name of the product. But humans do not need any bar codes to name products. When we see one, we know it is a car or a truck or a bus. When we hear the word "car," it brings to mind an understanding what that word means. We even assign properties such as "new car smell" to a car and can determine if we are in a car simply by smell or the tactile feeling by touch.

The meaning comes from our knowledge of what a car does, what it looks like, feels like, its function and other such things. It is as if we have templates in our minds that say if certain properties add up, then it must be a car. The specific configuration of those properties is what we can call a pattern. Thus, pattern can be viewed as an expression of a certain assembly of properties with some values. In some ways, we can view our world – that is, all the things we can name – as pattern configurations.

Humans are good at identifying patterns. For instance, when we use the word "car" and we are given two very different looking cars, for example, a Mini and a Mercedes, we are able to determine that both are cars. This means that our ability to name a car as a car is not specific to a particular instance of a car, but instead it is a general concept of what a car is. This means that our templates are not rigid. They are somewhat generalizable. It also means that when we assign meaning via pattern configurations, we do that in a class membership fashion. In other words, we can define a class based upon some properties and the class can have members – and we can form subclasses based upon different values of the properties. But every one of those classes are expressions of patterns with some properties and values of those properties. For example, Automobiles > Cars > Mercedes, each can be thought of as a class with some properties that generalize over some values.

Based on the above discussion, we can see that our pattern recognition falls under at least two concept categories. The first is about understanding general categories, that is, abstracting something to a level where we understand that members of that class represent a pattern (e.g., four wheels, steering wheel, seats belong to the class car) of some type.

Second, pattern recognition is being able to read the tealeaves. This means to get some related data about something and then based upon that being able to project. We do that intuitively by knowing the relationships between things. The pattern configurations are not limited to objects or things. They can also represent relationships between things. For example, when we see clouds forming, we can anticipate that rain is coming. In this example, both cloud and rain can be viewed as pattern configurations – each with their respective properties. When combined, they also possess a relationship pattern where we can observe that the presence of one can lead to the other. In some ways, we can view that the cloud-forming was a property of rain. We can add other factors to that as well. Other pattern elements could be temperature, wind, moisture, and so on. But how do we know what is temperature as a concept, what is wind, what is cloud formation, what is moisture? Well, we can use the same strategy, that is, to understand each of them by their properties. Clouds have a visual look – dark clouds, high clouds, and so on.

Here we run into a conceptual problem. The concept of pattern configuration as an assembly of properties and their values appears to be recursive and circular when we argue that properties themselves are pattern configurations of other properties, which are pattern configurations of other properties, and so on. It is as if nothing meaningful exists in the world except patterns, and perhaps that is why the human mind assigns meaning to things via pattern configuration. We can live with this recursiveness and circularity by consoling ourselves that it appears to be nature's strategy of achieving complexity from simplicity.

WHAT IS MACHINE LEARNING?

Based upon the above discussion, we discovered the following interesting concepts (see Figure 4.1):

There is something we are trying to predict. In the above example, it was rain. We can give it a name. Let us call it the **output variable** (also known as the dependent variable, target variable, or simply y).

We understood that there are properties or associations of rain that help us determine what is rain or help us predict if it will rain or not. For example, properties that might inform us whether it is rain or not could

Features, Attributes, or Dimensions

x1	x2	x3	x4	x5	x6	x7	x8	x9	x10	y
687	0.613	420.912	257.89	0.240	61.995	14.90	0.619	9.226	5.71	1
868	0.738	640.163	472.13	0.422	199.290	84.12	0.443	37.243	16.49	1
745	0.141	105.164	14.84	0.724	10.745	7.78	0.800	6.224	4.98	0
83	0.929	77.107	71.63	0.022	1.544	0.03	0.887	0.030	0.03	1
381	0.052	19.816	1.03	0.370	0.381	0.14	0.806	0.114	0.09	1
570	0.291	165.814	48.24	0.899	43.349	38.96	0.027	1.049	0.03	0
326	0.546	178.044	97.24	0.813	79.078	64.31	0.914	58.770	53.71	1
48	0.958	45.987	44.06	0.066	2.904	0.19	0.443	0.085	0.04	0
568	0.434	246.282	106.79	0.554	59.123	32.73	0.791	25.879	20.46	0
88	0.689	60.650	41.80	0.255	10.647	2.71	0.381	1.034	0.39	0
150	0.259	38.864	10.07	0.471	4.739	2.23	0.393	0.877	0.35	1
689	0.728	501.604	365.18	0.728	265.867	193.56	0.690	133.501	92.08	0
671	0.494	331.356	163.63	0.713	116.700	83.23	0.865	71.962	62.22	0
162	0.260	42.102	10.94	0.829	9.070	7.52	0.513	3.858	1.98	0
128	0.982	125.657	123.36	0.379	46.731	17.70	0.561	9.936	5.58	0
252	0.361	90.971	32.84	0.060	1.972	0.12	0.158	0.019	0.00	0
484	0.985	476.585	469.28	0.047	22.036	1.03	0.052	0.053	0.00	1
169	0.143	24.138	3.45	0.262	0.903	0.24	0.402	0.095	0.04	1
842	0.320	269.073	85.99	0.687	59.106	40.63	0.964	39.162	37.75	1
33	0.630	20.784	13.09	0.216	2.830	0.61	0.414	0.253	0.10	0
220	0.796	175.090	139.35	0.870	121.294	105.58	0.207	21.824	4.51	1
493	0.805	397.086	319.83	0.753	240.976	181.56	0.884	160.455	141.80	1
620	0.295	182.662	53.82	0.388	20.888	8.11	0.244	1.975	0.48	1
466	0.639	297.859	190.39	0.722	137.386	99.14	0.241	23.928	5.78	0
686	0.751	514.874	386.44	0.436	168.606	73.56	0.272	20.005	5.44	1
403	0.695	280.264	194.91	0.155	30.265	4.70	0.279	1.313	0.37	1
434	0.842	365.488	307.79	0.041	12.482	0.51	0.671	0.340	0.23	0
110	0.736	80.987	59.63	0.494	29.477	14.57	0.001	0.008	0.00	0
359	0.474	170.335	80.82	0.545	44.035	23.99	0.936	22.452	21.01	1
226	0.603	136.202	82.08	0.890	73.018	64.95	0.427	27.762	11.87	1
704	0.245	172.658	42.34	0.983	41.613	40.89	0.829	33.904	28.11	1
948	0.967	916.701	886.43	0.043	38.009	1.63	0.064	0.104	0.01	1
501	0.676	338.921	229.28	0.228	52.170	11.87	0.075	0.895	0.07	1
70	0.698	48.834	34.07	0.805	27.428	22.08	0.459	10.133	4.65	0
73	0.832	60.735	50.53	0.383	19.345	7.41	0.479	3.548	1.70	1
599	0.862	516.546	445.44	0.523	233.176	122.06	0.693	84.542	58.56	1
577	0.418	241.042	100.70	0.150	15.151	2.28	0.593	1.351	0.80	0
960	0.790	758.844	599.84	0.074	44.241	3.26	0.979	3.194	3.13	0
568	0.231	131.169	30.29	0.314	9.520	2.99	0.735	2.199	1.62	1
768	0.251	192.781	48.39	0.014	0.671	0.01	0.828	0.008	0.01	1
981	0.226	221.895	50.19	0.766	38.437	29.44	0.860	25.302	21.75	0
785	0.322	252.556	81.25	0.807	65.555	52.89	0.315	16.674	5.25	0
387	0.836	323.676	270.71	0.749	202.832	151.97	0.189	28.775	5.45	0
799	0.110	87.717	9.63	0.181	1.744	0.32	0.165	0.052	0.01	0
236	0.740	174.688	129.30	0.678	87.671	59.44	0.126	7.501	0.95	1
835	0.598	499.009	298.22	0.606	180.784	109.59	0.429	47.040	20.19	1
976	0.871	850.444	741.04	0.857	634.856	543.89	0.906	492.751	446.42	1
156	0.069	10.781	0.75	0.176	0.131	0.02	0.168	0.004	0.00	1
917	0.501	459.829	230.58	0.843	194.386	163.87	0.418	68.421	28.57	1
843	0.496	418.048	207.31	0.561	116.367	65.32	0.547	35.712	19.53	0
658	0.607	399.155	242.13	0.164	39.787	6.54	0.804	5.256	4.23	0
761	0.296	225.210	66.65	0.357	23.805	8.50	0.973	8.273	8.05	1
623	0.649	404.062	262.06	0.614	160.971	98.88	0.018	1.808	0.03	1
819	0.544	445.686	242.53	0.892	216.360	193.01	0.986	190.329	187.69	1
790	0.895	707.128	632.95	0.609	385.659	234.98	0.423	99.514	42.14	1
259	0.457	118.486	54.20	0.813	44.063	35.82	0.599	21.453	12.85	0
356	0.652	232.172	151.42	0.950	143.851	136.66	0.010	1.421	0.01	0
356	0.811	288.818	234.31	0.558	130.757	72.97	0.716	52.236	37.39	0
297	0.323	95.807	30.91	0.045	1.383	0.06	0.637	0.039	0.03	0
134	0.920	123.266	113.39	0.802	90.916	72.89	0.289	21.045	6.08	1

X = (x1, x2, x3, x4, ... xn)
These are independent variables, input

Many general problems have just one value of "y" e.g. Spam = Yes or Spam = No

This is the dependent variable, target variable, or output

FIGURE 4.1 Data, Features, and Target

be asking questions like: Is there water pouring down? Is it water? Is it coming from the clouds? etc. To predict if it will rain or not, we will use properties such as clouds, cloud type, moisture, or wind. Let us call these properties or attributes **features**. Features give us information about the target variable and are considered as the input variables or independent variables.

Each of the above features contains values. For example, temperature may contain a range of values, cloud type may be represented on a categorial scale (e.g., numbers 1 to 10, each representing a cloud type), and so on. This is obviously the **data**. We can think of it as the **training data**. Thus, features have data. Conceptualize a table with data in it such that each column represents each feature.

Imagine each row with values of features. Let us call that our **feature vector**.

Lastly, the most important thing is the relationship between features (the properties or attributes) among themselves and with the target variable. This relationship is what forms the patterns we are interested in. We can express this relationship as a mathematical function. Let us call this a **function** we are interested in finding. For example, it may look like:

$$\text{Will it Rain (Y, N)} = w_0 + w_1 * \text{Variable 1} + w_2 * \text{Variable 2}$$
$$+ w_3 * \text{Variable 3} + \ldots$$

Or written differently:

$$f(x) \text{ or } y = w_0 + w_1 x_1 + w_2 x_2 + w_3 x_3 + \ldots \ldots$$

Here "w" is the weights assigned to each variable. You can think of weights as importance assigners – variables with more importance in predicting the output get a higher weight. This means that if we are predicting whether it will rain or not, the variable (e.g., moisture) that has the highest predictive information will have a higher weight. Once we find the weights that can represent our data, we will have the representative function.

In general, machine learning is about finding that function – that is, the function that links the features (input or independent variables) to the output variables.

Notice that this problem is the reverse of what high school algebra trained us for. In algebra, equations (or functions) and the x values would be given to us and we were asked to find the y value. We plugged in the x values, made some adjustments, and then calculated the y value as our answer.

In machine learning, no one gives us the function (the equation). We discover it. We find the function from the data. We are given the x values, and in many cases the y values, and our job becomes to find the function that represents the data we are training it on.

MACHINE LEARNING IS REALLY SCIENTIFIC PROCESS ON STEROIDS

Beyond the human knowledge acquired through observation and direct experience, we also developed the methods that help us identify patterns and find relationships between them. We call it science. It is through scientific method that we are able to identify pattern configurations (i.e., conceptualize new things) and find new relationships between things. When such patterns are sustainable, that is, they do not change, we called them scientific laws.

Think about Newton discovering his laws of motion. His starting point for the laws of motion would not have been that he envisioned the equations and then simply started plugging in numbers. He would have conducted the experiments, collected the data, analyzed the relationship between variables in the data, and then come up with a representative equation. This is what scientists do. They collect data and then understand the mathematical functions that explain the data and the relationships between various variables in the data. Think about it: science discovers patterns in data.

Remarkably, machine learning does the exact same thing – except it does it faster and can find patterns that we can't find on our own.

Machine learning is teaching machines to develop the ability to recognize patterns. Through pattern recognition, machines can do the above mentioned tasks to (1) identify things and (2) identify relationships between things. Stated in terms of patterns, machine learning helps us identify pattern assemblies of things and their relationships.

The field of machine learning, therefore, has two goals. First, it focuses on understanding what learning is. Second, it focuses on figuring out how to embed the ability in machines to learn patterns efficiently and effectively.

THE LEARNING MACHINE

Let's say we are trying to see if the data given to us is about a refrigerator or not. One way we can embed intelligence to identify a refrigerator is by asking questions. We can ask a series of questions and based upon the answers the machine can conclude that we are referring to the refrigerator. For this to happen, we need to teach the machine the rules (i.e., answers to the questions) about the refrigerator. But this type of learning is inefficient. It will take us so many questions to get this right. Imagine the tedious job of programming thousands of if-then-else questions.

A machine that learns must be able to identify patterns. Identifying patterns implies that it learns beyond the specifics. For example, if we have a database of refrigerators with their associated properties, such as size or weight, and we want to search for a specific refrigerator by its properties, it is simple. We can query the database by providing the specific values of the properties (size, weight, etc.) and the database will tell us what refrigerator the property values belongs to. We are able to identify a refrigerator by the values of its properties. But, unfortunately, as you can tell, it is not the type of learning we are interested in. The reason is that if we are not able to provide the specific values, then the query will fail to identify it as a refrigerator. That is because it is unable to generalize the learning.

What if we don't even know it is refrigerator that we are looking for and all we have are the properties and values? Is it possible that we just look at the properties and say the pattern that emerges from these properties really points to a refrigerator?

We want the machine to learn a general pattern where it can develop some intuition about refrigerators. Then when we give it some test data, our learning machine can statistically determine whether the value of the properties adds up to a refrigerator or not.

Since the approach described above is based upon properties and their values lead to specific or general patterns, a learning machine needs the following:

1. An idea of what are the properties (i.e., preexisting simpler patterns).
2. The values of those properties.
3. A method to recognize pattern assemblies (i.e., identify things and identify relationships).
4. In many cases an idea of what we want the machine to do (i.e., do we want it to look at pictures and match people with pictures, or whether we want the machine to predict stock prices, or do we want it to help us discover a fraud).
5. A performance measure that shows how accurately the machine is performing.

In the machine learning world, the above five points are described as follows.

- **Features:** The properties or attributes are known as features. For example, a house can have the features such as number of bedrooms, number of baths, number of garages, size of the lot, size of the house, etc. An image's features could be the intensity of color as measured by pixels. A document's features are its words. This is the same concept that was presented earlier in the chapter.

- **Features Vector:** Once we have determined the features (properties), we need some type of values assigned to those features. Just knowing that a house has all the features listed above will not be helpful unless we have values assigned to those features. Only with those values we can tell the difference between two houses (e.g., the one with two beds and two baths and the one with three beds and three baths). The values assigned to a single pattern (e.g., one house) forms a feature vector. It can look like a configuration of values such as 3, 2, 2, 5, 6, 8, 9. Each value represents a value assigned to a particular feature of a particular house. For example, the numbers 3, 2, 2, 5, 6, 8 could mean the house has 3 beds, 2 baths, 2 garages, etc.

- **Method:** A method is the algorithm used by the machine to learn the task that it needs to do. The algorithm is not a set of instructions given to a computer to do something. For example, it is not a step-by-step recipe to cook something. It is more like a computer being given lots of ingredients and expecting the computer to learn to discover a particular recipe. More about this in the next section.

- **Goal:** In most cases we would like the machine to have a specific learning goal. For example, we would like the machine to tell us, based upon the features and feature values of a transaction, in which account to post a journal entry. In this case, the features could be the transaction details (e.g., supplier name, text from the invoice, amount, and P.O. details). Based upon the values in these features (i.e., the feature vector), classify it, first, to determine if the transaction belongs in the expense category or capitalization category, and then identify the specific account to which the transaction should be posted.

- **Performance Criteria:** The performance criteria specify the accuracy and precision of the ability of the machine (i.e., the task it has learned). The learning needs to have some level of reliability. For example, if we design a machine-learning solution to predict if a tumor is cancerous or not, its prediction performance could be a life-and-death situation. Performance criteria serve as a benchmark for us to know whether the machine is achieving its goals or not.

▪ ALGORITHMS

Algorithms are the methods by which machines learn to think. Unlike the computer programs where we give machines step-by-step instructions to do something, algorithms allow machines to develop the intuition to learn to do things on their own. They don't need to be given specific instructions. Think about a simple classification utility that helps you direct your legitimate email to your inbox and spam to your spam box. Now imagine you are writing a computer program to do that. One way to do that will be to identify a set of words that are used in spam email and write the code to direct the computer. The code will make decisions based upon if it sees certain words or word combinations and then based upon that decision send the email to spam or to your inbox. Under this strategy, to capture all such words and word combinations, you would need to write thousands, even millions of lines of code to consider all such combinations.

Clearly, a good solution does not seem to come from deterministic thinking. If, however, we can teach the machine to develop a statistical mindset to determine the likelihood of an email being legitimate versus spam, we have solved the problem without writing billions of lines of code. This is machine learning.

Recall from the previous section that we described machine learning as the ability to recognize pattern assemblies (i.e., things and their relationships) from other patterns (properties). From the email example, it is clear that the machine is using an inference mechanism to make sense of the pattern. It is developing intuition about email being spam or not spam.

The methods that help machines identify patterns and make inferences are known as algorithms. An algorithm has certain interesting properties:

- **It looks for a mathematical link or bridge:** It can be viewed as a mechanism to discover functions (as mathematical functions that express relationships between two or more variables). For example, a function can establish a relationship between the set of words (input features) and the output variable spam or not spam. (Note: some algorithms do not discover functions – more about this in the next chapter.)
- **It is goal oriented:** The goal of the machine-learning artifact is embedded in the function. That means that the function that expresses

the relationship between variables does that in accordance with some goal. The function to determine spam versus not spam has the goal to discriminate between spam and not spam. It will not be able to tell you about the mood or the sentiment of the author who sent you the email. For that, you will need a different function. The one that will tell you about the mood or sentiment will not be able to inform you about the writing style or educational background of the author of emails. For that, you would need another function to represent that relationship, and so on.

- **It has a performance benchmark – since it is not discovering any function, it is discovering the best one out there:** Here comes the really interesting part. The main idea of the algorithm is to find or discover that function that can meet or exceed the performance measure. In other words, an algorithm is not the function itself that solves your problem but instead it is a way of discovering the function that will solve your problem. In fact, in mathematical terms you can think of your problem as trying to discover a program from a large space of programs. The function you are trying to discover is the one that excels at your performance metric. In the spam classification example, there could be billions of functions that can make an attempt to establish a relationship between the input variables (text of the email) and output variable (spam or non-spam) but most of them will not be able to establish the relationship that can reliably perform the job. Some may be able to classify 10 out of 1000 emails. Some may be able to classify 100 out of 1000. Neither are the optimized solutions to your problem. You want the function that can at least classify 990 out of 1000 emails accurately. This means that in a large space of functions, there will be one that will be the best of them all. The goal of your algorithm is to find that function. To achieve that goal an algorithm must use some type of an approach. For example, the approach could be optimizing (i.e., selecting the best element from multiple possibilities given a certain criterion). Another technique could be genetic or evolutionary.

- **It starts its journey randomly:** To discover the best function, an algorithm's journey starts randomly. It doesn't know what the best function is. It simply starts somewhere and then changes the values of the parameters to determine the right combination that will get it to the right answer. In the spam example, the best combination of words and values of parameters that discriminates between legitimate and spam is the function you are seeking. The algorithm is trying to find the parameters that best represent the relationship. The journey of the algorithm that attempts to find the best or most optimized answer can be described as the algorithm's journey to accumulate experience. After all, its basic approach to find the best program from a large number of programs would necessarily involve some mechanism of moving toward the goal of finding that right program or function. In the absence of experience accumulation, the search can keep looking in the same places as previously searched and never move forward. In other words, as the algorithm is trying to optimize, it is accumulating experience by using a method to learn and by moving closer and closer to the best solution. It is converging. This means it contains a methodology and a feedback mechanism that tells it that it has to move forward and not keep looking in the same places.

▪ **Our algorithm must work efficiently:** Since we described our problem space as having many possible functions and one of those is the best or most optimized function, and that the goal of the algorithm is to find that function, it is helpful to know that more than one algorithm might be able to do the job. But the real issue is not just that we want to find the best function; we want to find it efficiently. The last thing we want is for our computer to go into weeks and weeks of processing frenzy while we wait to find the best function. This means it is not just the ability of an algorithm to be able to solve our problem that is important, but an equally important consideration is the efficiency of the algorithm. The criteria for the best algorithm is simple:

  ▪ It can do the job in accordance with the performance measure. Note these are two criteria in one sentence: (a) being able to do the job, since not all algorithms can solve all problems; and (b) being able to do the job effectively (i.e., to meet the performance measure).

  ▪ It can do the job efficiently, that is, it requires less computational resources (time, processing power) to do the job.

ACCUMULATING EXPERIENCE

In the previous section it was mentioned that the algorithm accumulates experience while trying to discover the best program or function. What does it mean to accumulate experience? There are two parts of accumulating experience:

1. The learning machine uses some technique to learn (make sense of the data that is being fed to it); and then

2. It uses some technique to come closer to the best and most optimized solution.

Note: While there are different ways, such as parametrized functional form, optimization, factorization, and simulation, we can consider the approach discussed here as optimization.

 ## TECHNIQUES OF LEARNING

To understand the techniques of learning, let us analyze how human children learn. One way that children learn is by watching others. They watch their parents, friends, and siblings do things and try to copy them. Thus, when a child observes how a parent makes coffee and copies the task, the child has received an example of how to do something. We can refer to that as *learning by example*.

The second way children learn is by exploring. For instance, a child may go in the backyard on her own and observe various flowers, insects, and birds. The child learns from her own experience and observation. In this kind of learning, she may not have expected to find something interesting, but once she was in the backyard, she not only observed insects and flowers but maybe also a bird that she had never seen before. This is *learning by exploring*. The goal for learning by exploring, hence, may not be to perform a specific task but instead the goal to explore becomes the primary goal. In other words, the goal to explore is embedded within the technique without any further specification of a goal. Notice that this is different from learning by example where the task being copied or emulated must be specific and the child knows what she is copying. In learning by exploring, however, the child may explore without knowing what she may find.

The third way that children learn is by reward and punishment. This learning can also be viewed as guided exploration as in this case the child gets feedback if she is moving closer to a learning goal or away from it. For example, if a child is learning about insects, she may get stung by a bee (punishment) or truly get fascinated by looking at a colorful and beautiful butterfly (reward). This learning method can be described as learning by reward and punishment.

When dealing with machine learning, the same three concepts of learning are applied. In the machine learning world, they are known as Supervised Learning, Unsupervised Learning, and Reinforcement Learning.

SUPERVISED LEARNING

Like the child who learns from examples, in supervised learning machines learn by the human (or computer) teacher-provided examples. Examples can be viewed as series of combinations of inputs and output(s). For example, an example of spam versus non-spam email could be composed of words (text) used in spam email and the output that elucidates that this is a spam email or not. In this scenario, the text can be viewed as the input and the binary classification spam or not-spam as the output.

Now imagine having thousands and thousands of examples of email text and the associated output classification as spam and not-spam. Our examples are complete; that is, they have the x-values and the y-values. The goal of the algorithm is to find the function that, when it is given text as input, will be able to classify an email as spam or not-spam.

Let us view all the email examples as our data set. We can then define a conceptual space composed of many functions that link the inputs with the outputs – but not all of them will be good at doing that. Out of many, there will be one that does the job better than all others. The algorithm's job is to help us find that function. It is simply finding a function that can successfully give us a reasonably correct output based upon a specific input.

Another example could be to classify documents based upon topics. You have a set of documents and you want to classify them based upon topics such as politics, sports, or science. Well, if you have lots of examples of documents that are already marked as politics, sports, or science, the algorithm will understand that words such as "Congress passed a bill" and "foreign policy" apply to politics and the word "touchdown" applies to sports. It will develop intuition about the topics. Just as documents and emails are classified, pictures and sound files can also be classified.

Let us now take a step back and quickly review what is happening here:

- We are giving the learning machine examples. The examples are related to the task we want the machine to do. The examples are labeled. The word "labeled" means that for each set of inputs the output is designated. For example, in the spam versus not-spam, the output designation of spam and not-spam will be the labels.
- Based upon the examples, the algorithm finds the best function.

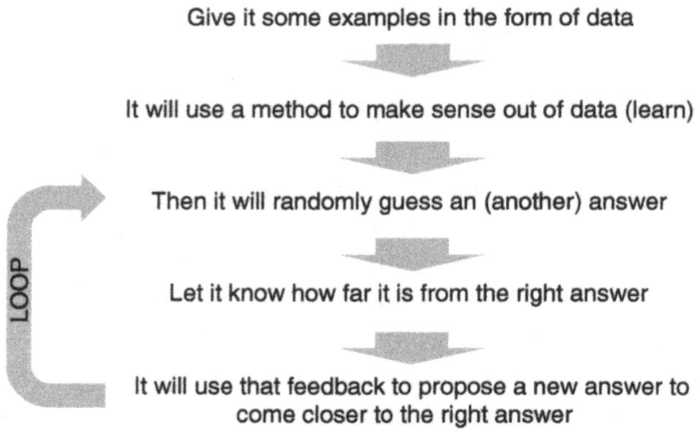

Give it some examples in the form of data

It will use a method to make sense out of data (learn)

Then it will randomly guess an (another) answer

LOOP

Let it know how far it is from the right answer

It will use that feedback to propose a new answer to come closer to the right answer

FIGURE 4.2 The Process of Using Examples in Supervised Learning

- We establish a performance measure for the task. For example, if our goal is to identify spam email, we can establish that our learning machine will successfully classify spam at least 95% of the time.
- When we give a new input to our learning machine, it will be able to correctly generate the spam versus not-spam 95 out of 100 times.

In practice, the following tasks are performed to accomplish the above (see Figure 4.2):

- The entire data is preprocessed. Preprocessing involves preparing the input in a form where it can be fed into an algorithm. The data is labeled. This means that the output is matched with the input for each example.
- An algorithm is selected to classify the data. Many choices are available.
- The algorithm is initiated via some initial parameters.
- The algorithm is based upon a specific technique, for example, optimization or evolution. In optimization, a cost function becomes the feedback loop that guides the algorithm in terms of whether the algorithm is moving closer to the best solution or stepping away.
- The cost function guides it to move toward the best solution.
- The data is separated into training data and testing data. Then the testing data is used.

Why is more data good? It must be clear that the more examples we have, the better for our algorithm. This means that we can get the algorithms to learn more effectively. Can you see why? Simply because more examples will be able to better tune the function parameters.

Supervised Learning Methods

Supervised learning includes two primary methods: classification and regression.

Classification uses the inputs to classify them into various classes of output. The spam versus non-spam example we saw above was of a binary nature where the input was classified as one of the two classes.

We can have problems where input is classified in more than two classes, for example, classifying images of fruits into pears, apples, oranges, and mangoes. This is known as multiclass classification. In multiclass classification the input can only be classified as one of the given classes. For example, if an image is classified as oranges, it is not classified as apples, mangoes, or pears.

It is also possible to have multilabel classification problems. In multilabel classification each set of inputs is classified into more than one label. For example, a document can have several topics (e.g., politics, religion, social, economic). This is known as a multilabel problem.

In classification the output is categorical. It means that the output could be 0 or 1 (binary), or 1, 2, 3, 4, and 5 (each representing a class). Another type of supervised learning problem is where the output is not categorical, it is continuous. It means that the output can take any number within a range, for example, temperatures, prices, and crop yields.

Prediction using regression involves estimating a continuous valued output. This means we try to estimate the expected value of a distribution on a continuous valued variable. In simple words, when you are trying to predict something where output can be over a range of values, you use regression. An example of using regression would be to predict the price of an asset based upon some data given about the asset. You can input factors such as number of bedrooms, number of bathrooms, Zip codes, size of lot, etc. to predict the value of a house. You will use regression to do that. You can enter the earnings, sector p/e multiple, revenues, etc. of a firm to predict its stock value. Again, regression will help you do that. To enable the algorithm to perform these and other time series-type analysis, you train the algorithm with that data of the inputs.

UNSUPERVISED LEARNING

Like the child discovering new things without any guidance, unsupervised learning is when machines find patterns from the data given to them as input. There is no example provided to the machine and therefore there is no external guidance. There is no expert or supervisor telling you how to label the data. There is no y-data – it is all x-data (features or input). Recall that the example has two sides to it – input and output. In unsupervised learning, we have the inputs but no outputs. That is why we cannot offer examples to the algorithm. Since our supervised learning algorithms are unable to learn without examples, we must do things differently in unsupervised learning. The underlying assumption here is that class membership is defined by commonly shared feature input patterns.

Unsupervised learning is an answer to many business problems in which we have lots of data and our objective is to discover new patterns in data that can illuminate new knowledge for us. For example, we want to figure out creative ways to segment our customers. Since we don't know what those segments are when we start the inquiry, all we have is data on our customers. We want the algorithm to identify those segments for us. Notice that we are not giving the learning machine the answers or output – and therefore our data sets are not labeled. Another example would be trying to group documents but not knowing which groups we would discover. Detecting fraud by discovering anomalies also uses unsupervised learning.

Some of the methods used in unsupervised learning are association rules, clustering, and self-organizing maps.

One way to get intuition about unsupervised learning is to think about data convergence due to proximity of features. For example, if we were teaching a machine to learn to classify fruits and we were using supervised learning, we would train it by providing examples of oranges, apples, bananas, and grapes from features of shape and size. So, for each combination of size and shape we would provide the algorithm with the right answer, that is, banana versus orange versus apple versus grapes. Once the algorithm learns, it will be able to classify the four fruits accurately. In unsupervised learning, we would only have input data and no labels. If size, color, and shape data are given to you about the four fruits, I am pretty sure that you (a human) would be able to tell the difference between bananas, grapes, oranges, and apples. The unsupervised learning methods aggregate the data into groups or clusters that are close to each other. Thus, apples will cluster around apples, oranges around oranges, bananas around bananas, and grapes around grapes. Here we did not tell the algorithm the right answers, but simply based upon the features the algorithm found the clusters.

REINFORCEMENT LEARNING

Reinforcement learning has recently shown miraculous success in various areas. It is a powerful form of learning that can be used in sustained strategic making areas. Reinforcement learning works on the basis of rewards and punishment where the algorithm learns through success and failure. Thus, agents in the reinforcement learning try to maximize their cumulative reward. It is based upon exploration and exploitation, where it explores the unknown territory and exploits the current knowledge while maximizing its reward.

Key Points

- Machine learning is finding the function that represents a link or a bridge between inputs and outputs.
- A learning machine uses algorithms and trains them with data.
- Features are the properties or attributes (independent variables). Feature vectors are fed to the algorithm.
- Algorithms find the optimized point where the function can optimally represent the data.
- There are three types of learning: supervised, unsupervised, and reinforcement.

CHAPTER FIVE

Machine Learning

C REDIT CARD BUSINESS is full of trepidations. Tired of fraud, many banks simply considered fraud as the necessary cost of doing business. Obviously, the losses from fraud are passed on to the customers, forcing banks to be less competitive in certain markets. Reducing fraud, therefore, is a direct driver of the bottom-line value creation and of enabling banks to be more competitive. Less fraud means less cost, and that translates into being able to offer more competitive credit cards to customers. Many banks are now tackling the problem of fraud by applying machine learning. Visa is one of the companies that decided to conquer the challenge by developing a deep learning – based fraud detection system (Castellanos, 2019). However, while this was not the first time that a fraud detection system was used by a bank, this was one of the first attempts to use advanced AI for that purpose. Visa's older systems were based upon more basic machine-learning and rules. Even though that system protected Visa from $25 billion of fraud attempts in the year ending in 2019, growing sophistication among the fraudsters required an even better system. The new system is a deep learning neural network. With higher sensitivity, the system can detect suspicious behavior with significantly higher precision.

The presence of fraud detection in credit card business is one application of deep learning in a firm. One can assume that based upon the success of that project, Visa will now develop and deploy more intelligent automation in other areas also. This means that slowly such innovative automations will start showing up in different areas, functions, departments, and business units.

To lead such powerful innovations, business executives must develop their skills in intelligent automation.

In this chapter I will equip you with the knowledge you need as a businessperson so you can envision, sponsor, and lead projects like Visa's deep learning fraud detection system.

In Chapter 4, the introduction to machine learning was informal. In this chapter, I will formalize the machine learning concepts and go into a little more detail. The chapter is a bit technical – but business readers will not have any problem understanding it. I have made sure that I simplify things so business readers can understand.

Machine learning is about teaching machines. It can also be viewed as helping machines learn from data. Many machine-learning methods are about extracting models from data such that we can extract patterns and make better predictions. Machine learning uses methods to accomplish the goal of extracting models. Another way to think about machine learning is to develop the viewpoint of fitting the model to the data.

MODELS

A model is a representation of reality that satisfies some goal. In other words, a model allows us to represent a reality so we can understand it better. Think of language as a model that allows us to understand the physical objects around us. We cannot place a physical car or an airplane in our head, but we can represent those objects with words, and words can serve as symbols that we can understand. Language can represent the reality and is therefore a model. A map, for example, is a model of the physical reality of roads, stores, buildings, etc. Financial statements are models of a business's performance.

A learning model attempts to predict something unknown. It uses some method (machine learning) to predict the unknown part of the reality that we are interested in. Let us give some relevant examples here:

- Predicting the potential for fraud in a company
- Detecting a fraud that has taken place in a company
- Predicting that a fraud is taking place

In general terminology, we tend to think about predicting as predicting some future event, but in the machine-learning world, the word "predict" signifies the formula to estimate some unknown value. Predictive modeling, therefore, focuses on predicting the value of interest, and doing it such that there is high level of trust in the prediction. A descriptive model can help understand what is going on. In contrast, a predictive model can help predict the unknown.

Specifically, the prediction can be viewed as using the feature vectors to estimate the value of the target variable. In other words, assuming there is some relationship between x and y, you ask the system: Given x, what do you think y will be? These concepts are further explained below.

The method helps make the prediction and the model the best possible representation that makes the goal of prediction successful.

 ## FEATURES AND TARGETS

Features are the attributes or properties on the target variable. Recall from the last chapter the discussion about how we understand things by looking at their properties. The properties or attributes of something are known as features. A feature can be viewed as data about something. Imagine we have data about customers. The data includes geographic, demographic, purchase, and behavioral information about customers. Those are all features. Say we are trying to predict how much business a customer will do with us, or whether a customer will respond to a specific marketing message; then the row of data that contains the information about the customer becomes the feature vector and each column that contains information about a specific informational element represents features.

What about the values that we are trying to predict? They are known as target values. From past transactions, we also know how much money customers have spent with us or how customers have responded to our marketing messages. These are the output values of our model, since they specify what we are trying to predict. They are also known as labels, output, dependent variables, or target values.

For example, if we had data on automobiles and we were trying to predict which data refers to private-use cars, we can find patterns where values of features could be used to predict whether it is a private-use car or not. The feature values could be about the size of the tires, windows, number of doors, size of the vehicle, presence of a light on the roof, etc. If I give you that data and ask you to predict what data applies to a private-use car versus a not-for-private-use car, it is likely that you will be able to tell simply by looking at the data. For example, trailer trucks will have more than four tires so you will eliminate them. A tractor may not have doors. A cab or a police car may have a flashing light on the top, etc. As you get to the final answer, you have used your cognitive skills to make that determination. A computer can do the same, except that it uses an algorithm to do the work.

As shown in Figure 5.1, the computer will use the values of features to predict the output value. The output value is private-use car versus not-private-use car. The input values will be the values of the features, that is, tires, windows, number of tires, and so on, that we discussed above. Since the system is statistical and not deterministic, it needs the ability to formulate a concept of what a car is by using the properties (feature values) of a car.

Let us say we call our features as x-values $(x_1, x_2, x_3 \ldots\ldots x_n)$ and our output or target variable as y; we need to discover a function that will be able to predict the y (car or not-car) when given the x-values (feature values).

The above example touched upon one of the methods used by machine learning (i.e., classification). In classification the machine estimates the output value by using the input values. More formally, we estimate the value of the output (dependent variable, target variable) as a function of the features.

 MODEL INDUCTION

There are so many different types of cars that can pass as being private-use cars – SUVs, sedans, sports cars, etc. This means there will be great deal of variability to recognize which are private-use cars and which are not. This means that our function is not deterministic. It cannot state the output with 100% precision; instead, it can guess with some high degree of reliability.

Teaching by Examples

VEHICLES

If you want to teach me how to recognize a car, tell me about the properties of a car

Many properties will apply to all vehicles shown above (FEATURES)

Tires, Windshield, Doors, Engine, others

The combination of properties and their values will help me determine if it is a car

FIGURE 5.1   Identifying a Car

Philosophy 101 courses inform us that inductive reasoning, in contrast to deductive reasoning, is where evidence is accumulated from premises to reach to some conclusion. While in deductive reasoning the conclusion is clear and certain, in inductive reasoning it is an estimate with some probability of its truth value. In machine learning, creating models from data is known as model induction. Just like philosophy, the induction part implies that some level of certainty is gained from the evidence accumulation process that glides over the features as we discover some rules that can be generalized. Induction learners or algorithms are the methods that create the models.

 ## DATA

It helps to think of data in terms of tables. Tables are structured representations of features where we list the feature names up at the top. The values of the features are filled in the rows below. Each row forms a record. We call it a feature vector. Now imagine a column at the end of the table (or view it as the last column of the table) that is not part of the features but instead is the target variable or the dependent variable we are trying to predict. Collectively, your data table now includes both input or independent variables and your output or dependent variable(s).

For instance, in Figure 5.2 we have 10 x-variables (input variables) and one y-variable with the binary value of 0 or 1. In our car example, that value could represent private-use-car versus non-private-use car and is stated as 0 or 1 (binary).

 ## STOP AND THINK!

Now take a step back and think what you are trying to do and from what. Your toolkit includes the features and feature values. You also have the labels or the known outputs (the dependent variables) for these feature values. You are trying to determine a relationship between the input variables and the output variables in the form of a function (you can think of it as an equation with parameters and coefficients that you are trying to identify). You also have methods that can help you establish that function. The function is the bridge between data and the output. It is the pathway that links the two – inputs and output. That is why machine learning can be viewed as fitting a model to the data. Once that bridge is established, when you input the feature data the

Features, Attributes, or Dimensions

x1	x2	x3	x4	x5	x6	x7	x8	x9	x10	y
687	0.613	420.912	257.89	0.240	61.995	14.90	0.619	9.226	5.71	1
868	0.738	640.163	472.13	0.422	199.290	84.12	0.443	37.243	16.49	1
745	0.141	105.164	14.84	0.724	10.745	7.78	0.800	6.224	4.98	0
83	0.929	77.107	71.63	0.022	1.544	0.03	0.887	0.030	0.03	1
381	0.052	19.816	1.03	0.370	0.381	0.14	0.806	0.114	0.09	1
570	0.291	165.814	48.24	0.899	43.349	38.96	0.027	1.049	0.03	0
326	0.546	178.044	97.24	0.813	79.078	64.31	0.914	58.770	53.71	1
48	0.958	45.987	44.06	0.066	2.904	0.19	0.443	0.085	0.04	0
568	0.434	246.282	106.79	0.554	59.123	32.73	0.791	25.879	20.46	0
88	0.689	60.650	41.80	0.255	10.647	2.71	0.381	1.034	0.39	0
150	0.259	38.864	10.07	0.471	4.739	2.23	0.393	0.877	0.35	1
689	0.728	501.604	365.18	0.728	265.867	193.56	0.690	133.501	92.08	0
671	0.494	331.356	163.63	0.713	116.700	83.23	0.865	71.962	62.22	0
162	0.260	42.102	10.94	0.829	9.070	7.52	0.513	3.858	1.98	0
128	0.982	125.657	123.36	0.379	46.731	17.70	0.561	9.936	5.58	0
252	0.361	90.971	32.84	0.060	1.972	0.12	0.158	0.019	0.00	1
484	0.985	476.585	469.28	0.047	22.036	1.03	0.052	0.053	0.00	1
169	0.143	24.138	3.45	0.262	0.903	0.24	0.402	0.095	0.04	1
842	0.320	269.073	85.99	0.687	59.106	40.63	0.964	39.162	37.75	1
33	0.630	20.784	13.09	0.216	2.830	0.61	0.414	0.253	0.10	0
220	0.796	175.090	139.35	0.870	121.294	105.58	0.207	21.824	4.51	1
493	0.805	397.086	319.83	0.753	240.976	181.56	0.884	160.455	141.80	1
620	0.295	182.662	53.82	0.388	20.888	8.11	0.244	1.975	0.48	1
466	0.639	297.859	190.39	0.722	137.386	99.14	0.241	23.928	5.78	0
686	0.751	514.874	386.44	0.436	168.606	73.56	0.272	20.005	5.44	1
403	0.695	280.264	194.91	0.155	30.265	4.70	0.279	1.313	0.37	1
434	0.842	365.488	307.79	0.041	12.482	0.51	0.671	0.340	0.23	0
110	0.736	80.987	59.63	0.494	29.477	14.57	0.001	0.008	0.00	0
359	0.474	170.335	80.82	0.545	44.035	23.99	0.936	22.452	21.01	1
226	0.603	136.202	82.08	0.890	73.018	64.95	0.427	27.762	11.87	1
704	0.245	172.658	42.34	0.983	41.613	40.89	0.829	33.904	28.11	1
948	0.967	916.701	886.43	0.043	38.009	1.63	0.064	0.104	0.01	1
501	0.676	338.921	229.28	0.228	52.170	11.87	0.075	0.895	0.07	1
70	0.698	48.834	34.07	0.805	27.428	22.08	0.459	10.133	4.65	0
73	0.832	60.735	50.53	0.383	19.345	7.41	0.479	3.548	1.70	1
599	0.862	516.546	445.44	0.523	233.176	122.06	0.693	84.542	58.56	1
577	0.418	241.042	100.70	0.150	15.151	2.28	0.593	1.351	0.80	0
960	0.790	758.844	599.84	0.074	44.241	3.26	0.979	3.194	3.13	0
568	0.231	131.169	30.29	0.314	9.520	2.99	0.735	2.199	1.62	1
768	0.251	192.781	48.39	0.014	0.671	0.01	0.828	0.008	0.01	1
981	0.226	221.895	50.19	0.766	38.437	29.44	0.860	25.302	21.75	0
785	0.322	252.556	81.25	0.807	65.555	52.89	0.315	16.674	5.25	0
387	0.836	323.676	270.71	0.749	202.832	151.97	0.189	28.775	5.45	0
799	0.110	87.717	9.63	0.181	1.744	0.32	0.165	0.052	0.01	0
236	0.740	174.688	129.30	0.678	87.671	59.44	0.126	7.501	0.95	1
835	0.598	499.009	298.22	0.606	180.784	109.59	0.429	47.040	20.19	1
976	0.871	850.444	741.04	0.857	634.856	543.89	0.906	492.751	446.42	1
156	0.069	10.781	0.75	0.176	0.131	0.02	0.168	0.004	0.00	0
917	0.501	459.829	230.58	0.843	194.386	163.87	0.418	68.421	28.57	1
843	0.496	418.048	207.31	0.561	116.367	65.32	0.547	35.712	19.53	0
658	0.607	399.155	242.13	0.164	39.787	6.54	0.804	5.256	4.23	0
761	0.296	225.210	66.65	0.357	23.805	8.50	0.973	8.273	8.05	1
623	0.649	404.062	262.06	0.614	160.971	98.88	0.018	1.808	0.03	1
819	0.544	445.686	242.53	0.892	216.360	193.01	0.986	190.329	187.69	1
790	0.895	707.128	632.95	0.609	385.659	234.98	0.423	99.514	42.14	1
259	0.457	118.486	54.20	0.813	44.063	35.82	0.599	21.453	12.85	0
356	0.652	232.172	151.42	0.950	143.851	136.66	0.010	1.421	0.01	0
356	0.811	288.818	234.31	0.558	130.757	72.97	0.716	52.236	37.39	0
297	0.323	95.807	30.91	0.045	1.383	0.06	0.637	0.039	0.03	0
134	0.920	123.266	113.39	0.802	90.916	72.89	0.289	21.045	6.08	1

X = (x1, x2, x3, x4, ... xn)
These are independent variables, input

Many general problems have just one value of "y" e.g. Spam = Yes or Spam = No
This is the dependent variable, target variable, or output

FIGURE 5.2 Data, Features, and Target

machine should be able to estimate the output. Note this machine will output or predict the dependent variable not as a specific, but as a generalized function. It has developed an instinct for what the right answer should be. It may not be right all the time, but the function has learned from the data and can provide estimates of values. Now that we understand what we are trying to do, we need to figure out the "how" part, and that comes from understanding the methods.

Let us turn our attention to the methods.

 ## SUPERVISED: CLASSIFICATION WITH TREES

In this section we will discuss decision-tree-based classification methods. Recall that supervised learning is based upon learning from examples.

Supervised: Decision Trees

A decision tree is a structure that looks like an upside-down tree where the top is known as the root and the bottom nodes are known as leaf nodes. Starting at the root node, a question is asked about a feature and depending upon the answer the data set is split into branches. Then another question is asked about the next feature and the data set is again split. This question/answer continues till a point is reached where the data is segmented such that all members of the node carry the same label or that no more features are left to classify. The beginning point of the decision tree is a labeled data set of features.

Let us say we are trying to predict whether citizens of a certain area will vote with Party A or Party B, and we are using features such as education, age, income, etc. We can start building a decision tree by asking questions about the data, for example, "College educated? Age above 40? Makes above $100,000?" and based upon the answers we get to the bottom of the tree. The split at each question establishes a different path. At the bottom of the tree, we get information about how many people for each path voted for Party A versus Party B. In fact, if at the leaf node we are left with a mix (impure) where some voted for Party A and some for Party B, we can calculate the probability.

Notice that each path gives us some rule paths also – for example:

IF (Education = College, Age = 40+, Income = 100,000+)
THEN Class = Party A

Notice that sometimes full paths may not exist. If our second question informed us that all "College educated" and "Age above 40" voted for Party A, then there is no need to further explore that path. We have made that path pure.

Which questions get asked first does matter. Some questions may carry more prediction-worthy information (i.e., information that contributes most to the prediction). Not all the features will provide the most prediction-worthy information. Nor would all features provide equal information about whether a citizen will vote for Party A or Party B. Clearly, some features may give us more information than others. Can we find out which ones? There are processes that are employed (e.g., entropy) that can help us identify the most prediction-worthy participant features in the data set. Therefore, a better way to build decision trees is by segmenting the data in a manner that increases the accuracy of the prediction and that means to identity the features that carry most information and then structuring the order of questions in accordance with that. More advanced models of decision trees allow us to determine which features are more informative and, hence, allow us to choose more useful features first near the root.

Supervised: Random Forest[i]

Decision trees sometimes overfit the data. That means they too closely resemble the data and therefore lack the ability to predict new examples. In other words, the model is emulating the data so precisely that it accepts the data set as gospel and thinks that the whole world is like that data set. It doesn't generalize to new situations. It happens because it is picking up both noise (due to outliers and randomness) of the data and the signal (the insights obtained from the sample data). Since the data set you use includes both noise and signal, instead of picking up the signal, your model picks up noise.

Random forest is an ensemble method that takes the average or vote of more than one decision tree where each tree represents a subsample of features (Ho, 1995). At training time, random forest creates multiple decision trees and then calculates mode for classification, or median for regression. The averaging of multiple trees increases the quality of the result. This tries to solve the overfitting problem and generalizes the model so that it is applicable in other situations.

 CLASSIFICATION USING MATHEMATICAL FUNCTIONS

In the decision trees, we discovered models that predict target output based upon other descriptive attributes (inputs). The trees enabled that by subdividing

---

[i] Random Forests is trademark of Minitab, LLC https://trademarks.justia.com/786/42/random-78642027.html

the set of all instances into more informative subsets (purer), which enabled our ability to predict. They contained more information (a better, stronger relationship) between the output and the inputs. The decision tree gave us the structure and the parameters of the model. The structure was the specific tree model and the parameters were the probability estimates that we discovered at the leaf nodes. Using those, we were able to make better predictions.

Another way to develop a predictive model is to specify a mathematical function (Figure 5.3) where the structure of the model and the parameters represent the data set. Think of it as the tree (structure and parameters) that is embedded in an equation and our job is to calculate the values of the parameters. The model is set up by choosing the parameters. This is done either by the modeler knowing something about the data set from domain expertise or by using some mathematical concepts (like entropy) to develop some insights into the data. Then the parameters are tuned such that the learning can take place. This process, known as parameter learning, is the process where the model searches for the best parameters from the space of all parameters that describe the data set.

The general idea of the classification via mathematical functions is to split the data in a manner that can predict the output better. What splits the data can be thought of as a straight line (in a two-dimensional system) that cleanly partitions the data such that its predictive value can be improved. This is known as a linear classifier. It is explained in the next section.

Many problems require us to think in terms of binary answers. For example, is there a fraud or not; should a person get the credit or not; should

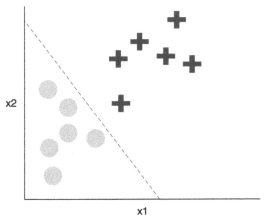

FIGURE 5.3   Function-Based Split

an investment be made or not. Using the data of the attributes that describe those scenarios, we can think of a way to split the data set such that we can identify the parameters that are most important predictors and their values (probability estimates) of contributing to the prediction.

Thinking of linear separation as a line limits us to splitting the data where there are only two variables. What if we have three, four, hundreds, or even thousands of attributes? We will deal with that later in the chapter, but for now, it can be visualized that for a three-dimensional system (i.e., three variables) we can use a plane to divide the data, and for four and more dimensions a hyperplane that can segment our data.

SUPERVISED: SIMPLE LINEAR CLASSIFIER

Let us return to our previously used example of classifying citizens as likely to vote for Party A or Party B based upon two variables of Education and Income. Note, since we are using a linear model here, we are only using two variables and not three as in the decision tree example. Again, the linear classifier can be viewed as a line that tries to split the data nicely into two classes. The reason I said "tries to" is because sometimes (in fact, in most cases) it is unable to split the data precisely, and some values may end up on the wrong side. Like any line, however, the divider line can be viewed as having a certain slope and a y-intercept. This means we can represent this line as an equation. Let us say we discover that the equation is as follows:

$$Income = (-1.75) * Education + 100$$

Here −1.75 represents the slope and 100 represents the y-intercept. In fact, we can move the Income on the other side of the equation and set a simple rule that says if the value of the function is above zero, this means the point resides above the line, and if it is below zero, then it is below the line:

$$Class(x) = Party A \ if - 1 \times Income - 1.75 \times Education + 100 > 0$$

$$Party B \ if - 1 \times Income - 1.75 \times Education + 100 <= 0$$

Recall our target variables (output variables) are Party A or Party B. Think of them as classes. What are the above equations trying to accomplish?

We are trying to split Party A voters versus likely Party B voters based upon two attributes of income and education. We capture Education from 0 to 20 (years of education) and Income from zero to $200,000 as 0 to 200. Our plotted data therefore gives us points where each point is a mixture of (education, income) or (x1, x2). Based upon our known information, each of those combinations produced a Party A or a Party B. We are trying to divide the data set into two regions where, hopefully, our data can be nicely split between Party B and Party A based upon the two attributes of Income and Education (Figure 5.4). To split the data, we take the weighted sum of the values of the two attributes and based upon that determine a line that splits the data into two regions of Party A and Party B. In Figure 5.4, they are shown as plus sign and circles.

The line was represented by an equation and the equation when viewed as a function gave us the ability to segment our data by calculating the value of the function and figuring out if the value is above or below/equal to zero. Of course, we can have more than two features and hence we can think of a general function as:

$$f(x) = w_0 + w_1x_1 + w_2x_2 + w_3x_3 + \dots$$

Here the weights of the function are the parameters and the classification is based upon negative or positive value of the function. The higher the weight, we can generally assume that attribute (input) is better for predicting the output. We now have both the structure and the estimates embedded in a mathematical function. We have successfully fit our model to the data by representing it mathematically. This is our parametrized model.

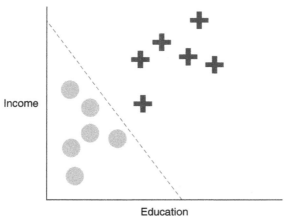

FIGURE 5.4 Predicting Vote

The function $w_0 + w_1x_1 + w_2x_2 + w_3x_3$ .... . shows that in addition to income and education we can use other attributes, such as age, or number of times previously voted, for classification.

Also, the data used above was numerical. What if we had text or descriptive data or categorical data? How will we manage that? Finally, the parameter values can turn out to be vastly different if there is a wide difference between the numeric values of the variables. For example, in the above example, while the education scale runs between 0 and 20, the income scale runs between 0 and $200,000. To eliminate that problem, we normalized the data before using it in the classification algorithm.

Picking the Right Line

Picking the right linear classifier is not easy. Observe the space between the two types of features. Many lines can qualify as the partitioning line (Figure 5.5). Which line then represents the best line that truly partitions the data sets most effectively can be considered as an optimization problem. Here you are asking, of all the lines that can part my data into regions, which line is the best line?

If you are trying to classify between two labels (y-values), ideally your data splits such that you can place a line between the data. The way you fit model for data is by estimating a dividing line. A line can separate the data into two sections.

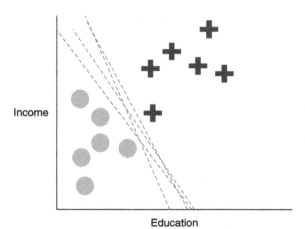

FIGURE 5.5   Solution Space, Many Lines Possible

Recall that we only included education and income as the input variables. We can also include age as a feature input. This creates a three-dimensional space and visually you can imagine a plane that will separate the data space in three ways. Similarly, a four-dimensional or more system will have a hyperplane.

One way to think about it is that based upon the features, the data will show that there appears to be some natural partition between the data. As shown in Figure 5.3, we hope that based upon the feature vector provided (i.e., X1, X2) the data points will clearly occupy separate areas in the space. Hence, the problem of classification can be defined as finding the line, plane, or hyperplane that can separate the data into segments of the output variable (target). The word "hyperplane" is generally used. A hyperplane in a two-dimensional system is a line. A hyperplane in a three-dimensional system is a plane.

As shown in Figure 5.5, the line that separates the data has a certain equation (in this case linear). Finding that function that nicely separates the data is the core problem of classification.

What if your data had three or more classes? For example, you wanted to divide data between large, medium, and small, or the desired output was to classify between more than two political parties. Notice that in the above function, while we considered several inputs, our classifier was only doing binary classification (i.e., two outputs – Party A or Party B). A more advanced system (multi-classifier) will be able to classify among several classes (e.g., Party B, Party A, Party C, Independents, etc.). Those problems are known as multi-class classification problems. In a multi-class classification problem feature vectors are classified in three or more classes.

There is another type of problem in classification and it is known as multi-label classification, in that each feature vector can be classified into two or more classes. Notice that in both binary and multi-class classification, each feature vector belongs to only one class. If a feature vector belonged to Party A, it did not belong to Party B. But in multi-label classification, you can have feature vectors belong to more than one class. For instance, you are looking at articles and you want to classify them in classes of politics, economics, and social. Some articles may have an overlap and they may be about both politics and economics or society and politics. In such cases, you use multi-label classifiers.

While simple classifiers can address some trivial problems, some more complex problems can be solved with more advanced and powerful methods explained below. These methods display different levels of effectiveness for different types of problems.

 ## SUPERVISED: SUPPORT VECTOR MACHINE

In machine learning, our goal is twofold. We want our algorithm to learn from the data set we provide it, but we also want it to develop an intuition about the data so that it can generalize its learning. If all it can do is to just replicate the data set on which it is trained, it will not be very useful when it sees new data. In order to avoid those types of scenarios, we make sure that prior to starting the training, we randomly divide the data into two sets. One set (say about 80% of the data) is used as our training set and the rest (20%) we keep as our test set. Once we train our algorithm with the 80% data, we can then test its performance using the test data. Recall that in supervised learning we know the correct answers for the test data.

In addition to being able to part your data set into class regions, think for a moment about what is the real goal of the exercise. The real goal is that you are trying to predict. Prediction implies that there are some test cases that you will run through your trained model. Running your test case means that you will give the function the test inputs for the features and the function will tell you which class this input belongs to. In our example, when provided the input values for education and income, the function will provide the output class as Party A voter or Party B voter. Our goal is to make this prediction more reliable. This means that the separating line should be such that it can maximize its ability to classify properly.

One way to increase the reliability is to first consider a band or a bar between the data instead of a line. This band will have two boundaries, one on one side and the other on the other side. In a way it is the best boundary drawn closest to the data. Now we can draw a line that runs right in-between the two boundaries and that becomes our separation line. The distance between the two boundaries of the corridor (stripe, band) is known as the margin. See Figure 5.6.

A support vector machine (SVM) is a classifier (Ben-Hur et al., 2001) that separates data into classes by establishing a boundary space between the data (Boser et al., 2010). The boundary space can be viewed as a street with a line in the center (Figure 5.6). The street is laid out in the middle of the data such that the distance between the closest points and the central line of the street is maximized. Maximizing that achieves the goal of finding the optimal hyperplane. Margins are the perpendicular distance between the hyperplane

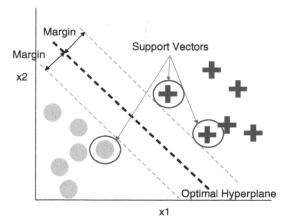

FIGURE 5.6 Support Vector Machine

(i.e., the middle line) and the lines on the side. The lines of the side are defined by the class that contains support vectors. Support vectors are the vectors (points) that are closest to the hyperplane on all sides of the plane.

If we drop a test vector and it falls on either side of the plane, we can be reasonably confident that it belongs in those categories. What if the test vector falls very close to the middle line or on it? One thing is clear. The closer a value is to the margin, the more suspect it becomes. It can go either way. Assuming you have a reasonable divider-line in between the data, the further away a point is from the margin, the more likely you are to belong to that class.

But regardless of the separation, clearly some values of inputs may end up on the wrong side of the line. For example, we may have a Party A voter whose attribute values indicate that she should be a Party B. She will be classified as a Party B by the classifier (misclassified). Her misclassification raises an important issue: What should we do about misclassifications? A related question is, wouldn't misclassifications decrease the predictive ability of our function? To measure that, we can define something that is central to these models and it is known as the loss function. The loss function can be measured by calculating the distance between the misclassified values and the margin. In fact, we can have a simple rule:

- There will be no loss if the values fall where they belong, that is, the predictor gets it right.
- If the values fall inside the boundary but have not crossed the margin, we will not penalize them.

- But if the values end up on the other side of the margin, we can penalize them by calculating the distance between the values and the boundary of the margin.

The above two-dimensional vector is shown as an example. That means that each vector has only two features (X1 and X2). Real problems will involve more than two dimensions (i.e., N-dimensions). In those problems, the feature vectors are mapped to an N-dimensional space and a hyperplane is discovered that separates the vectors into two classifications.

Here is another problem. What if our training data is mixed as shown in Figure 5.7? Try putting a partitioning line through that. In fact, if we drop a text feature vector (represented by the triangle) in the middle of the data, we will have a hard time determining if it belongs to Party A or Party B.

Notice in this case it is hard to get a line (hyperplane) to divide the data precisely into two camps (Figure 5.7). They are known as non-separable (linear) cases since the data is not easily separable with a straight line. The triangle is the test vector and clearly it is hard to determine if it belongs with the circles or the plus signs. In that case advanced versions of SVM give us some creative ways to handle those situations. One is simply tolerating a few misassignments.

The dissenters or rebels are tolerated as the necessary evil. The misclassified can be in the margin area, even if they are on the wrong side of the decision boundary or they are deep inside the wrong territory. The algorithm tries to make sure that it is optimizing the tradeoff between maximizing the margin and minimizing misclassification.

The second way to achieve better classification for tough cases is to transform the existing features by using mathematical transformations. For

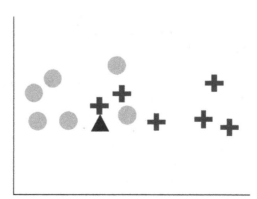

FIGURE 5.7 Non-Separable

Close-Ups, Weird Ones

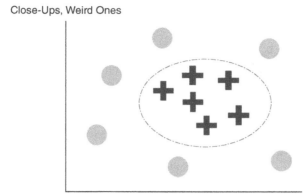

FIGURE 5.8 Inseparable

example, you can square, multiply, or a create a mathematical transformation to alter the state of features in a manner where they become more separable.

Figure 5.8 shows that it is virtually impossible to separate the data since it is right in the middle surrounded in a manner where you cannot easily separate Party A voters and Party B voters. What do you do now? Well, a mathematical transformation can help split the data as shown in Figure 5.9. A new dimension (Z) was introduced and calculated by squaring x and y and adding them. When we plotted this new data, the transformation made the data separable so we could easily part the data into two segments.

Close ups, Weird Ones

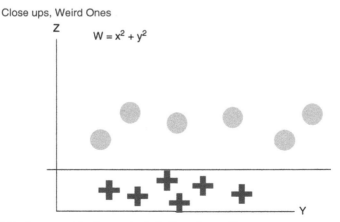

FIGURE 5.9 Inseparable Separated via Transformation

SUPERVISED: NAïVE BAYES

The Naïve Bayes algorithm performs classification by calculating the probability of different classes or outcomes. The probabilities are determined based on previously known examples presented in the training data. This algorithm is based upon the Bayesian theorem. It assumes that each feature is independent of the other feature. The core strategy of the algorithm is to assume that the features are independent. Then it estimates the probability (think of it as the relative participation) of the feature in a class. The probabilities are then multiplied to determine the influence of features in a class.

 ## SUPERVISED: BAYESIAN BELIEF NETWORKS

Bayesian Belief Networks (BBNs) are also based upon Bayesian Theorem, except unlike the Naïve Bayes model, which assumes that features are independent of each other, BBNs consider the probabilities and dependencies among features.

 ## SUPERVISED: K-NEAREST NEIGHBOR

Just as the name states, this algorithm looks at the nearest neighbors of the instances being classified and classifies in accordance with that. An analogy could be that you are asked to classify a family by its income. One way you can estimate the income is to find out the income of, say, ten neighbors, and based upon that you can estimate a family's income. Just as a person is known by the company he or she keeps, data tells us a lot by the surrounding points in the decision space.

If we had taken only one neighbor to estimate the family income, we may have gotten it wrong. But just by looking at the ten neighbors, we are more likely to get a reasonable estimate. The k in the k-nearest allows us to specify how many nearest data points we want the algorithm to look at. We can represent our test data as a triangle. Test data is in the form of feature vector that is used to test if our algorithm works. As shown in Figure 5.10, we are trying to see if the triangle belongs in the plus class or in the circle class. When we use k=4 (the inner circle), it looks at the 4 nearest neighbors and determines that there are more plus signs (i.e., 3 out of 4) than circles (1 out of 4) and therefore classifies the triangle as a plus. However, if we increase the size of k to 7, the 7 nearest neighbors of the triangle give a different picture: 4 out of 7 are circles and 3 out of 7 are plus signs, so we classify the test (triangle) as a circle.

k Nearest Neighbor Classifier

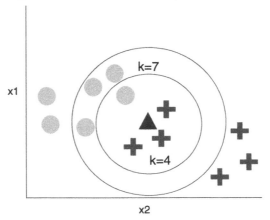

FIGURE 5.10 k-Nearest Neighbor

Teaching a machine involves a general strategy of using examples from the data. Recall that examples consist of two parts, feature values (input) and target (output). This data is fed into the algorithm and the job of the algorithm is to learn to recognize and separate data.

 ## SUPERVISED: REGRESSION

Supervised learning is applied in areas such as classification and regression. Classification is when the output is composed of discrete values, such as spam or no spam, cancer or no cancer, type of car, or selecting a person from an image. Regression is when the output has continuous variables such as prices, temperatures, or stock prices. Unlike classification, where you have clear buckets or pigeonholes in which you can classify the input, in regression you have range of possible values.

For example, see Figure 5.11, where we are trying to predict the GPA of students based (y-values) upon their SAT scores (x-values). Hypothetical data is provided on both sides and the middle is empty space. That space is for the function we are trying to discover.

Recall from the previous chapter the problem of having the data and trying to discover the function that connects the data. How do we go about doing that in regression? We can start by plotting the data (Figure 5.12).

When we look at the plotted data, we can see that it would be nice if we can find a best fit line that passes through the data and if we can discover the

PREDICT GPA BASED UPON SAT

SAT		GPA
850		2.8
900		2.9
950		2.9
1000		3.0
1050		3.1
1100		3.4
1150		3.5
1200		3.5
.		.
.		.
.		.

FIGURE 5.11   Finding the Function

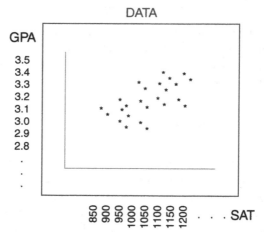

FIGURE 5.12   Plot

equation for that line, we will be able to supply the SAT values (input) and the output will come out to be close to the projected GPA. But how do we find the best fit line? We can do that by arguing that the best fit line through the points will be the one where the average squared distance between the points and the line will be minimized.

Well, we have to start somewhere. So, we start by randomly placing a line and then calculating the average distance (squared, to eliminate the negative and positive values from being above or below the line) between all the points

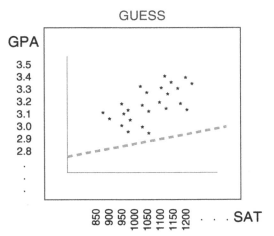

FIGURE 5.13 Random Placement of a Line

and the line (Figure 5.13). But that doesn't tell us much. We need a few more lines to figure out if we have minimized the average squared distance.

As we place a few more lines by nudging our first line (Figure 5.14), and calculate the average distance, we can then determine if we are moving closer to the ideal line (where the distance is minimized) or moving away from that. With great determination, we keep on nudging, moving closer and closer to finding that ideal line (Figure 5.15).

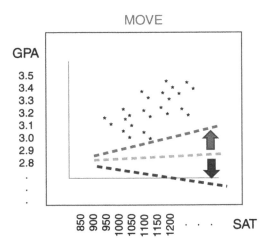

FIGURE 5.14 Adding Lines

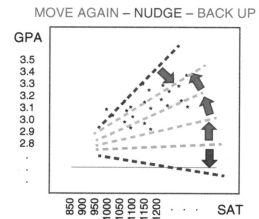

FIGURE 5.15 Finding the Best Fit Line

If we pass that ideal line, we will know, as the average squared distance will start increasing again. When we reach that point where the average squared distance is the lowest, that is the line we are looking for. Now, this line will have both a slope and the y-intercept. Remember, this is a linear system. The job of the algorithm is to find the best line and it does that by iterating through various possibilities.

Since it is linear, this line is of the form: $y = a + bx$

We are saying:

$$GPA = a + b * SAT$$

where

a = the y-intercept
b = the slope.

We are trying to find a and b. Finding that best-fit line happens when we minimize the "cost function" where the cost function is the mean squared error, which we measured by calculating the average squared distance. More formally, we can define it as the squared distance between an observation's actual and predicted value. We use the gradient descent method to minimize the cost function. It simply means exactly what you saw in the figures above. We started with a random line – which means some random values for the coefficients (a and b) in the above equation were used – and then based upon that we calculate the gradient by plugging in those numbers and repeatedly iterating till we minimize the mean squared error.

Every time we plug in a combination of a and b, we get a new line. Our goal is to reduce the error, or – in other words – of minimizing the cost function. When the cost function is minimized, we have found the best fit line and discovered the function that we were seeking.

SUPERVISED: MULTIDIMENSIONAL REGRESSION

What we saw above was one x-variable, that is, SAT scores to predict the y-value GPA. What if we want to use more features? For example, to improve our chances of predicting the GPA values, we can add variables, such as how many hours a student spends on social media daily, male versus female, hours spent on extracurricular activities, or plays active sports. That will give us many x-input values and our discovering of the function will become a multivariable problem. The overall concept, however, of minimizing the cost function, will remain the same.

UNSUPERVISED

Unsupervised: Clustering

Unsupervised learning is both highly strange and extremely interesting because in many cases you do not know what you are looking for or what you will find. You take the data and allow it to form natural groupings. It is as if data will accumulate around other data with which it has some type of affinity. Once the data groups together, you can then start looking at the groups and see if you find something interesting. For example, you can take a large data set related to your customers or suppliers and then run clustering algorithms to see if you discover interesting, in many cases previously unknown, information about them.

I teach clustering by introducing the concept of "conceptual proximity" (i.e., data has a conceptual affinity to cluster around other data). We take the total data population and divide it into multiple groups based upon data points having greater affinity to those with whom they are grouped.

One of the clustering algorithms known as k-means clustering (MacQueen, 1967; Lloyd, 1982) works by randomly placing a certain number (k) of datapoints (known as centroids) in the middle of the feature datapoints and then calculating distance between feature datapoints and the centroids. Each feature vector is considered a datapoint and the centroids are dropped at random locations in the middle of the datapoints. The (Euclidian) squared distance is calculated from the points to the centroids and those points that are closer to each of the centroids are grouped together. Then the process is iteratively repeated till the position of the centroids is optimized.

Let us say we have two features X1 and X2 about customers and we want to find out how to group customers based upon those features. We start by dropping two centroids (the dark triangles) at random locations as shown in Figure 5.16. We didn't think about their positions, we simply dropped them in the midst of the feature vectors – centric data points. Based upon Euclidean squared distance we start by identifying points closest to them and then establishing two groups (Figure 5.17).

Now we have split our data into two groups – notice the line parting the two groups. But we shouldn't stop there. Let's calculate the average of the data points in each group and force our centroids to move to those new average positions.

You can see in Figure 5.18 that the new positions (darker triangles) are identified for the centroids. They left their original positions (white triangles) and moved to the center of their respective clusters. But their moving does

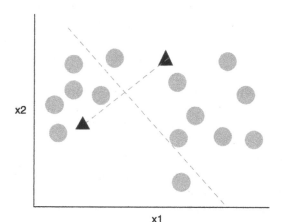

FIGURE 5.16   Step 1 of Clustering k-Means

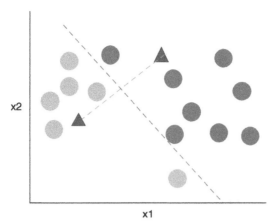

FIGURE 5.17 Step 2 k-Means Clustering

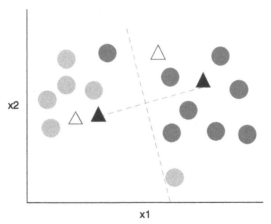

FIGURE 5.18 Step 3 k-Means Clustering

something we didn't expect. The Euclidian distance between the original points and the centroids has now changed. This means we can now re-divide the clusters – shifting members based upon the new division.

As shown in Figure 5.19, now they are redivided into new clusters. We can now calculate the new average for the points and once again force our centroids to move. And we can keep on iterating till our average position of center of the cluster does not change memberships of the data. This means that we now have

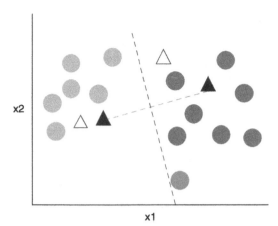

FIGURE 5.19 Step 4 k-Means Clustering

our final clusters. We can no longer split the data into any more clusters. Notice that data needs to be numerical to do this.

Now we can look into these clusters and see if our clusters represent meaningful information.

In real life, you will not have just two features. You will be working with many features. Take the example of fraudulent transactions. Let us say we have accumulated data on fraudsters and fraudulent transactions. We can cluster the population to discover some unique features of the fraudsters that we did not know before. Perhaps when the data got clustered, we realized that the group of younger fraudsters committed fraud in high-frequency, low transaction size versus older, who did low-frequency, large-transaction-sized frauds. Perhaps we can analyze the logs (metadata) to determine the presence of people with certain attributes who are showing up in a cluster that indicates irregular or anomalous communications or logins for some systems.

Clustering is used extensively in fraud detection and we will see several examples of that in later chapters.

NEURAL NETWORKS

Unlike the methods that I have explained up until now, neural networks is not only a different method, it is a different way of approaching the problems. It emulates how the human brain functions.

It can be viewed as a specific configuration of neurons, where neurons are divided into layers. There is an input layer where data comes in. There is an output layer where the result comes out. And there are hidden layers in between. This forms the network of neurons.

Think back to how I explained that machine learning tries to find a function that links the input with the output. Remember the diagram we looked at earlier, shown again in Figure 5.20? Well, what if we change seeking the function to a network structure that can embed the patterns of the data in its structure versus in variables.

For two input variables, it may look something like that shown in Figure 5.21. All we did was to replace seeking a function with seeking a neural structure in which we can get what we could have gotten from the function and more. So, what exactly does this structure do for us? Let's first understand how it works.

When the training starts, each neuron (also known as nodes) is a blank slate. It is dumb as a rock. As we pass feature vector data to the input layer, the neurons get activated. They quickly pass the data to the next layer. But before passing the data to the next layer, they tune themselves in relation to the data they just received. This tuning is pretty random. After all, at this stage all they can do is to arbitrarily pick some numbers for themselves and then hope for the best (I will explain later what "best" means). Now the next layer receives the data and, just like the previous layer, this layer, too, tunes itself and then sends the data to the next layer. This goes on till the data goes to the output layer and is then sent out of the network in the form of a predicted value.

PREDICT GPA BASED UPON SAT

SAT		GPA
850		2.8
900		2.9
950		2.9
1000		3.0
1050		3.1
1100		3.4
1150		3.5
1200		3.5
.		.
.		.
.		.

FIGURE 5.20 Predicting with a Function

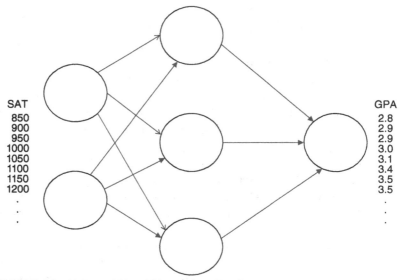

FIGURE 5.21 Using a Neural Network to Predict

At this stage, the predicted output is compared to the actual target value (the y-value, the dependent variable). The difference between the two is seen as the feedback that must be provided to the neurons so they can tune themselves a little better.

Let us repeat the above in a slightly different form. When the network starts, all neurons are ignorant. As the data comes in, each neuron in the first layer takes the data and assigns a weight to it such that its value becomes:

$$\text{Input} * \text{weight} = \text{guess}$$

The weight is assigned randomly. Each neuron in the first layer will calculate the guess. And the sum of guesses from the first layer will be passed on to the neurons in the next layer. This becomes the input for the next neuron. Here we ask the question whether this neuron should be activated or not. Just like the human brain, certain neural pathways are better to solve a specific problem. To make that determination, we taper our "guess" by multiplying it with something known as an activation function. The activation can be viewed as something that can turn the guess from a number of any size to a number between 0 and 1 (think probability) and then serve as a gateway where we can specify whether to pass the numbers to the next neuron or not. Passing values from one neuron to another neuron in the subsequent layer is known as firing

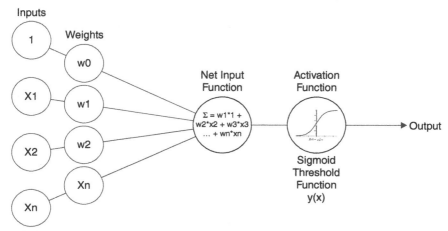

FIGURE 5.22 How a Neuron Passes the Output to the Next Layer

the neuron. If it passes on the next node (neuron), the node becomes activated and does the same exact thing. It takes in the input, assigns weight, and then tapers it with the activation function to take it to the next layer, and the next layer, and the next layer, till it reaches the output.

What you see in Figure 5.22 is repeated for each neuron. As the output layer is reached, a final answer is spitted out of the network (Figure 5.23).

This output represents the output of the entire network. So, the output is compared to the actual or the correct answer such that:

Correct (Actual) answer–guess = Error

This error is now fed back into the network so that it can be used to adjust the weights such that on the next try the network learns to close the error gap.

Error ∗ weight's contribution to error = Fine − tuning

This back-feeding into the network to fine-tune the weights is known as back propagation. Based upon the fine-tuned weights, the network once again goes through the forward propagation process (i.e., nodes from each layer passing the fine-tuned calculations to the next layer) to make another attempt at guessing the answer and based upon the error generated once again back propagates.

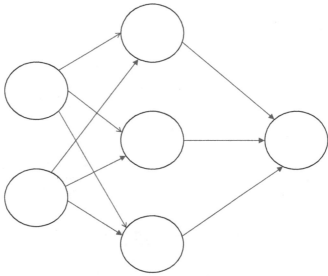

FIGURE 5.23 A Neural Network

This back-and-forth continues till the error is minimized. Once minimized, we can declare that our neural network is now trained. Now the structure of the network is such that it has learned the data on which it was trained. If we give this network the input test data, it now has the capability to give the right answers.

Deep Learning

Unlike an ordinary neural network, deep learning is a neural network that has several hidden layers (Figure 5.24).

This upcoming technology is so extremely powerful that it is being used to teach machines how to perform sophisticated tasks such as analyzing pictures, videos, and voice for patterns. Unlike other neural networks one thing that is profound about deep learning is that the network develops the ability to understand which features are more relevant for predicting the output. Deep learning uses multiple layers and systematically extracts features. This means that the deep leaning network will take the raw input and can extract different details about the data at different levels. The word "deep" in deep learning stands for several hidden layers.

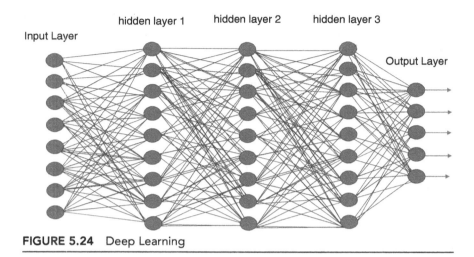

hidden layer 1   hidden layer 2   hidden layer 3

Input Layer

Output Layer

FIGURE 5.24   Deep Learning

PREPROCESSING THE DATA

Before we finish this chapter, it is critical that we go over one of the most important processes performed before we run any algorithms. Data needs to be prepared before it can be fed to the algorithms. This means that data needs to be converted to digital form. In addition to numericalization of data, many other operations are also performed at the preprocessing stage. In the following discussion I will discuss those processes.

Converting the Data to Numbers

Algorithms use numerical data. All data needs to be efficiently converted into numbers. The data is organized and structured in a format that it can feed into the algorithm. Rows with missing values are either removed or data filled in for them. Data quality is analyzed.

Feature Extraction

Our ability to understand pattern configurations is immensely powerful. Going back to the template concept, it is likely we do not match every property to determine what everything is. It would take too long to do that. When we see a book or hear the word "book," we do not go through a checklist of every property a book possesses to determine if it is a book or not. It is as if intuitively we know it is a book. That could be because we are hardwired to ignore all the possible properties of patterns and focus on the most important ones to determine if it is a book. If I see a book, I can tell it is a book by focusing on the most important visual elements relevant to make that determination. I could be wrong, as someone could have given me a fake book, like the ones used for home decoration. But simply by observing the high-level information, I know it is a book. Thus, we can process information selectively and choose to focus on important elements while ignoring everything else. This makes us very efficient. The same way it is far more efficient for the algorithm to focus on those features that add most predictive value to the output. The process by which we determine which features are important and which are not is part of the preprocessing exercise. Typically features with low variance and highly correlated features are removed.

Dimensionality Reduction

Sometimes combining the variables to reduce the number of variables speeds up the solution. It is done by transforming the features via mathematical operations. This is known as dimensionality reduction.

Data Normalization

Sometimes features may have large differences between the sizes of numbers. For example, one column may have data in thousands while another column may have it in tiny decimal numbers. Data normalization is achieved by making numbers across columns (features) comparable. Also, sometimes extreme values in the data are removed.

Key Points

- There are several methods that are used in machine learning.
- Machine learning finds a function that links the input with the output.
- Machine learning is about minimizing the cost function.
- There are several classification algorithms.
- Another form of supervised learning is regression. Regression is used to predict continuous variables.
- Clustering algorithms fall under unsupervised learning.
- Deep learning is a neural network with several hidden layers.

▓ REFERENCES

Ben-Hur, A., Horn, D., Siegelmann, H., and Vapnik, V.N. (2001) "Support vector clustering". Journal of Machine Learning Research. 2: 125–137.

Boser, B. E., Guyon, I. M., and Vapnik, V.N. (2010) *A training algorithm for optimal margin classifiers.* [online] Available from: http://findit.dtu.dk/en/catalog?utf8=✓&locale=en&search_field=all_fields&q=training+algorithm+for+optimal+margin.

Castellanos, S. (2019) Visa to test advanced AI to prevent fraud: A cloud-based platform set to roll out this year will test deep-learning algorithms to better detect unauthorized transactions. *The Wall Street Journal.* [online] Available from: https://www.wsj.com/articles/visa-to-test-advanced-ai-to-prevent-fraud-11565205158.

Ho, T. K. (1995, August). Random decision forests. In Proceedings of 3rd international conference on document analysis and recognition (Vol. 1, pp. 278–282). IEEE.

Lloyd, S. P. (1982) Least squares quantization in PCM. *IEEE Transactions on Information Theory*, 28 (2): 129–137.

MacQueen, J. (1967) Some methods for classification and analysis of multivariate observations. *Proceedings of the Fifth Berkeley Symposium on Mathematical Statistics and Probability, University of California Press, Berkeley, Calif.*, 1281–1297. [online] Available from: https://projecteuclid.org/euclid.bsmsp/1200512992.

CHAPTER SIX

Building an IAA Audit Firm
The Planning Toolkit

I N THE PREVIOUS TWO CHAPTERS we observed the power of machine learning. We saw that machine learning offers a host of methods, approaches, and models to develop powerful solutions. We also recognized in Chapter 4 that machine learning is only one of the four tools of automation for audit. The other tools are robotic process automation (RPA), process mining, and expert systems. In this chapter we build the basic design and analysis toolkit that will enable us to know how to develop intelligent audit automation (IAA) solutions and it will also give us an understanding of intelligent agents.

WHY PLAN AND DESIGN?

Imagine the alternative to not having a structured process for performing design activities. Recall the times when expert systems were presented as the greatest thing since sliced bread.

Expert systems were viewed as the ultimate solution to a wide spectrum of accounting problems (Meservy et al., 1992). Their eventual decline reveals our inherent inability to predict the future. In some ways, we paint the future in terms of what we would like it to be rather than what it can be. In a journal article, Alles and Gray (2016) touch upon an important historical lesson. Referring to the Ellis report from 1993, they remind us regarding our euphoric optimism about new technologies. The Ellis report predicted that by 2013, audit fees would swell from $14 billion to $21 billion. Just the e-commerce assurance part was estimated to contribute up to $6.25 billion. The actual number turned out to be $8 billion for 2013, far less than what the Ellis report had predicted. Alles and Gray also remind us that the artificial intelligence promise for audit automation has been around for decades.

It wasn't that long ago when expert systems were expected to revolutionize audit and in 1991 Brown (1991) identified 43 expert systems in use by the Big 6, of which Gray et al. claim (Gray et al., 2014) that none are in use. The sudden deaths of promising technologies raise some questions. Is it possible that the audit firms' setup and focus contributed to their inability to automate? For instance, did audit firms focus on short-term profitability, and after making some initial investments decided that it is better to keep things simple and old-style, and instead of investing in new technologies, it makes more sense to distribute the money among partners?

Another question could be whether the audit technology was so complicated and tedious and expensive to maintain that the return on investment was not worth it.

I believe the real answer is that both factors were at play. The real issue is that without a design toolkit or body of knowledge that gives a clear strategy and process for automation, automation remains directionless. It happens in a sporadic and chaotic way. Systems refuse to scale or work with each other. Some processes are automated, others are not. Design initiatives do not consider interdependent elements. Millions are invested but no return is realized. Disappointed executives lose hope (and their jobs). New teams are brought in with expectations that they will be able to fix things with a magic wand. The wand is used but no magic happens. Hype dies down and technology-related return on investment does not materialize.

Despite being in consulting and advisory roles, we tend to be not very good with planning. During the new-technology-hyping period, market research firms, consultants, and even some academics play a nonconstructive role. Instead of fully understanding client problems or developing a more strategic perspective, consulting firms try to rush clients into adopting new technologies. Adoption without planning is a sure recipe for disaster.

As companies are rushing to implement intelligent automation, the above mentioned chaotic scenario is unfolding again. Many companies that implemented artificial intelligence are failing to realize return on investment (Vanian, 2019).

In the audit world, we observe growing interest in intelligent automation. The current dynamics have introduced new challenges for audit firms. First, the secondary and tertiary stakeholders who silently benefited from the accounting information have emerged from the shadows and have become the primary stakeholders of the audit information. This includes not just investors, but also regulators, government, public interest groups, Congress or Parliament, ethics groups, and others. Second, the emphasis on data and information has placed audit and accounting at the center of all corporate activity and decision-making. Third, the external reliance on data produced by a firm has increased tremendously. The data analyzed is not just numeric (financial data) and disclosures, but also nearly all communications by a firm are under full scrutiny. All that information is picked by algorithms and incorporated into some potential actions. Fourth, the audit field has recognized that the innovations in finance and economics have created new risks for the profession. The Great Recession of 2007–2009 showed that the profession needed to be ahead of the complexity introduced by the sophisticated derivative products. Fifth, the profession recognized that traditional assurance services and other services (e.g., valuation, risk management, and forensic accounting) required audit firms to be more responsive to the client needs. These developments imply that the design of audit automation cannot be done in isolation. It requires careful planning.

I want to equip you with the design and planning tools so that when you think about audit automation, you do so in a disciplined and structured way. At the conclusion of this chapter we will be fully prepared to take on Part Two, which will focus on the end-to-end audit automation.

 ## STUDYING AGENTS

An intelligent agent is a goal-directed synthetic artifact that interacts with its environment by receiving information through its sensors, and by acting back to the environment via its actuators, and makes decisions using its knowledge and learning capabilities.

The study of intelligent automation in business is the study of exploring optimal ways to create shareholder value by adopting intelligent systems. This definition therefore places the field in the realm of planning and management of intelligent automation but also in the area of conducting such activities in a manner that maximizes the shareholder value.

Here, the term *intelligent automation* is defined as using machines that autonomously perform the type of work that requires purposeful resolution of uncertainty. Also, in this context uncertainty can be viewed as the complexity of a task and includes both physical (for example, a moving robot or flying drone) and cognitive (for example, making decisions). Higher complexity tasks can be viewed as pursuing goals in more complex, and therefore uncertain, environments. In that regard, the practitioner of IAA engages in activities that help design, evaluate, envision, manage, lead, plan, and implement intelligent automation projects.

In the context of intelligent audit automation, or IAA, we study the design and development of intelligent agents used in audit work.

We address questions such as:

- How do we structure the audit process for IAA?
- How do we then break the audit process down into subprocesses?
- How do we determine what types of agents will be needed?
- How do we design agents?
- How do we determine the interaction of the agents?

To answer the above questions, I will offer the process developed at the American Institute of Artificial Intelligence. This process is composed of the following six tools, where each tool represents one degree of planning. To design and develop new AI products, you need Six Degrees of Planning:

1. First Degree of Planning: VIGOR (Value, Intelligent Design, Governance, Organization, and Responsiveness)
2. Second Degree of Planning: APA (Automation, Activities, and Processes)
3. Third Degree of Planning: DTCM (Do, Think, Create, Model)
4. Fourth Degree of Planning: SADAL® (Sense, Analyze, Decide, Act, Learn)
5. Fifth Degree of Planning: ELCAD (Efficient Learning Capability Automation Design)
6. Sixth Degree of Planning: Life-cycle Planning

First Degree of Planning: VIGOR

VIGOR has five dimensions: Value, Intelligent Design, Governance, Organization, and Responsiveness.

Value

An intelligent automation – aspiring organization must first focus on value. The value focus means that it looks at its entire value cycle and determines how the entity creates value. VIGOR does not consider value creation as a chain but instead as a cycle. This cycle is driven by two drivers. The first are value drivers and include factors such as revenues, costs, and cost of capital. The second are behavioral and include factors such as expectations, opinions, evaluations, appraisals, sentiments, attitudes, and emotions of various stakeholders. Value prediction and measurement becomes a process of understanding value creation as a dynamic and cognitive process that results from a firm's ability to efficiently and effectively automate. Besides analyzing the value creation process, you must also study the alternative value creation frameworks to develop an optimized and synthesized version of the automation strategy. To perform this activity, you need to analyze the total work value chain (business model plus what work creates value) of the firm and answer the following:

Value = Financial Value + Social Value

Automation Value = Innovation Value + Execution Value

Innovation Value comes from deploying automation to create extraordinary and unexpected innovation in both R&D (research and development) and customer service.

Execution Value comes from being able to execute current strategies better.

Understanding the business problem to solve is one thing, developing the strategic perspective of business model redesign another. In intelligent automation, a firm must spend significant time and effort to fully understand the business problems as well as the business model. Review the first chapter to see the considerations for developing the cognitive product or service. At this stage, your intelligent automation team will not just look at how the current process happens but also what is possible. For instance, your current processes are often designed around human participation. In other words, the human is a critical part of the workflow. In many automatable processes, human presence or participation is unnecessary. I explain this phenomenon by giving the analogy of a manufacturing plant. The old-style manufacturing plants were built around humans conducting several parts of the manufacturing (e.g., packaging, moving goods from one point to another, bringing in the raw material). In order to make that possible, plants were designed with the mindset that a large number of humans would work there. When manufacturing plants were fully automated, their designs did not require elaborate consideration for large-scale human presence in the plant. Similarly, intelligent automation processes are not necessarily designed around humans.

Intelligent Design

Intelligent design includes three parts. In the first part a firm's total work chain is analyzed based upon core value creation processes. In the second part work chains and cognitive chains are obtained by breaking down the preferred value cycle into various process and task-centric configurations. Work chains are composed of task automation and skill automation. Tasks are the work steps, whereas skills are the necessary human skills needed to complete the task. In part three cognitive chains are analyzed to understand if processes can be improved or innovated. Let us take an example from audit:

> **Step 1. The Audit Work Chain:** A key concept is to analyze how an audit firm creates value for clients and identify the audit process. For instance, based upon current practices we know that it is composed of preplanning, risk assessment, audit procedures, and reporting.
>
> **Step 2. Work Analysis:** We recognize that value creation in each step in the audit process is a function of audit quality and cost. We take an inventory of human skills needed to accomplish the audit process steps. We map each audit process step to one or more human skills needed for that task to be completed.
>
> **Step 3. Envision Process Modifications:** We try to expand, modify, and creatively think how the process can be expanded to increase its overall value. For example, in addition to other methods, we can propose to perform risk assessment of revenues by looking at the social media updates of customers about the products and services that the firm sells. Another example will be to add continuous monitoring to audit as a process step that follows the reporting.

Governance

Governance is a comprehensive process to ensure that the automation will be used responsibly, that it is bias free, and its impact on humans, human institutions, and human civilization has been analyzed and determined. This ensures that the artificial intelligence technology is being deployed for the benefit of humankind and that the artifact will sustain its goals and will be safe for use.

Organization

The organizational planning includes three parts: (a) managing the modern "digital + human" organization effectively, (b) developing human skills for the new era, and (c) ensuring that despite automation human dignity stays intact. This is the change management part and it needs to be included in any intelligent automation project.

Responsiveness

The modern business is not static. Changes in market conditions and competitive dynamics require rapid change response. In today's world, a firm's intelligent automation architecture should be such that it can analyze signals from the market and then prepare an effective operating response. Such a responsive architecture also includes the performance measurement features that analyze whether the entity is achieving its goals or not. To stay competitive a firm needs metacognition that enables it to understand its network of activities and actors, and the relationships between actors and activities. Responsiveness means that the enterprise architecture must be designed to incorporate the ultimate reality of modern competitive dynamics; that is, dynamic and responsive measurement of strategy and execution changes is key to transformation.

Second Degree of Planning: Activities and Processes Automation

The second degree of planning expands the intelligent automation step of the VIGOR tool (discussed in the previous section). This focuses on understanding the activities and subprocesses. They are derived from the base value creation processes discovered in the previous exercise.

For example, the base process of audit was identified as Preplanning, Risk Assessment, Procedures, and Reporting. The subprocesses in Risk Assessment would be (a) Inherent Risk Assessment and (b) Internal Controls Assessment. Both of those subprocesses are analyzed for activities performed within each process.

As shown in Figure 6.1 the activities are composed of work tasks. For example, internal control assessment may require asking and analyzing questions; thus the key activities will be developing, sending, and reviewing

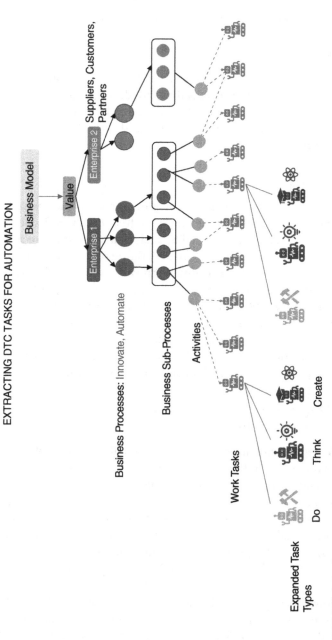

FIGURE 6.1 Extracting DTC Tasks for Automation

the questionnaire. The work tasks for the first activity, that is, developing the questionnaire, will be (1) identify the client industry, (2) determine the client specific risks, (3) determine which questions should be asked, (4) prepare the questionnaire, and (5) send the questionnaire to the auditee.

On the cognitive scale, task automation is a low-skill and repetitive task that can be automated by using robotic process automation. Skill automation requires greater intelligence and can be automated by deploying machine learning and expert systems. Finally, cognitive chains are analyzed to understand the decision dynamics in a firm.

At this step analyze what cognitive work is performed by humans. It starts by looking at each node in the work process and then determining what nodes represent human decisions. For example, determining how large a sample should be analyzed in audit is a human-centered decision. Another example is deciding to do physical inventory in a warehouse would be a human-centered decision.

Third Degree of Planning: The DTC Model of Intelligent Artifact

An intelligent agent is a goal-directed synthetic artifact that acts on its environment by receiving information through its sensors and acting via its actuators and makes decisions using its knowledge and learning. It can be a simple agent that performs a simple atomic task, or it can do very complex things, such as performing a sophisticated audit. However, when we divide work tasks, we realize that the task could be composed of any combination of three types of work – doing, thinking, and creating.

As shown in Figure 6.2 the DTC model stands for Do, Think, Create and it refers to relative degree of intelligence needed in an intelligent artifact to perform work. Let us consider an example. Say we want to design an agent to make restaurant reservations. We can designate three levels of progressively increasing intelligence levels for this artifact:

1. **Doing:** "Doing" is where the artifact performs a single atomic task when it receives some stimulus. Let us say you are designing an agent to make restaurant reservations. The work needed to accomplish the restaurant reservation can be broken down into calling the restaurant, conversing to make the reservation, and understanding and responding to unexpected situations. At the most basic level of work task you can ask your agent to make the calls. It has one single clear task to do: make the call. You can

		UNCERTAINTY	EXAMPLE	TECHNOLOGY
	Do	Absolute clarity on what needs to get done, zero to no variability, high repeatability	Pick oranges (anything that comes on the conveyer belt)	Robotic Process Automation, Machine Learning, Expert Systems
	Think	Variability due to randomness or inability to process information, multiple possibilities and paths, less repeatability	Identify oranges and apples. Separate them. Recognize good vs. bad, large vs. small	Machine Learning, Expert Systems
	Create	Unlimited set of possibilities, unlimited paths, no repeatability, novel and innovative	Develop the ability to identify new types of fruits, packages, target to customers, etc.	Machine Learning

FIGURE 6.2 DTC Model

experience that with Siri on your phone where you can command Siri to make a call. This is an atomic structure where instruction generates a single response. Often, the response may depend upon the task criteria.

2. **Thinking:** The next level of intelligence is where an artifact is able to have a sustained conversation with the reservation staff member of the restaurant. The thinking agent will be able to have a brief sustained conversation to make a reservation; however, its interaction will be limited to handle only a moderate level of uncertainty. This will include informing the person on the other end that the agent is calling to make a reservation, provide information about the name, seating requirements, date and time, and receiving feedback. This agent performs some thinking. It needs some flexibility in understanding that the person on the other end of the call may say things differently, in different accents, or ask some questions.

3. **Creating:** The creating agent will be able to develop a more sophisticated strategy on making restaurant reservations. For example, the agent may know your requirements so well that you may not even have to ask the agent and the agent will know that you need to make a reservation. The agent can then call the restaurant and, if declined due to capacity constraints, can try to negotiate. If the negotiation fails, as an alternative it can follow up with another restaurant. This agent is using its creativity as it is responding to more complex uncertain situations.

The DTC model helps us break down the work-tasks into the types of agents that will be needed to get the work done. Some of the agents may be simple Do agents only. Others could be Thinking agents. Yet others could be a combination of Do and Think. Today companies are developing Create agents for work processes. For example, one of the most fascinating upcoming buildings, the Future Museum in Dubai, was designed by using algorithms. Trading algorithms can explore and create strategies. Pharmaceutical companies are using agents to develop new molecules.

Fourth Degree of Planning: SADAL®

Notice that by the time you complete the third degree of planning, you have already identified the agents that you will be needing to automate the work process.

The Fourth Degree of Planning involves two steps:

1. Detailed analysis of the internal structure of each agent. It is performed by using the SADAL® framework. See Figure 6.3.
2. Performing multi-agent analysis to model the interaction of multiple agents.

At this stage, we will develop the high-level analysis needed to design the various components of each agent. The SADAL® framework is used to develop a design structure for the agent. The acronym SADAL® stands for Sense, Analyze, Decide, Act, and Learn. The use of verbs to identify components of the agent is intentional as it forces designers to think in terms of actions performed by the agent.

Sense: The first component is Sense and its job is to give the agent a sense of the external environment. The Sense component is like the eyes and ears of the agent and it brings in the external data. The description of Sense includes the types of sensors the agent uses to perform its function. It also includes the types of data that is captured by the sensors.

Analyze: In the Analyze component, we determine the goals, performance measures, knowledge components, and how the agent maps internal state to the environment.

SADAL				
Sales forecasting using product reviews, sales data, media chat about firm and products and service.				
SENSE	ANALYZE	DECIDE	ACT	LEARN
Product reviews (social media) Market share by markets Social media chat about firm Social media chat about product	Uses data from social media and internal sales data. Clean and preprocess data sets.	Forecast the sales	Notify upon changes.	Learn to do it autonomously and constantly.

FIGURE 6.3 The SADAL® Process

Decide: In the Decide component we analyze the decision made by the agent in response to the data received by the sensors. The decisions could be from a stored knowledge base (for example, RPA or expert system) or from a learned process (for example, from machine learning).

Act: This component determines how the artifact outputs or actuates actions back to its environment.

Learn: The Learn component determines if the agent is a learning agent and what type of learning method will be used by the agent. Any intelligent agent will have some level of knowledge representation, but the learning part in the SADAL® framework is specifically designed to be a machine learning system. At this stage, the designer determines whether the system will perform classification or regression, if it will use a neural network, etc.

Fifth Degree of Planning: ELCAD (Efficient Learning Capability Automation Design

ELCAD is composed of five steps and they are intended only for systems that are learning systems and use machine-learning. It has five parts:

1. **Preprocessing:** This was covered in the previous chapter. This part includes preparing the data to be fed into the algorithm.
2. **Algorithm Selection:** This includes understanding which algorithm works best for the type of data you have and the problem you are trying to solve. In some cases, you may not know which works best and you have to try multiple models.
3. **Training:** This is where you train your algorithm. In certain cases you may need to train multiple algorithms so you can test results.
4. **Evaluation:** Evaluation is using various tests to determine how accurate and relevant your model is to the data. Note that performance expectations will be clarified in the Analysis part of SADAL®.
5. **Architecture:** Architecture refers to the IT infrastructure-related design concerns that include integration, deployment, and other such issues.

Sixth Degree of Planning: Life-Cycle Planning for Agent

The Sixth Degree of Planning refers to life-cycle planning for the agent. In addition to ensuring that the agent stays relevant, effective, and efficient, it also looks at the stability of the agent. A learning agent's environment or goals can change. From a machine-learning perspective new features may be needed for better quality product or the underlying data distributions of the data used to train the original model may have changed. For example, we trained our model to detect fraud based upon the fraud strategies employed by fraudsters and that are known to us. But fraudsters can evolve their strategies and our system may not be able to catch that. In the Sixth Degree of Planning we deploy methods that can make our systems turn into continuous learners.

CONCLUSION TO PART ONE

With this chapter we have finished Part One. Part One was about building the foundational knowledge. We began our journey by understanding the importance of the artificial intelligence revolution. We learned about the new challenges for audit and then took a deeper dive into artificial intelligence as a field. We learned about various types of machine-learning approaches and the methods.

By now you can appreciate that data science or artificial intelligence are not like rest of the IT. It is a different skillset. It is not engineering the system for data – instead it is engineering the system from data. It is all about data. Generally, the more data you have, the better you can train your algorithm. The better trained your algorithm is, the better its ability to solve your problem effectively and efficiently.

We now have a clear path forward on how to take the audit firm from AIS to Autonomous, as shown in Figure 6.4. We will not get there overnight – or even in a decade. But we must begin the journey now. Our journey needs to have clear objectives and it must be guided by a pragmatic but inspiring plan. In Part Two, we will develop the plan and vision that will move our audit firms to intelligent audit automation.

AIS	Automated	Augmented	Autonomous
Computerization	Basic repetitive tasks automated	Several parts of the process automated	Total process automated
Transactions	Some level of variability	Machine-human joint control	Machine has control over the process
Deterministic Tasks	Human fully in charge of	over the process	Machine makes decision
Reports	major parts of the process	Human makes decision	
ERP/BI/BA	Robotic Process Automation	Machine Learning	Agents/Multiagent
	ERP/BI/BA	Robotic Process Automation	Machine Learning
	(Light ML)	ERP/BI/BA	Robotic Process Automation
			ERP/BI/BA

FIGURE 6.4 The Journey Forward

Key Points

- To successfully automate, we must plan.
- Our planning methodology includes six degrees of planning.
- It begins by analyzing the business model and the related work processes.
- It breaks down process into subprocesses and activities.
- Each activity is broken down into an atomic work-task and one or more agents are identified for automating the work-task.
- The agent's internal structure is developed using the SADAL® method.
- The machine-learning component of the agent is further expanded.
- The overall architecture for the artifacts is designed.
- Finally, the life-cycle planning is performed for the intelligent agent.

 REFERENCES

Alles, M. and Gray, G. L. (2016) Incorporating big data in audits: Identifying inhibitors and a research agenda to address those inhibitors. *International Journal of Accounting Information Systems.* [Online] 2244–2259. Available from: http://dx.doi.org/10.1016/j.accinf.2016.07.004.

Brown, C. E. (1991) Expert systems in public accounting: Current practice and future directions. *Expert Systems With Applications.* [Online] 3 (1), 3–18.

Gray, G. L., Chiu, V., Liu, Q., and Li, P. (2014) The expert systems life cycle in AIS research: What does it mean for future AIS research? *International Journal of Accounting Information Systems.* [Online] 15 (4), 423–451. Available from: http://dx.doi.org/10.1016/j.accinf.2014.06.001.

Meservy, R. D., Denna, E. L., and Hansen, J. V. (1992) Application of artificial intelligence to accounting, tax, and audit services: Research at Brigham Young University. *Expert Systems With Applications.* [Online] 4 (2), 213–218.

Vanian, J. (2019) Why most companies are failing at artificial intelligence: Eye on A.I. Fortune.com [online]. Available from: https://fortune.com/2019/10/15/why-most-companies-are-failing-at-artificial-intelligence-eye-on-a-i/. https://fortune.com/2019/10/15/why-most-companies-are-failing-at-artificial-intelligence-eye-on-a-i/

PART TWO

Building the Automated Audit Function in the Enterprise

W E OWE OUR GRATITUDE TO Henry Ford for introducing the power of successive and sequential processes connected with the goal of producing a final product. Since then, the twentieth century saw an upsurge in innovative assembly lines. The assembly line concept jumped from manufacturing into the services sector and the last quarter of the century saw the rise of services assembly lines. In the communal furnaces of consulting and audit firms, crude and segregated tasks were made malleable, hammered and forged into clean wrought processes. What came out was a neat linear assembly line that streamlined various service deliveries. One of those services was audit.

The audit process is composed of several interdependent steps that lead to the audit report. Despite the linearity and process orientation, major problems have beleaguered the audit profession. The fact that audit is quite an unswerving annual ritual, often augmented by internal audits that are supposed to add another degree of credibility, and that the reported financial statements are released wrapped in the protective shield of audits, one should expect audit quality to be impeccable and ironclad successful. Nothing should go wrong, as the shield of assurance is the last anchor on which investors and other stakeholders rely to keep their financial boats afloat and ground them when storms of uncertainty strike. The global economic performance rests on those audit reports.

Despite such immaculate expectations, audit failures seem to have become the new normal. And that is when the bar is kept significantly low. After all, many auditors approach audits as verifying the presentation of the financial statements. They couldn't care less if the firm they are auditing is clinging to that little bush at the edge of the cliff – as long as they can feel good about the assertions used to manufacture the historical financials. Ignoring the underlying economics and the systems used to map the economic activities to the financial statements is often accepted as the pragmatic approach. If the bars were raised to include early stage fraud discovery, or sudden and major value loss, or the inclusion of operational performance and decision-making as subject to auditable assurance, the failure of audits would be even more prevalent.

The problems with audit are behavioral and not procedural. In most cases procedures exist but are not applied or are intentionally ignored. Where procedures don't exist, intentional ignorance (you know you don't know and still proceed) is applied to move forward. Both are behavioral issues. At the core of these behaviors is the human behavior. Our decisions and pursuits are not independent of our emotions and feelings. Professional skepticism is a behavioral attribute.

Machines do not exhibit these fears. But machines can learn to adapt human biases. After all, if they are being trained on data that we provide, they learn our biases and fears. We will cover this more in the ethics chapter.

Our audit automation process is based upon five processes:

Automated Preaudit Evaluation,

Automated Risk Assessment,

Automated Audit Procedures,

Automated Post-Audit Management, and

Automated Assurance, Forensic, and Valuation.

The IAA model assumes that the design of the automation will incorporate continuous, intelligent, and automated.

In this part we will cover the first four areas. Part Three will focus on Assurance, Forensic, and Valuation. We will follow the methodology developed in Chapter 6 and describe the automation in audit.

CHAPTER SEVEN

Obtain, Retain, and Preplan with AI

C AN ARTIFICIAL INTELLIGENCE (AI) be used to assess and compare the cultures of companies? MIT researchers think so. MIT Sloan launched a study to measure and compare culture across various companies (Sull et al., 2019). Known as Culture 500, MIT researchers used natural language processing to evaluate values like agility, collaboration, customer, diversity, execution, innovation, integrity, performance, and report. Using data from Glassdoor, the research study focused on classifying words (sentences) written by employees or former employees in Glassdoor. These words became the hunting grounds for the researchers to identify patterns that can help evaluate the culture of a firm. The researchers wanted to understand how to classify words into cultural categories. To make it work they trained the algorithm by developing custom hand-coded features. The results turned out to be fascinating, as they were able to study and compare cultures of hundreds of companies. The lesson here is that audit firms can deploy tools that can provide rapid and continuous assessment of a prospective client in creative ways. Just as the Culture 500 artifact has been trained to identify and measure the cultural elements of firms, new AI-based artifacts can be developed to study, analyze, and warn about many areas that are part of audit preplanning. This chapter introduces you to those opportunities.

SOLVING THE BEHAVIORAL PROBLEMS IN AUDIT

One of the values measured by MIT study was integrity. It is important to recognize that in MIT's model integrity is a cultural value; however, culture is a product of how individuals, especially leaders, of a firm conduct themselves.

KPMG's audit problems are not new. The audit firm has been a target of investigations, fines, and allegations of misconduct for several years. While much of this chapter is about using technology to improve the ethics and governance frameworks of audit firms, the irony is that KPMG offers an example of where the AI technology was used to do just the opposite. KPMG, it was revealed, contracted Palantir, a Palo Alto – based firm, to apply a model to predict which engagements would be inspected by the regulator (McKenna, 2018). Furthermore, it was alleged that KPMG hired a former Public Company Accounting Oversight Board (PCAOB) employee and tried to probe him to disclose which of KPMG's audits would be audited by PCAOB (the regulator). As the saga unfolded, it was further pointed out that the compliance issues were widespread and extensive. KPMG ended up firing several employees. PCAOB's report on KPMG LLP 2016 audits found deficiencies in 43% (22 of 51) of audits (PCAOB, 2019). Deficiencies related both to testing controls for purposes of the ICFR opinion and to the substantive testing performed for purposes of the opinion on the financial statements. In response to the audit quality and misconduct allegations and investigation, KPMG responded with a letter (Ostrom, 2015).

In the letter, KPMG agreed that the firm had not satisfactorily addressed the quality control issues within the one-year period of the report publication. KPMG claimed that the remediation efforts were led by people who violated the firm's code of conduct and also inappropriately used PCAOB confidential information. Once the firm discovered that, it was reported to PCAOB and those employees were fired. To take proper remedial steps, KPMG reported that it had now hired and deployed new people who were chosen for their "sound judgment, professionalism, ethics, integrity, and ability to inspire the trust." KPMG also claimed that an enterprise-wide cultural assessment was performed by cultural change and ethics experts. To improve the audit quality, KPMG said that it was deploying a new technology and a new methodology that would focus more on internal controls and that the technology platform would be fully operational by 2020. The technology will enable workflow-centric improvements. Furthermore, the firm said that it is focusing on professional skepticism, supervision and review, and engagement quality control by enhancing training, clarifying roles, modifying processes, increasing accountability, and improving workflow. To improve monitoring, the firm will also move the Inspections Group from Audit Practice to the Legal, Risk and Regulatory department. The company also declared that a process for root-cause analysis will be invoked if an issue is reported based upon internal monitoring or external inspections.

While all of the above remediations are important steps toward improving the process, it is important to recognize that systems that are inherently dependent upon human intervention and decision-making are not necessarily foolproof. For example, the same scandal that rocked KPMG also led to the disclosure that the violations at KPMG went beyond the few who had been fired and were widespread and endemic (McKenna, 2019). The U.S. Securities and Exchange Commission (SEC) discovered that auditors (even senior-level employees) cheated on internal ethics, integrity, and compliance tests and intentionally manipulated the system to change the limits needed to pass the exam. So much for training, processes, and root-cause analysis!

Here are some interesting questions:

- Could KPMG have determined the personality traits or judgment of various auditors before the misconduct or quality compromises affected the client engagements?
- If KPMG could have used Palantir to predict which audits would be investigated by PCAOB, this implies that audit data has significant predictive power. Why couldn't KPMG have used the audit data to predict if the audit was effective or not while conducting the audit?
- Can KPMG deploy machines that monitor audits and auditors for professional skepticism?

Whether picking a new team member or a replacement member of the audit team, it is preferable to use a rational and data-oriented perspective to make those decisions. As pointed out previously in the book, the problems in audit – from both client and auditor side – are predominantly behavior related. Thus, when we think about automation, we must pay attention to both numbers and human behavior. Since significant problems that happen at the later stages of the audit can be avoided with better planning, the goal of preplanning automation is to improve both the quality and efficiency of audit.

AUTOMATED PREPLANNING SUBPROCESSES

The intelligent automation preplanning (aka Preaudit Evaluation) has two major subprocesses. The first subprocess is Automated Pre-Engagement Planning and the second is Automated Audit Planning (see Figure 7.1).

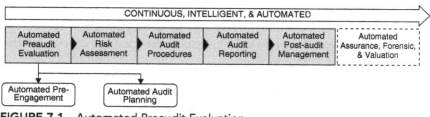

FIGURE 7.1 Automated Preaudit Evaluation

AUTOMATED PRE-ENGAGEMENT

The goal of pre-engagement activities is twofold: (1) to understand client desirability, and (2) to develop the engagement letter and agreement.

Understanding client desirability means to assess whether the audit firm wants the prospect as a client or not. There are many reasons why an audit firm wouldn't want a firm to become a client. For example, if the previous auditor abruptly resigned from the engagement, or the client has entered a new highly risky business, or the client has promoted or hired a management team that has a record of bad management and ethical compromises, or the client's management team has criminal record, or if the audit firm has a significant independence issue, then an audit firm may pass on the opportunity. In addition to those factors, the client may have legal or regulatory issues, an overly complex business model, or other such issues that may make it unattractive for the audit firm to conduct business with.

Once the audit firm has overcome the desirability issue and has determined that it will be acceptable for the firm to be the auditor of the prospective client, the audit firm can proceed to develop the engagement letter. In addition to the traditional items like objectives, responsibilities, etc., the engagement letter identifies constraints or limitations in the engagement and the expected financial arrangements (i.e., the auditor's fee).

AUTOMATED AUDIT PLANNING

This subprocess includes staffing, early stage analysis of risks, internal assessment, schedule development, specialist assessments, and most importantly understanding the financials, risks, and strategy of the firm.

While risk assessment is part of audit preplanning, from an automation perspective it is a broad area that I cover in the next two chapters.

AUTOMATED PRE-ENGAGEMENT ACTIVITIES AND WORK TASKS

As shown in Figure 7.2, automated pre-engagement subprocess is composed of three primary subprocesses and activities:

Activity 1: Automated Acceptance and Continuance of Audit
Activity 2: Automated Ethics and Independence Evaluation
Activity 3: Automated Contractual Agreement

Each of the three activities can be further segmented into lower level tasks:

- **Acceptance and Continuation of Audit:** This activity is based upon determining if the client is desirable and the audit firm will accept or continue with the client. This includes specifically looking at the following work-tasks:
  - **Management team background checks:** This agent performs background checks on the prospective client management team and uses public information to do that.
  - **Client financial background check:** This agent specifically looks at the financial performance of the firm. Most of the analysis is numerical (i.e., it uses financial information such as ratios and data from the financial statements); however, some of the more insightful parts are also based upon analyzing textual information such as analyst reports, news, articles, online comments, and general sentiments of various stakeholders. The agent also looks at the industry benchmarks.

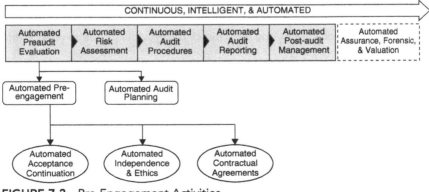

FIGURE 7.2 Pre-Engagement Activities

- **Client culture assessment:** Like the MIT Culture 500 product mentioned above, this agent performs various cultural assessments.
- **Client conflict patterns (e.g., lawsuits):** This agent looks at the various lawsuits the client is involved in as well as the general level of conflict that exists with various stakeholders (e.g., climate change or human rights activists).
- **Relationship assessment:** This agent compares the cultures of the audit firm and the culture of the client to observe if a reasonably sound relationship potential exists or not. If based upon the relationship assessment agent and other agents, the audit firm discovers that the client will not allow the auditor to perform audit with confidence and tenacity that is needed for a quality audit, it will be better to pass on the opportunity.
- **Extraordinary business risks:** This agent looks at the extraordinary or abnormal risks faced by the client.
- **Fraud index:** This agent uses the information from various sources (including the financial data) to assess the likelihood of fraud in a firm.
- **Ethics and Independence Evaluation**
  - **Independence in form evaluation:** This is an inward-looking agent that evaluates the audit firm to assess whether the firm is independent in all respects. It also focuses on the auditors.
  - **Independence in appearance evaluation:** This is also an introspective evaluation agent that looks at whether the audit firm or any of its auditors have violated the independence in appearance requirement.
  - **Ethics:** This agent ensures that ethical standards are maintained, that ethics trainings are completed, and that ethical conducted is pursued in all matters.
- **Contractual Agreement**
  - **Special requirements assessment:** This agent understands the special needs of a client and determines the type of extra help or specialist needed.
  - **Cost assessment:** This agent helps evaluate the cost of the audit.

As you can observe above, our concepts from Chapter 6 about planning have come in handy. We now have the entire process segmented into subtasks, activities, and work-tasks. The work-tasks are where automation materializes.

PRE-ENGAGEMENT *SADAL*

In the fourth stage of planning, we take each of the work-tasks and develop the structure of the intelligent agent by analyzing Sense, Analyze, Decide, Act, and Learn. While in the actual implementations of intelligent audit automation each of the above work-tasks will require a comprehensive evaluation, in this book I will present only few examples for illustration purposes. The ones I explain below will cover large areas and other SADAL analysis can be patterned after them.

Pre-Engagement SADAL for Background Analysis

Here, I will present a higher-level SADAL model for background checks. From this higher-level model, you can extract many applications of background checks. Background checks can apply to individuals (management teams of prospective clients, audit staff, partners, etc.) and can apply to entities (firms, business units, etc.). The goal of a background check is to give us a profile of the individual that can help answer the question: Is this person credible for the purpose he or she is being placed in charge or being held responsible for? It can also answer a related question that if a certain responsibility is assigned to a person, what could be the areas in which he or she is most likely to fail (intentionally, for example, due to moral weakness, or unintentionally, that is, due to being unskilled, incompetent, or negligent). At this stage the background check is performed using only publicly available information.

In addition to formal data available on individuals (e.g., credit, criminal, legal), these days we leave a trail of our activities on the web. This may include our articles, speeches, presentations, social media updates, organizational memberships, photos, comments, likes or dislikes, reviews, and so on. Our residential addresses can also reveal data about our estimated monthly mortgages or rents. All of that data is minable and becomes a source of providing great information.

For illustration purposes, I will present a general agent analysis. Readers can abstract the concepts to develop more customized applications for their specific uses. While audit firms are familiar with the criminal background checks, the SADAL agent presented in Table 7.1 takes those checks to the next level. We are designing an agent that will perform continuous background checks. Recall that such background checks can be performed for employees, management

TABLE 7.1 SADAL Analysis for Background Checks

Sense	Analyze	Decide	Act	Learn
▪ Data: Criminal, legal data (publicly available) ▪ Previous employment data ▪ Previous publicly disclosed sale/purchase of equity ▪ Previous legal data ▪ Social media ▪ LinkedIn ▪ Articles ▪ Interviews	▪ Look for criminal behavior and activity ▪ Identify deception-related personality traits ▪ Identify fraud-related personality traits	▪ Decision to hire or not hire OR decision to accept a client or not ▪ Recommendation to investigate more	▪ Provide ongoing feedback to the audit leaders ▪ Provide feedback to the engagement staffing/HR department	▪ Learn to perform the background checks ▪ Learn to classify candidates on various output dimensions of criminal behavior, deception traits, fraud traits

teams, etc. These capabilities should be deployed in audit firms on a proactive and preemptive basis. This means to preemptively start building such analytical capability as soon as the firm believes that a company may become a prospective client.

Pre-Engagement SADAL Analysis for Management Profile

Creating and keeping a management profile of prospective clients is an important consideration. It enables auditors to develop a deeper understanding of client executives' motivations, behaviors, and personalities. As stated before, it can give the auditor warning signs for potential misconduct. Using the language from molecular biology, these analyses are in vitro and noninvasive. The invitro part signifies that they can be conducted outside the client organization, in a lab. The noninvasive means that only public data is used to perform them.

Building a management profile requires analyzing publicly available information about the management teams. Some of the nonstandard signals hide in the communications given out by the management teams. Many communications, for example, earnings calls, interviews, articles, and others, give out significant information about the management team. It is better that these analyses are performed first at an individual level, if possible, and then the team dynamics can be explored to identify if the management team risks are augmented by the combination of traits that could indicate trouble. For instance, the following rules can guide risk assessment:

An extremely aggressive *CEO* + Extremely aggressive *CFO*

= Higher risk of fraud/misconduct

Extremely controlling *CEO* + Overly compliant *CFO*

= Higher risk of misconduct

Unethical and aggressive CEO + Ethical CFO

= Interal conflict

The deception analyzing agent shown in the SADAL analysis in Table 7.2 is built using the earnings call data (note that similar agents can be built for disclosures, financial statements, or other communications analysis).

Natural language processing methods are used to analyze the text. The text or communications are analyzed for patterns of language and then classified based upon either previously known usage of certain words, styles of speaking, and vocal features as being associated with deception and lying, or a sample of communications is taken from known cases of management fraud. Once the agent learns how to spot deception, it can be used to analyze earnings calls (or other communications) to identify deception.

TABLE 7.2 SADAL Analysis for Deception Analysis

Sense	Analyze	Decide	Act	Learn
Data: Earnings calls data Sensor: Voice recorder, digital file, text	The words that indicate deception or obfuscation The language patterns The vocal features	Determine if the vocal, linguistic, and financial information indicates fraud	Update the profile of the prospects Send results to agent that analyzes team dynamics	Learn the language and vocal patterns that indicate deception

TABLE 7.3   SADAL Analysis for Audit Team to Client Matching

Sense	Analyze	Decide	Act	Learn
Resumes Project requirements Client-related data Communications by the staff member Previous audit reports Previous audit reviews (internal and external)	Using NLP establish a profile of candidate and a profile of client/audit and determine if the right match: Qualification Deceptive Impression Management Situational Industry Client type Personality Interest	Determine if the candidate is the right match for the client assignment. Predict quality of work/audit. Identify special areas of weakness.	Notify the engagement leader.	Learn the various capabilities to be able to perform the analysis on an ongoing basis.

EXAMPLES OF MACHINE LEARNING TO IDENTIFY DECEPTION

Larcker and Zakolyukina (2012) performed a study where they used a classification model to classify deceptive discussions during quarterly earnings conference calls. They labeled the data based upon subsequent financial restatements and severity of accounting problems. In their model, language is analyzed for deceptive words. The model found that it predicted better than or equal to prediction by financial and accounting variables. They found that the words used by a CEO and CFO indicate if the executives are trying to hide something. The methods employed include searching deceptive words as included in a custom dictionary and then looking at the frequency of their usage in statements. Another method employed is to use Bayesian classifier (introduced in Chapter 5). While evaluating disclosures, researchers Humpherys, Moffitt, Burns, Burgoon, and Felix found that "fraudulent disclosures use more activation language, words, imagery, pleasantness, group references, and less lexical diversity than nonfraudulent ones. Writers of fraudulent disclosures may write more to appear credible while communicating less in actual content." (Humpherys et al., 2011).

In addition, Support Vector Machine algorithms have been used for detecting fraud (Pai et al., 2011), Researchers found that artificial neural networks (ANNs) perform better than other methods. As technology has advanced, now deep learning is being applied to the deception problem. In addition to linguistic characteristics, psycholinguistic features and syntactic complexity were used. As micro-expressions, hand gestures, and other visual features are now analyzed from videos, multimodal features are being used to train deep learning neural networks (Mendels et al., 2017; Krishnamurthy et al., 2018). This means that in addition to language, body language and gestures can also be analyzed to detect deception. That takes the deception evaluation to the whole new level. In fact, financial fraud detection effectiveness may increase by simultaneously considering vocal, linguistic, and financial cues (Throckmorton et al., 2015).

 ## AUTOMATED AUDIT PLANNING ACTIVITIES AND WORK TASKS

The audit planning happens after the client and the auditor have contractually agreed for the audit. The goals of planning in audit are:

- To evaluate and understand the target client's business and industry
- To develop insights into business, organization, and strategy
- To understand the operations and operational methods
- To examine the accounting and financial systems

The preplanning process sets the tone of the audit engagement and enables the auditor to discover important issues early on and includes the following activities: Staffing, Project Management, and Strategic Review, and Intelligence (Figure 7.3).

Activity 1: Staffing

For as long as humans are relevant for the audit, assessing staff competency and ensuring that the project is staffed with the best people will continue to be relevant. The automation focus for staffing is on the following three work-tasks:

1. **Competence and Capability Assessment:** This agent looks at the competence and capabilities of the audit staff and also determines if they are

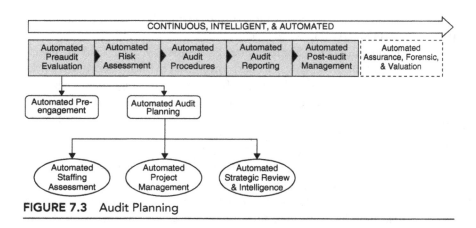

FIGURE 7.3 Audit Planning

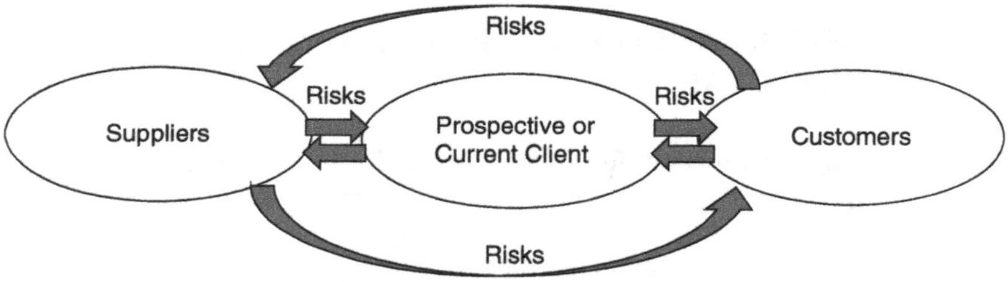

FIGURE 7.4 Value Network

the right match of the client needs. Note, this implies that client needs are determined and expressed in a detailed manner.

2. **Independence Assessment:** This agent evaluates the independence of the auditor staff that begins work on the audit. Unlike the independence evaluator in the pre-engagement evaluation (which used public information for evaluation), this agent constantly evaluates the audit staff to identify if risk of independence compromise is increasing.

3. **Professional Judgment Assessment:** This agent looks at the professional judgment and professional skepticism as personality traits. It evaluates personalities of the auditors to understand the propensity of compromising professional judgment.

Activity 2: Project Management Automation

This activity involves general project management. Notice that while these tasks seem to be more manual, significant automation efforts are being applied to automate project management.

- **Partner Management:** This agent helps manage the partner relationships. This includes the planning of audit components, allocation of work, setting expectations, resolving issues, etc.
- **Work Management:** This agent is a project management and work management agent. It works with Partner Management in areas where external coordination with third-party experts or partners is needed.
- **Scheduling:** This agent manages and schedules tasks.

Activity 3: Strategic Review and Intelligence

This activity involves performing a comprehensive review of the client's business, industry, strategy, and financials. In addition, it can involve other audit-related evaluation (e.g., understanding the audit framework).

 AUTOMATED AUDIT PLANNING *SADALS*

The intelligent automation preplanning environment is composed of several agents working together to enable rapid and comprehensive assessment and effective proposal, preplanning, and understanding of an audit. In this environment, the auditor must gain insights about herself and her team, as much as about the client. The environment is subdivided into four broad capability areas:

1. Competence and Capability Assessment
2. Independence Assessment
3. Professional Judgment Assessment
4. Preplan Intelligence

Competency and Capability (C&C) Assessment Toolkit

As the Big Four were rocked by scandals and audit quality disasters in the UK, Marriage and Ford analyzed the problems and stated that price gouging was not as big of a worry as the dominance of the Big Four leading to "slapdash audits conducted at minimal cost by inexperienced staff" (Marriage and Ford, 2018). Selecting competent and capable individuals as members of an audit team is critical for audit success. Despite the technological advances, the human auditor is expected to stay relevant and important for audit success. Many audit failures happen when, either due to time pressure or resource availability issues, wrong team members are picked and deployed. Competency is related to factors such as work ethics, personality, trustworthiness, and managerial capabilities. Capability refers to the experience and educational experience that qualifies the auditor to conduct an audit. Competency and capability are assessed from education, experience as an auditor, experience in an industry, experience with a client, and experience with the specific type of audit needed. The goal of competency and capability assessment toolkit is to ensure that the auditors are capable, knowledgeable, and competent to conduct an audit. The artifacts that accomplish this are composed of several components and use multiple agents to:

- Identify specific attributes of competency and capability by using natural language processing.
- Determine if these factors can predict the audit performance risk.

The first problem area strictly deals with evaluating the experience of a covered or uncovered member of an audit or assurance team. Various intelligent utilities check for different dimensions that contribute to competency and capability. The analysis performed goes beyond the overly simplistic analysis performed in many firms that use resume, employee reviews, and recorded experience from a firm's databases. The core idea is to enable a firm to identify such patterns that are not easy discernable from rudimentary analysis.

The history of previous audit and audit teams includes binary or class data on the success of audits and auditors. If such data is not available, it will be helpful to label that data by asking partners or others to report on the relative (categorical) or binary success of the audit. Regulators, such as PCAOB, can also provide such information. The starting point is to discern which of the audits were successful and which were not. That information can be considered as the output variable or the dependent variable to the wide set of inputs that go into making audit successful or not. For the specific utility under discussion in this section, the input variables are focused upon the human element (i.e., the human auditor). Once we know which audits were successful versus unsuccessful, several types of information can be extracted from them.

Previous successful/unsuccessful audits provide a plethora of information on the firms in which the audit was conducted and of the people involved in the audit. When unsuccessful, the general response of audit firms is to fire the people involved and then try to forget as if it didn't happen. In reality, each audit gone bad or good provides some critical information about many dimensions of the audit. That information can be used to plan future audits. Specifically, we can learn about the type of the resources used – hence the capability and competence evaluation.

This agent is multimodality automation (i.e., deterministic and machine-learning–based automation). In deterministic evaluation it looks for some specific criteria – for example, using RPA to identify if the potential staffing candidate has a CPA or not, years of experience, client-specific experience, audit area experience, or industry experience. On the machine learning side, the agent should be able to conduct far deeper evaluation about both the client needs and the candidate's competency and capabilities.

Agent Adds Details to Experience

Situational experience implies the experience of an auditor from handling business circumstances, states, and situations that were encountered in client audits. For example, knowing that an auditor audited Company A from 2008–2010 is one thing. Understanding that the audit was conducted when the firm was undergoing restructuring, was being run by new management team, and had suffered huge losses another. Situational experience looks for such patterns. The situational categories refer to a state that a company was in when the audit was conducted. The state implies the presence of business conditions that prevailed during the time of the audit.

Situational classification determines categories such as pre-IPO, post-IPO, bankruptcy, reorganization, new leadership, and new product launch.

The C&C agents use data from various internal and external sources and determine if the auditor has the relevant experience for an audit engagement. Using natural language processing, the C&C Assessor evaluates the patterns of interest. It seeks to classify the unique client situations from the past and relate them to the times the auditor was involved with the client.

Notice that while the situation is specific to a client, the role played by the auditor in the engagement is specific to the auditor.

Situational inputs include details about the audit client. Such details might include factors such as industry, client type, complexity of client, challenges of client, and other details such as unique situation of clients, including factors such as pre-IPO, post-IPO, or bankruptcy. As previously mentioned, some of the data (e.g., client industry) could be pre-classified and can be directly extracted from the databases. But to learn about the specific situations of the audit, workpapers or other areas where such strategic insights were recorded can become an excellent source of information. The attributes (inputs) for this could be notes from previous client engagement, or information (news, articles, commentaries, analyst reports) published about the client during the timeframe when the audit was conducted.

The audit team members who participated in that audit can be asked to comment on the specific parts that were applicable to their specific assignment in the audit. Senior members, especially partners, are usually part of the entire audit and hence knowledgeable about such situations.

Another issue of matching a client with a candidate is industry classification and candidate experience. Such experience is often stored in the database of the firm where client companies are classified by industries. Since these days firms can have many different business segments and units, it is important to make sure that the candidate had experience in the exact area where prospective client audit needs help. Hence, just because client information is maintained in a firm's company records does not imply that an industry match can be established. Experience from previous audits must discern specifics of the industry. For example, if GE was the client, we need to identify the exact areas of audits – business unit, department, functional area – that the employee worked in. If such records are not kept, or the degree of depth is not maintained, machine learning can be used to establish such details by datamining documents from previous audits.

Agent Looks at the Qualifications

Qualification assessment is performed by using the data from resumes, certifications, and internal testing. The goal of the agent is to determine if the candidate or potential audit staff member is qualified or not. The learning environment set up to perform these analyses is typically composed of the following features:

- Target staffing description
- Applications by candidates to staff a position
- Candidate background and experience
- Candidate resume
- Client description
- Client industry

- Candidate skills (candidates and skill tags relations)
- Generic skill tags

Skills are often taken as a collection of skills represented in text where a person can have many skills and one skill can be described by many words. One way to capture skills is to form canonicalized sets of skills as representatives of skills required to perform a job (Matos Pombo, 2019). A specific combination of skills can be consolidated to represent such a collection of skillsets. For example, it may include factors such as skill tags, experience level, extracted skills, or extracted additional skills. Other data, such as about compensation, educational background of the candidate, distance between residence and client audit site, and other such factors are preprocessed to be used as inputs. This can be used to match the client with the audit staff.

Note that since audit team members may update their data as they acquire new experience, and the HR system may only have the most recent data, if we are using the experience generator from prior years, we may have to shave off some of the recent experience of the audit so that his or her experience is rolled back into the time when he or she performed the audit that is being included in the training data.

Agent Looks for Deceptive Impression Management Sanitize and De-DIMing

DIM refers to Deceptive Impression Management. DIM, in the context of employment and project assignment, happens when job or project candidates engage in deceptive practices by intentionally distorting their experience and qualifications on resumes, records, interviews, and other documents that are used to make sense of their educational and experience background. The de-DIMing agent uses natural language processing to understand the use of words that indicate deceptive practices. Misstatement or distortion can be intentional or unintentional.

Unintentional distortion happens when a candidate believes that he or she has experience in doing something but he or she hasn't done it, or done it at the level he/she believes. Misstatement happens when a person intentionally claims that he or she has experience when they have not performed the required tasks to acquire the experience. It can happen when someone embellishes or decorates experience, or when the auditor creates stories about experience they don't have, or when a person configures their experience to the specific requirements of the recruiter regardless of the veracity of the claims, or when a person conceals important facts about their experience (Levashina et al., 2009; Levashina and Campion, 2006; Levashina et al., 2014; Levashina and Campion, 2007). Research shows that deceptive tactics, including exaggeration or lies, on resumes are a function of word usage. For example, usage of fancy or too exciting words used to represent achievements or family are often used as proxies or markers to identify distortion.

There are two ways to build the agent to track this (Auer, 2018). The first way is using dictionaries in which predefined content (words) is used to analyze resumes. This is a closed-vocabulary approach where word lists (user-defined dictionaries, lexica) are developed based upon psychological factors, and word counts (total word frequency) in text are analyzed based upon those to determine the pattern. The obvious constraints in this approach are, first, that the context of the usage of a word is not reflected in the analysis and, second, when you build a dictionary you already assume that you know the features (a priori).

The second method is to use open-vocabulary techniques to predict words and phrases (n-grams) relevant to the topic. A method known as latent Dirichlet allocation (LDA) is used (Blei et al., 2003, 2010). This method is based upon understanding the relationships between words by calculating their distance from each other by looking at the usage patterns. For instance, the word *mug* is closer to *coffee* than *water*, and the word *glass* is closer to *water*, *juice*, and *milk* than *coffee*.

Using the above methods, agents can extract patterns from resumes to determine if the candidate is using deception in the resume.

Agent Evaluates Independence

Many large company audit committee chair positions are staffed by Big Four alumni. Nearly all large audit firms provide consulting services to audit clients. The independence assessor is a utility that tests for an auditor's independence. The utility takes input from various sources, including social media (e.g., LinkedIn, Facebook), to evaluate whether the auditor has made comments about the firm, the management team, or products of the firm. Using frequency of words, one can measure whether the auditor has expressed personal opinions about the client or its management team, had relationship with the client, or has any other ideological connection with the auditee. The approach can expand to include relatives of the auditor for evaluating conflict of interest – if needed. The agent can also identify relationships between the auditor and the audit committee. AI is now being widely used in performing background checks. Similar concepts can be applied to identify such relationships. The vast amounts of data these days can be used to track relationships between related parties.

Note: A regulator (e.g., PCAOB) can also use similar agents to scan the Internet to pick up news, comments, social media entries, or press releases about the auditor conducting consulting business with the client.

Besides performing searches or deploying closed-vocabulary dictionary-based models to evaluate occurrences of joint mentions or words, a more reflective system can also be designed. For example, data can also provide insights about "values and orientation" matches. For example, these days companies often take positions on social or political issues. Understanding those positions and then evaluating whether the auditor may have a conflict with the political or social positions is a major concern for evaluating independence. The Independence Assessment may reveal that a member of the audit team is either too conservative or too liberal, or too religious or anti-religion, and may hold a too accepting or rejecting attitude toward the client. For instance, the Vatican hired PwC in 2015 for audit and then in 2016 suspended the audit. The Vatican's chief auditor, Libero Milone, informed the *Financial Times* that he was forced to resign because he requested information about assets held by Vatican in Switzerland and that some people in the Vatican felt uncomfortable about that (Johnson and Mancini, 2019). Vatican representatives denied the allegations and counter-alleged that Milone was accused of spying on the private lives of cardinals and others, and that is why he was asked to leave. The *Financial Times* reported that audit was part of the efforts by Pope Francis to bring transparency to the church; however, his efforts were being resisted internally. One can appreciate the internal conflict an auditor might face if he or she has to be placed in this situation and has to tread through the complexities involved. Can one maintain independence?

While search algorithms are used to scan the networks for independence assessment, data from previous engagements can be extremely valuable to develop an agent to evaluate independence.

Professional Judgment

Autonomy, an upcoming UK firm, was sold to Hewlett-Packard in 2011 for $11.7 billion. Soon after the purchase, HP had a write-down of $5 billion. A fraud investigation followed. From the United States to the United Kingdom, courts got involved and after years of investigation the FRC (Financial Reporting Council) claimed that they found that Deloitte auditors had "oneness" with Autonomy leaders and Richard Knights, the partner who was in charge of Autonomy audit, "consciously lost his objectivity," and was "reckless" and "seriously misleading" (Kinder, 2019). Clearly, over a period of five years of the engagement, Richard Knights may have made several comments, written emails and reports, and covered for the client. Was it possible for the firm to know that he was getting too close to the client? Was it possible for the firm to get an early warning sign that his behavior indicates that he is losing his independence? Was it possible that the firm may have recognized that due to his personality he was more inclined to lose professional skepticism? The combination of the agents discussed in the previous section and this, achieves that. It is possible to get early warning signs when an auditor begins to lose his or her independence.

The emails, articles, and almost all words, either said verbally or written, can provide tremendous insights into the personality of a person and his or her judgment in various situations. Tausczik and Pennebaker's early ground-breaking work using closed-vocabulary (dictionaries) to classify various personality states can be applied to evaluate professional judgment (Tausczik and Pennebaker, 2010). However, open-vocabulary–based models can work wonders. The professional judgment agent uses the written communication to categorize the speech pattern of people to determine their personality traits. While this is by no means a science, it can provide some level of assurance to determine if the person possesses behavioral traits that give the person the right professional attitude toward audit. As covered in research by Mairesse, Walker, Mehl, and Moore (Mairesse et al., 2007) the language used by people in general can provide some information along the following personality traits (Mairesse et al., 2007):

- Extraversion vs. Introversion (sociable, assertive, playful vs. aloof, reserved, shy)
- Emotional stability vs. Neuroticism (calm, unemotional vs. insecure, anxious)
- Agreeable vs. Disagreeable (friendly, cooperative vs. antagonistic, faultfinding)
- Conscientious vs. Unconscientious (self-disciplined, organized vs. inefficient, careless)
- Openness to experience (intellectual, insightful vs. shallow, unimaginative)

Mairesse et al. classify along the above traits. However, in addition to classification, they used regression (see Chapter 5) and ranking models.

Add to the above the data from auditor's calendar (time spent, calls, timing of calls, dinners, etc.) with a client and the expense reports (type of travel and entertainment activities charged to the project) and emails to the client (management teams) and the firm can start to get an indication if the auditor is crossing the independence redline.

Personality

Determining personality is a classification exercise where management teams' or auditors' personality assessments are made from using text data. Using the data from their speeches, written texts, and other sources, various personality classifications can be made.

A 2011 study from neuroscience revealed a close relationship between written communications and regions of brain that exhibit personality traits (Adelstein et al., 2011). That provided a physiological (brain regions) link between personality traits and written communications and therefore enables us to link written communications directly with personality traits.

Imagine the sources of textual data that we can have these days, from articles to interviews, and social media to emails. Several studies have attempted to extract personality traits from social media text and classify them along the Big-Five personalities (openness, conscientiousness, extraversion, agreeableness, and neuroticism) and Eysenck's Three Factor personality mode (Mairesse et al., 2007; Sewwandi et al., 2017; Tandera et al., 2017). While text-based features show promising results, adding other features, such as hashtags, avatar choices, and other text features, provides even deeper insights (Wei et al., 2017).

Going beyond pictures, facial images are also being used to predict personalities (Ilmini and Fernando, 2016). Both ANN and support vector machines were used by Ilmini and Fernando to classify facial image to discover personality.

In 2017, Stanford research focused on using deep learning to classify structured written content by Myers Briggs Personality Type (MBTI) (Ma and Liu, 2017). Using novels as the input, and the known personalities of the authors by MBTI, they used neural networks to discover authors' personalities from their work.

With the advances in technology, deep learning can enable multimodal data to predict personality (Kaya and Salah, 2018). Multimodal data includes text, video, and audio to get a sense of personality. Videos and images can provide significant feature inputs like facial expression, facial attributes, gestures, and age/sex of a person.

Understanding Client Strategy

When scandal after scandal erupted in UK Big Four audit firms, the UK Parliament decided to take action (Parliament, 2019). The idea was to create more competition and improve the quality of audit. As the search for solutions continued, suggestions were made to include the next-tier firms to perform group audits. In the January 2019 hearing organized by Parliament, two separate sessions were held. The second session was when the Big Four were called to testify about the various proposals on improving audit quality. The first, and perhaps more interesting, session was with the next-tier firms and included BDO and Grant Thornton. The parliamentarians were interested in understanding the criteria that audit committees are interested in evaluating when they hire audit firms. Scott Knight, head of Audit and Assurance at BDO, answered that question by stating that the audit committees seek audit firms that can choose "the right team and right personalities," and that can "understand the business," and go "under the skin of the business" and develop "industry benchmarks." I believe his answer pretty much sums up the importance of understanding the business, business model, business strategy, and financials of the client. Such an understanding cannot be superficial or at a surface level. Scott Knight's words, "under the skin of the business," imply developing a truly comprehensive and deep understanding of the client's business.

The agents I introduce in this section do just that. As you can tell, understanding a client's business is not an easy task. There are so many avenues of developing that understanding. As we develop these analyses, it also enables us to identify patterns that can show us the overall complexity of the organization and/or identify risks.

 ## CLIENT BUSINESS STRATEGY AGENTS

I will focus more on this in Chapter 8, but I would like to provide some context to how to accomplish this. The Client Business Strategy includes three agents:

1. Agent that helps understand the financials
2. Agent that helps identify the value chain
3. Agent that can help understand the competitive dynamics and industry benchmarks

Understanding risks is an important part of this exercise; however, it is discussed in the next two chapters.

Agent for Identifying the Value Chain/Network

In 2016, three professors (from Georgia Tech and Boston University) and a researcher from Instacart develop a computational model of risk diffusion in global supply chains (Basole et al., 2016). Their study had two objectives: "1) Assess and visualize the impact of network structure on risk diffusion and supply network health. 2) Determine the impact of subtier visibility on reduction and potentially mitigation of cascading risks." They built their data sets using four sources. First, they identified a list of electronics businesses by revenues using EB300. Then they got data on the businesses they had identified from Thomson Reuters Securities Data Company (SDC). This database contains information on relationships such as alliances, supplier, R&D, licensing, marketing, and manufacturing. They then augmented that with data from Connexiti, which also has information on suppliers and customers of companies. Finally, they got the financial data from Compustat. Using these data sets, they developed a two-tier supply network of the supply chain. Using the AB agent-based simulation they performed the risk analysis. Basole et al. (2016) used z-scores and simulated the environment composed of agents (companies, customers, suppliers) using a model borrowed from biology (epidemiological model).

This offers a great example of the data-centric modeling that audit firms need. A similar concept can be deployed to first build the value chain of the prospective and current audit clients. This value chain represents the value creation process in a firm. The process starts by first capturing the broad network of key relationships the firm has. A separate modeling exercise is used to model the internal operations of the firm. Once the network is established, additional risk drivers such as supply-side risks, process-side risks, demand-side risks, operational risks, disruption risks, and other risks can be added to the model.

Once the network structure is set up using tabulated historical data, many deeper insights about the firm and its value chain can be obtained. The model works as follows:

- Each firm is an agent.
- Using features such as Financial (current ratio, quick ratio, working capital, turnover, etc.) Operational (inventory, inventory turnover, margins etc.), Supply (supply characteristics, prices, etc.) and many other such features.
- The output variable can be viewed as adding risk or reducing risk.
- Your machine-learning algorithm will predict the risk for your network configuration.
- As an added benefit, meta-analysis of your client's network can give you other information about your client. For instance, the competitive position of your client in the network, the number of nodes your client has, or the vulnerabilities.
- You can add to this text data from various players in the network. The specific focus of the text data will be to understand communications about various strategies.

Agent That Helps Understand the Financials

While a lot of this will be discussed in the upcoming chapters, in this chapter, I will introduce the power of machine learning to analyze and predict the financials. As early as the 1980s, researchers have pointed out the value of having expectation-based account estimation (Peters et al., 1989). It begins with financial statements from time t, and then looks for quantitative factors that may have impacted a change in accounts; an estimate is produced; and an adjustment is made to develop a financial statement at time t + n. A somewhat related idea explored by some researchers is to use agents to model shadow accounting (Chesney et al., 2017). Shadow or counter-accounting is when external parties to a company try to create accounting estimates of those things that either the company is trying to hide or is unintentionally not reporting. Activists often use shadow accounting for understanding the environmental or human rights impact of a firm's activities. Both of these examples shed light on something important. It is possible to build a reasonable estimate of a company's financials (and accounting) by external parties who don't have direct access to internal information. This becomes an extremely valuable tool for audit firms. This means that to provide an estimate of expected financials, an alternative accounting system can be developed outside the client firm. In a way this can be viewed as reverse engineering the accounting system.

This agent is responsible for providing information about the target client business. Since this agent can perform this task constantly, it is not efficient to solely focus it on one firm. To accomplish its task, the agent scans through various types of information and tries to help develop important aspects of expectations adjustment about the client. The core conceptual architecture of the machine learning agent is composed of the utility using input data from various sources, and then classifying it to various outputs.

The input comes from various sources, including news, analyst reports, financial statements, PR announcements, social media, lawsuits, patent filings, or regulator reports.

Output variable is either a binary expected increase or decrease classification, or a more useful estimate of the increase or decrease percentage as a continuous variable from a regression (see Chapter 5).

Note that the output variables can also include other items, such as asset types, culture, management, issues, incentives, or risks. Each of these will be different classifications/regression problems.

Machine learning plays an extremely important role in reverse engineering the accounts based upon the public data. For instance, using social media data one can estimate if the sales (revenues) of the firm may have increased or decreased. In fact, social media is great source of developing key insights into companies. The insights go beyond analyzing the culture and can be used to understand factors such as quality of sales, innovation, new product launches, strategies, management styles, financial performance, and many other areas. When other sources, such as analyst reports and news, are added to social media, even greater insights can be obtained. Several machine learning artifacts can be designed to enable such ongoing analysis, to:

- Augment existing analytics based upon financial metrics using machine learning to identify unseen risk from management disclosures, communications, earnings calls, and other information released by the firm.
- Enhance insights into the company using content from social media. Evaluate risks and performance potential but also about the management team.
- Develop a learning system to understand and study the competitive structure of the industry based upon various drivers such as capabilities, access to capital, innovation potential and other such factors.

Finally, the above information can also be used to determine the complexity of a client. While the drivers of complexity can refer to the business model or asset characteristics of the client, many factors determine that complexity. For example, culture of a firm, leadership style, personalities of leaders, specific situations (e.g., shareholder activism), incentive structures, and financial returns.

Key Points

- Audit preplanning and planning are critical steps for audit. The success or failure of an audit greatly depends upon these steps.
- Automating these steps requires two types of automations: (1) Automated Preplanning; and (2) Automated Audit Planning.
- Automated preplanning focuses on developing capabilities that can help develop information about the desirability of a client included in Automated Acceptance and Continuance of Audit, Automated Ethics and Independence Evaluation, and Automated Contractual Agreement.
- Automated audit planning develops insights into business, industry, organization, and strategy of a client, understands the operations and operational methods, and examines the accounting and financial systems and frameworks. At this stage (i.e., early stage of the audit), a sanity check system also works in background and in parallel to formal financial reports, which uses public information to produce expected financial statements.

REFERENCES

Adelstein, J. S., Shehzad, Z., Mennes, M., DeYoung, C. G., Zuo, X. N., Kelly, C., Margulies, D. S., Bloomfield, A., Gray, J. R., Castellanos, F. X. et al. (2011) Personality is reflected in the brain's intrinsic functional architecture. *PLOS ONE*. [Online] 6 (11).

Auer, E. M. L. (2018) Detecting deceptive impression management behaviors in interviews using natural language processing. Master of Science (MS), thesis, Psychology, Old Dominion University, [online]. Available from: https://digitalcommons.odu.edu/psychology_etds/70.

Basole, R. C., Bellamy, M. A., Park, H., and Putrevu, J. (2016) Computational analysis and visualization of global supply network risks. *IEEE Transactions on Industrial Informatics*. [Online] 12 (3), 1206–1213.

Blei, D., Carin, L., and Dunson, D. (2010) Probabilistic topic models: A focus on graphical model design and applications to document and image analysis. *IEEE Signal Processing Magazine*. (November), 55–65.

Blei, D. M., Ng, A. Y., and Jordan, M. I. (2003) Latent Dirichlet allocation. *Journal of Machine Learning Research*. [Online] 3 (4–5), 993–1022.

Chesney, T., Gold, S., and Trautrims, A. (2017) Agent based modelling as a decision support system for shadow accounting. *Decision Support Systems*. [Online] 95110–116. Available from: http://dx.doi.org/10.1016/j.dss.2017.01.004.

Humpherys, S. L., Moffitt, K. C., Burns, M. B., Burgoon, J. K., and Felix, W. F. (2011) Identification of fraudulent financial statements using linguistic credibility analysis. *Decision Support Systems*. [Online] 50 (3), 585–594.

Ilmini, K. and Fernando, T. (2016) Persons' personality traits recognition using machine learning algorithms and image processing techniques. *Advances in Computer Science: An International Journal*. 5 (1), 40–44.

Johnson, M. and Mancini, D. P. (2019) Ousted auditor says he got too close to secret Vatican accounts. *Financial Times*.

Kaya, H. and Salah, A. A. (2018) Multimodal personality trait analysis for explainable modeling of job interview decisions. In *Explainable and Interpretable Models in Computer Models and Machine Learning* (eds. H.J. Escalante et al.), 255–275. Switzerland: Springer Nature.

Kinder, T. (2019) Deloitte was too close to Autonomy, regulators claim. *Financial Times*. 11 October.

Krishnamurthy, G., Majumder, N., Poria, S., and Cambria, E. (2018) *A Deep Learning Approach for Multimodal Deception Detection*. [Online]. Available from: http://arxiv.org/abs/1803.00344.

Larcker, D. F. and Zakolyukina, A. A. (2012) Detecting deceptive discussions in conference calls. *Journal of Accounting Research.* [Online] 50 (2), 495–540.

Levashina, J. and Campion, M. A. (2007) Measuring faking in the employment interview: Development and validation of an interview faking behavior scale. *Journal of Applied Psychology.* [Online] 92 (6), 1638–1656.

Levashina, J., Hartwell, C. J., Morgeson, F. P., and Campion, M. A. (2014) The structured employment interview: Narrative and quantitative review of the research literature. *Personnel Psychology.* [Online] 67 (1), 241–293.

Levashina, J. and Campion, M. A. (2006) A model of faking likelihood in the employment interview. *International Journal of Selection and Assessment.* 14 (4), 299–316.

Levashina, J., Morgeson, F. P., and Campion, M. A. (2009) They don't do it often, but they do it well: Exploring the relationship between applicant mental abilities and faking. *International Journal of Selection and Assessment.* [Online] 17 (3), 271–281.

Ma, A. and Liu, G. (2017) *Neural Networks in Predicting Myers Brigg Personality Type From Writing Style.* 1–9.

Mairesse, F., Walker, M. A., Mehl, M. R. and Moore, R. K. (2007) Using linguistic cues for the automatic recognition of personality in conversation and text. *Journal of Artificial Intelligence Research.* [Online] 30, 457–500.

Marriage, M. and Ford, J. (2018) An illusion of choice: The conflicts that mire the audit world. *Financial Times.* August 8, 2018.

Matos Pombo, L. (2019) *Landing on the right job: A machine learning approach to match candidates with jobs applying semantic embeddings.* Universidade Nova de Lisboa. [online]. Available from: https://run.unl.pt/bitstream/10362/60405/1/TAA0024.pdf.

McKenna, F. (2018) KPMG turned to Palantir to help predict which audits would be inspected. MarketWatch [online]. Available from: https://www.marketwatch.com/story/kpmg-turned-to-palantir-to-help-predict-which-audits-would-be-inspected-2018-06-26.

McKenna, F. (2019) The KPMG cheating scandal was much more widespread than originally thought. MarketWatch [online]. Available from: https://www.marketwatch.com/story/the-kpmg-cheating-scandal-was-much-more-widespread-than-originally-thought-2019-06-18.

Mendels, G., Levitan, S. I., Lee, K. Z., and Hirschberg, J. (2017) Hybrid acoustic-lexical deep learning approach for deception detection. *Proceedings of the Annual Conference of the International Speech Communication Association, INTERSPEECH.* [Online].1472–1476.

Ostrom, E. (2015) *Public Company Accounting Oversight Board.* [Online] 53 (9), 1689–1699.

Parliament, U. (2019) Big 4 accountancy firms questioned on future of audit inquiry [online]. Available from: https://www.parliament.uk/business/committees/committees-a-z/commons-select/business-energy-industrial-strategy/news-parliament-2017/big-4-accountancy-firms-questioned-on-future-of-audit-inquiry-evidence-17-19-/.

Pai, P. F., Hsu, M. F., and Wang, M. C. (2011) A support vector machine-based model for detecting top management fraud. *Knowledge-Based Systems.* [Online] 24 (2), 314–321. Available from: http://dx.doi.org/10.1016/j.knosys.2010.10.003.

PCAOB (2019) *Report on 2016 Inspection of KPMG LLP. Public Company Accounting Oversight Board.* PCAOB RELE.

Peters, J. M., Lewis, B. L., and Dhar, V. (1989) Assessing inherent risk during audit planning: The development of a knowledge based model. *Accounting, Organizations and Society.* [Online] 14 (4), 359–378.

Sewwandi, D., Nugaliyadde, A., and Thelijjagoda, S. (2017) Linguistic features based personality recognition using social media data. *Proceedings of the 2017 6th National Conference on Technology and Management: Excel in Research and Build the Nation, NCTM 2017.* [Online] (January), 63–68.

Sull, D., Sull, C., and Chamberlain, A. (2019) *Measuring culture in leading comapnies* [online]. Available from: https://sloanreview.mit.edu/projects/measuring-culture-in-leading-companies/.

Tandera, T., Hendro, Suhartono, D., Wongso, R., and Prasetio, Y. L. (2017) Personality prediction system from Facebook users. *Procedia Computer Science.* [Online] 116604–611. [Online]. Available from: https://doi.org/10.1016/j.procs.2017.10.016.

Tausczik, Y. R. and Pennebaker, J. W. (2010) The psychological meaning of words: LIWC and computerized text analysis methods. *Journal of Language and Social Psychology.* [Online] 29 (1), 24–54.

Throckmorton, C. S., Mayew, W. J., Venkatachalam, M., and Collins, L. M. (2015) Financial fraud detection using vocal, linguistic and financial cues. *Decision Support Systems.* [Online] 7478–87. Available from: http://dx.doi.org/10.1016/j.dss.2015.04.006.

Wei, H., Zhang, F., Yuan, N. J., Cao, C., Fu, H., Xie, X., Rui, Y., and Ma, W. Y. (2017) Beyond the words: Predicting user personality from heterogeneous information. *WSDM 2017 – Proceedings of the 10th ACM International Conference on Web Search and Data Mining.* [Online] 305–314.

CHAPTER EIGHT

Automated Inherent Risk Assessment

N A DYNAMIC AND CONSTANTLY CHANGING WORLD, the risk assessment function in an audit is continuous. Businesses are exposed to risks. The risks that are from the nature of a business are known as inherent risks. Rapid changes in technology, new business entry, regulatory changes, and other such factors can change the inherent risk of a firm. From an audit perspective, inherent risk is part of the total audit risk.

 ## TOTAL AUDIT RISK

The total audit risk is composed of inherent risk, internal controls risk, and detection risk. Inherent risk refers to the risk that an error or fraud will penetrate the financial system without internal controls. The internal control risk comes from management's failure to place, or override, proper controls. The detection risk is specific to the auditor and comes from the failure to detect an error or mistake in an audit. The value of Detection Risk often depends upon the value of Inherent Risk and Controls Risk – the higher the Inherent and Controls risks, the more auditor's testing and vigilance are needed to improve the chances of detection. In this chapter, we will cover various ways to build an Inherent Risk assessment system. The primary design of the system is composed of multiple agents working together to analyze and measure the risk. Each agent is supported by several other agents that produce the baseline

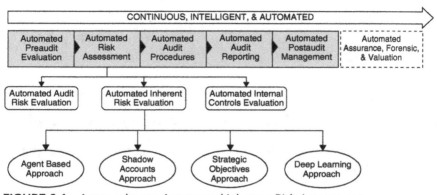

FIGURE 8.1 Approaches to Automated Inherent Risk Assessment

data both as inputs to develop the agents and also as the user of the system (explained later).

The equation for the Total Audit Risk is:

$$TAR = IR * CR * DR$$

where

> IR = inherent risk
> CR = controls risk
> DR = detection risk

I am presenting four methods to estimate inherent risk – agent-based approach, shadow accounts approach, strategic objectives approach, and deep learning approach (Figure 8.1). The first method (agent-based approach) is the most comprehensive as it provides measures at the assertion level of each major account. Which approach to use depends upon many factors, including the time and investment available for a firm, if the company is developing the system for internal audit versus external audit for various clients, how automated the system needs to be, and the level of sophistication the firm needs.

INHERENT RISK

As the word *inherent* signifies, inherent risk is the risk of error or fraud penetrating accounts in the absence of internal controls. The risk therefore is inherent or embodied in the nature of the account and comes from factors such as the form, frequency, size, transactions, training, incentives, business model, and the need for making qualitative assessments.

When we say "inherent," the term seems to imply characteristics or properties of something. Is a leaf inherently green? Is water inherently wet? A leaf is green based upon what the observer perceives as green and water is wet because the observer (human) finds it wet. The same way, are there properties of something that make it inherently risky – just as water is inherently wet?

For instance, in accounting concepts, cash is viewed as an inherently riskier asset than a building because one can easily steal the cash but not a building. The inherent risk is based upon the characteristic of "ease of transporting a valuable asset." That characteristic increases the risk for the owner of the asset. From an auditor's perspective, measuring the inherent risk is critical because it is directly tied to the assertions being made by the management related to the financial statements. For instance, the assertions of existence and completeness may make cash more risk prone versus the same assertions for a building. However, consider the same assertions being made about a firm declaring that it is in possession of various buildings on an island that few have heard of. Can we know that the buildings exist as asserted by the company just by looking at the financial statements? Of course not.

Hence, while an account may exhibit in its nature high or low inherent risk, circumstances surrounding the business also impact the inherent risk. The nature of inherent risk varies for accounts by the industry, the type of firm, the accounting systems used, the business model, and the processes. Furthermore, as the nature of the business changes, the inherent risk for specific accounting systems can change. For instance, if a business does not accept cash and then switches to accepting cash, it has increased the inherent risk of cash.

 ## UNDERSTANDING THE BUSINESS PROBLEM

The process of inherent risk identification is typically a function of the industry, business model, and the operating dynamics of a firm. Experienced auditors are familiar with the risk characteristics of industries and recognize the areas where firms have greater risk. The cognitive work performed by the auditors is composed of understanding the nature of transactions in an industry and then evaluating whether errors or frauds associated with such transactions are more likely to be included in a financial report or assertion made by the firm.

The inherent characteristics of such transactions can be determined by factors such as the following:

- **Nature of the Account:** A more liquid account, e.g., cash, is more vulnerable to fraud.
- **Account Balance Size:** Accounts with a larger balance can have a bigger impact on material misstatement and can be more error and fraud prone.
- **Transaction Estimation:** Transactions in which human subjectivity is used – for example, allocations across different accounts – can be more likely to have fraud or errors.
- **Business Model:** Business models of companies can create more risk for errors and fraud.
- **Transaction Volume:** Accounts with a large number of transactions can be more likely candidates for inherent risk.
- **Transaction Complexity:** Transactions that are more complex (for example, derivates) can have greater risk. This risk comes from inability to value or understand the transaction, which can lead to errors and fraud.
- **Transaction Treatment:** Some transactions can be recorded in ways where they may appear fine but if explored further would show that the transaction should have been recorded in a different account.
- **Past History:** Past history of mistakes and frauds/errors.
- **Financial Condition as a Motivator:** The financial condition of a business that motivates management to commit fraud.

When these risks reach an account level, inherent risk manifests in recording invalid or fictitious transactions or omitting to record factual and legitimate transactions. It can arise from inaccuracies in the transaction amounts and account balances or from classifying transactions in the wrong accounts. It can happen from wrong posting or wrong accounting of the transactions. It can happen from misleading or incomplete disclosure. It can also arise from when transactions are recorded in wrong time period. All of these can happen as errors or intentional frauds.

The nature of inherent risk is such that the auditor does not control or impact it. It exists and is embedded in the DNA of the firm. An auditor's knowledge of the industry and the firm helps in evaluating the inherent risk. For example, certain accounts may be more prone to management discretion and subjective treatments in certain industries. And, based upon the auditor's previous experience with a client, the auditor may possess information about some accounts having greater risk than others. Automating inherent risk measurement implies we need to somehow model the thought process of the auditor.

AUDITOR'S THOUGHT PROCESS

Based upon the various criteria presented in the previous section, the auditor makes assessments about the risk inherent in the assertions related to the financial statements of the auditee. As such, identifying and measuring inherent risk can be approached in terms of a risk identification, assessment, evaluation, and management problem.

Cognitively, therefore, the auditor processes information about the industry, the firm, and the firm's management team and practices, and all such information is intuitively, or mathematically, translated into a risk estimate (Peters et al., 1989). The measurement could be qualitatively determined and based upon auditor's experience or it can be estimated by applying very rigorous mathematical criteria. Regardless of how it is estimated or determined, the risk estimate can be viewed as the cumulative measurement of values of risk drivers.

Risk drivers are individual risks that collectively lead to the measure of the total audit risk. Recall that the risk manifests in the accounting system and eventually finds its way into the financial statements.

Breaking down the auditor's cognitive thinking, the risk assessment part implies that that auditor maps the financial statements to accounts and accounts to risk factors (Shailer et al., 1998). The risk factors, in this case, are based upon the economic and operating environment of the firm, upon industry dynamics, and upon the management decision-making (Figure 8.2). More practically, for our purposes, the problem can be viewed as this: the inherent risk impacts the financial statements and comes from the accounting system and is driven by the risk factors that emanate in the nature and operations of the firm, and its management and industry, processes, and the transactions.

Thus, risk drivers are a function of business model, industry dynamics, regulatory changes, etc., *and* of the firm-specific dynamics *and* of the management.

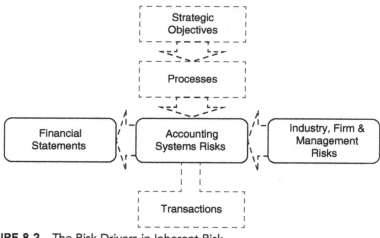

FIGURE 8.2 The Risk Drivers in Inherent Risk

 ## GENERAL APPROACH FOR AUTOMATION

There is a dynamic side to evaluating inherent risk. Typically, auditors use their experience and training to manually estimate the inherent risk. This is usually estimated by the auditors during the engagement. The vibrant and volatile nature of today's business constantly creates new opportunities and risks. In many cases it may even impact the business models of firms. This implies that the nature of inherent risk also evolves the business dynamics and is impacted by both strategic and operational execution decisions.

To automate measuring inherent risk constantly, we use the following general approach:

- Start by developing a stationary model of inherent risk. This model is composed of identifying the relationship between assertions and accounts in terms of risks. The beginning state (i.e., static) of the model will establish a relationship between accounts receivable and various assertions.
- Each assertion contributes to the risk to an account in different ways. Some assertions may have a lower contribution to the risk than others. For each assertion we identify four assertion risk factors, and then we assign a risk contribution weight to each risk factor. We then rate each risk factor in terms of magnitude (high, medium, low).

- Separately, drivers of assertion risks are identified. There are the exogenous and endogenous variables that drive the assertion risk higher in a dynamic risk assessment model.
- Consider each of the variables as output variables of a learning system.

Approach 1: The Inherent Risk Intelligent Automation

In addition to an established body of knowledge auditors are guided by experience to determine the inherent risk in an audit situation. The inherent risk is an indirect result of the operational dynamics of a business where an error or fraud can creep into the financial statements in the absence of internal controls. For example, a business which deals with large cash amounts is more prone to problems (mistakes, errors, fraud, etc.) in cash accounts. The inherent risk is therefore based upon the industry and the business model of a firm. The changes in business dynamics can result from changes in the general economic conditions and a firm's participation in new industries.

When approached from an automation perspective, the goal of intelligent automation is to develop an automated learning system that can track, identify, and measure the inherent risk in a firm's audit environment. This learning system should be able to adapt to the changes in the firm's business environment.

This intelligent agent can reduce the time and effort needed to identify and measure areas where a firm has greater inherent risk. It can streamline the process and enable an audit team to quickly assess the inherent risk. It can also be a part of the continuous audit. The value comes from increase in audit efficiency and effectiveness.

As shown in Figure 8.3, where the example of an Accounts Receivable (AR) account is given, the primary model of intelligent automation to measure inherent risk is based upon identifying the relevant assertions to the account, and developing risks factors, drivers, and values for the assertions.

Building an automated inherent risk manager requires the following three steps:

Step 1: Set up the base model

In Step 1, we prepare a base static model of inherent risk. This model links key accounts with assertions and deploys a risk-based model that identifies the initial states of the risks as understood by the auditors at an initial time t_0. The process begins by identifying the relevant assertions to an account. Not all assertions are applicable to an account.

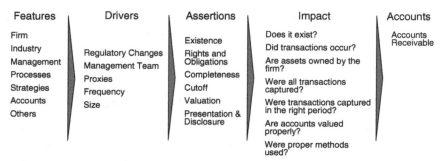

FIGURE 8.3 Accounts Receivable

For each assertion for an account, the risk is measured by the assertion risk factors: Likelihood, Impact, Velocity, and Vulnerability (Table 8.1). Likelihood measures how likely the specific assertion is of impacting the account; impact assesses the impact of potential dollar impact; velocity can be viewed as a subjective measure of how quickly a misstatement can become material (in other words how rapidly a situation can turn into a major problem, in minutes, days, weeks, or months); and vulnerability implies the susceptibility of an account to be impacted by special, largely unknown, situations.

For each of the four risk measurements (Likelihood, Impact, Velocity, and Vulnerability), we assign weights to signify the importance (Risk Importance) of each for an account on a scale of 0% to 100%. For example, Velocity could be least important for an account and hence may contribute only 10% to the risk versus Impact and Likelihood could be the most important elements and are estimated at 100%. As shown in Table 8.1, each of the Assertion Risks can be valued as Low, Medium, High (i.e., a scale of 1, 2, and 3). For example, for a major account, "Accounts Receivables" we can identify the assertions

TABLE 8.1 Measuring Risk

Assertion	Likelihood	Impact	Velocity	Vulnerability
Weights	100%	100%	10%	20%
Existence	H	H	M	L
Cutoff	H	M	L	L
Valuation	H	H	L	L
Rights & Obligations	L	L	L	L
Presentation & Disclosure	L	M	L	L
Completeness	H	H	L	L

Valuation, Existence, Completeness, and Cutoff as of high risk for Likelihood and Impact, with Rights and Obligations and Presentation and Disclosures as low risk.

Once those risks are defined as High, Medium, and Low, we can replace the values as 1 for Low, 2 for Medium, and 3 for High (Table 8.2). The total score for each assertion risk can be calculated by multiplying each of the risk scale entries by the Risk Importance and adding across (Table 8.3). For example, the Existence Risk would be 3X100% + 3X100% + 2X10%+ 1X20% = 6.4. The total highest possible risk for that Existence Risk is 6.9 (i.e., 3X100% + 3X100% + 3X10%+ 3X20%). Dividing the calculated risk by the total risk gives the value for Existence Risk.

This model gives us the first state of inherent risk model in a firm. As each major account is linked with assertion risks, it allows us to understand which accounts have higher inherent risk and why. Clearly, as business changes, a dynamic model is needed to study the changes in risk.

TABLE 8.2 Risk Scale Assignments

Weights	100%	100%	10%	20%
Existence	3	3	2	1
Cutoff	3	2	1	1
Valuation	3	3	1	1
Rights and Obligations	1	1	1	1
Presentation and Disclosure	1	2	1	1
Completeness	3	3	1	1

TABLE 8.3 Risk Calculation

	Likelihood	Impact	Velocity	Vulnerability	Sum Risk	Total Risk	Risk
Existence	3	3	0.2	0.2	6.4	6.9	93%
Cutoff	3	2	0.1	0.2	5.3	6.9	77%
Valuation	3	3	0.1	0.2	6.3	6.9	91%
Rights and Obligations	1	1	0.1	0.2	2.3	6.9	33%
Presentation and Disclosure	1	2	0.1	0.2	3.3	6.9	48%
Completeness	3	3	0.1	0.2	6.3	6.9	91%

Step 2: Identify a set of drivers for assertions

Each risk of each assertion can be impacted by various exogenous and endogenous factors. For instance, a sudden surge in frequency of transactions can change the likelihood, magnitude, and velocity of the account. A significant regulatory change can influence the firm's revenues. A winning spree that highlights management achieving shareholder expectations milestones can make management psychologically wired to the idea of continuing the trend even if that means fudging the numbers. These developments can add or subtract the values of four risk factors for each assertion. In fact, it can even change the importance weights to each. In other words, the risk value of an assertion changes based upon some exogenous or endogenous developments.

In Step 2, we identify those drivers that can increase or decrease the assertion risk. This exercise uses the existing data sets based upon the risk drivers and assertions. These data sets can also detail the errors that can lead to assertion risk increase.

For example, the following factors: obsolescence in inventory, previous misstatements, previous audit results, client operational risk, conflict of interest in management team, non-routine transactions, litigation, patents, earnings management, profit smoothing, management incentives, management credibility, culture, or ethics.

Step 3: Deploy agents

Each of the exogenous and endogenous factors is monitored by an agent. The agent operates in the relevant environment and learns to study the environment to predict if the changes in the environment will increase or decrease the risk of an assertion. For some agents, the design could be very simple – for example, an agent that can look at the number of transactions in an account can assess whether the transaction frequency is increasing more than the normal or expected transactions. Other agents can be more complicated and may require analyzing complex environments to assess what conditions will impact which assertions.

For example, an agent can use regression to predict the impact of sales forecast on the overall risk. For instance, using regression the agent tasked with the job to analyze the sales of a firm determines the sales volatility to be high. It makes this determination based upon analyzing the social media data about the products sold by the firm. Based upon that, the sales agent predicts that sales can fall in a broad range of plus/minus 28%. This implies that the existence assertion risk for sales could be higher. If the firm's sales are done on credit, this implies that AR's existence assertion risk may also go up. In the sales example the chain of automation will be as follows:

1. Predict sales volatility using features from social media.
2. Determine the assertion-risk that it impacts and by how much.
3. Make adjustments to the Assertion Risk Factor values.
4. Recalculate the inherent risk for an account.

Another, perhaps more sophisticated, agent can be viewed as a multilabel classification problem where the input features for each agent will be used to perform classification into multiple risk drivers. This means that if the agent considers risk to be high, it will use the features to learn to classify the output into one or more classes.

Approach 2: Shadow or Parallel Account

In the previous chapter we discussed about the shadow account. The purpose of the shadow account is to create a parallel account where we can develop financials using external data. Such financial statements can be reverse-engineered into approximate account values (for major accounts). Each of the accounts in the shadow account provides a range of possibilities for the actual value. For example, the shadow account may indicate that the sales could be significantly different than anticipated, thus impacting the assertion risks (existence, completeness, valuation) of misstatement.

The process of shadow account development was discussed in the previous chapter. In this chapter I would like to emphasize the importance of using external public information (e.g., social media) to create a map of the actual financial performance of a firm. It is best explained by an analogy of similar use. In 2012, the United Kingdom was hit by severe storms, which led to flooding. It is hard to develop models for surface water flooding due to the variation in the sources of flooding, the structure of the cities (e.g., buildings, street designs, drainage), and many other factors. The lack of hydrodynamic models to study real-time flooding in urban areas posed a problem in planning for surface flooding. In the UK flooding, as cities and towns were flooded, people provided live accounts of that flooding on social media. By capturing the social media data, researchers were able to develop a real-time model of flooding, which closely resembled the actual flooding and, hence, had the predictive power (Middleton et al, 2013). The actual urban flooding dynamics were analyzed using the data reported by the citizens who were in the path of the flooding. This is a great example of how data can be used to create shadow accounts for firms.

It is a form of predictive auditing (Vasarhelyi and Kuenkaikaew, 2013) but the difference is that the data used to construct the shadow financials is all acquired from external sources.

Approach 3: Strategic Objectives, Inherent Risk by Firm

Another approach to modeling inherent risk is to directly use the feature data to model inherent risk (Wu et al., 2014; Calderon and Cheh, 2002). Unlike developing agents for each of the assertion risk drivers, in this approach features vectors are directly fed into a neural network to understand the inherent risk in various firms. Modeling the inherent risk is achieved by breaking down the problem into multiple sections, where each section attempts to evaluate the risk related to an engagement. The problem sections raise the questions:

- Does a "specific firm" carry greater inherent risk than other firms?
- Does a management team imply greater inherent risk?
- Do certain accounts lead to greater inherent risk?
- Does the industry in which a firm operates increase inherent risk?
- Can we measure inherent risk by account?

The problem can be viewed as a classification problem where based upon various inputs, the learning algorithm will give a classification output of High Risk versus Low Risk. The problem can have many different versions. For example, data about the industry can be used as the input, or management-team–related data can form the input variables, or firm-specific data can be the basis of discovering the function. Ideally, all of the above are integrated and represented either as a collection of separate calculations that are mathematically linked and consolidated or as a single large deep learning implementation where numerous features can be represented.

The general approach to the problem can be viewed as:

Input Risk Drivers => Output Risk Classification (High vs.Low)

The firm-level inherent risk is a function of the industry in which a firm operates, the firm's business model, its management team, and its operating dynamics. The utility we are trying to develop will perform such that if we provide data about a firm, our intelligent artifact can assess for us a high versus low inherent risk client. In advanced versions, the artifact will conduct this surveillance continuously and notify when the inherent risk increases or decreases. An advanced version can also establish a link between business model, strategic objectives, processes, and accounts impacted. Firms constantly evolve and their risk profile changes accordingly.

We will start with a lighter version and then add more complexity. The added complexity will come from adding features and depth to the model.

We can start by building a basic model where we provide the following features as input features (with target output labeled by high vs. low risk):

- Profitability of a firm (can be measured as geometric mean or CAGR of returns; note if it contains negative numbers, transformation will be needed)
- Other financial ratios
- Regulatory change (nominal value)
- State of the economy (nominal value or numerical value by using economic volatility indicators or CBOE index)
- Access to financing (nominal value)
- Intellectual property expiration (nominal or binary)
- Management team competence (nominal value)
- Prior discrepancies (numbers or size of discrepancy)

The output or target variable is high risk versus low Risk. Based upon prior history, the data can be labeled for companies for which knowledge exists about inherent risk of audit being high risk versus low risk. Once training is successful, the classifier will classify the test data to predict high risk versus low risk firms.

Another version of the above model can be developed as a predictor of inherent risk measure – meaning that instead of binary classification the model outputs continuous variable value for inherent risk. That model uses regression to predict the inherent risk. For each of the above features, an estimate of likelihood (implying the likelihood of the variable impacting the outcome, with the outcome being meeting or not meeting the company objectives, and measured by a percentage value) and its impact (a nominal measure from high to low impact on meeting the company objectives) is calculated. The labeling of the target variable in this case involves using examples of companies whose inherent risk was calculated and properly assigned in the previous audits. In other words, you are estimating the contribution of each of the above variables to the overall risk of a firm to miss its objectives.

As the network is trained, it will be able to predict the inherent risk for a firm. Note that from an auditor's perspective, while helpful, this information will not clarify how the firm-level inherent risk translates into inherent risk at the account and assertion level (see Approach 1).

Approach 4: Deep Learning – Deepening the Model

In the previous rendition of the model, we focused on the direct link between a select number of features used to predict the inherent risk being high or low from classification or to estimate in the case of continuous target variable from regression. We can broaden the model by approaching it as a multilabel classification problem.

Strategic Objectives

The strategic objectives assessment argues that the inherent risk can be viewed as the risk that emanates from the strategic objectives laid out for the firm; therefore, inherent risk is embedded in its business model and therefore processes. This line of reasoning will focus on features that are tied to strategic objectives where a firm is viewed as a combination of strategic objectives. Each strategic objective is tied to a certain capability-centric process of a firm and each process is represented by certain accounts in the firm. The strategic objective and processes link with various accounts can be used to identify high risk accounts.

The data set for building that artifact is composed of strategic objectives, processes, and accounts. For example, a strategic objective could be to increase sales by a certain percentage. The processes invoked to achieve that goal could be a new marketing program, a new product launch, and changing the management incentive system. Each of the processes will impact associated accounts and those accounts could be identified. Overall, we are making an assumption that a company's economic performance is a function of its capabilities and strategies, and that those capabilities and strategies lead to the design and deployment of specific processes, and those processes form patterns of transactions and events that are captured by various accounts. Therefore, if we can have an input data set that is composed of strategic objectives, processes, and the related accounts, we can teach a network to perform multilabel classification to predict if the inherent risk will increase in certain accounts or not. Adding a layer of assertion risk in this setup will truly help fully automate the process of dynamic inherent risk measurement.

 ## UNDERSTANDING THE FEATURES USED IN VARIOUS APPROACHES

In this section I will provide some further explanation on features used in the various approaches presented above.

Note that while management risk can be considered as a firm-specific risk, and can be modeled with the firm risk, there are advantages of modeling the management risk separately also. Its benefit will become clearer below.

Firm Risk

This involves factors unique to a firm, which include capital structure type, shareholder characteristics, profitability (represented by various ratios), relative profitability, revenue type, capital expenses, regulatory environment, position in the industry, complexity of business model, complexity of supply chain, stock volatility, analyst sentiment, shareholder sentiment, customer sentiment, board characteristics, and management characteristics that can indicate if a firm is high risk or low risk.

The target variables could be a history of errors, frauds, and misstatements where the number of issues identified by an audit team (or publicly reported) are modeled as the output variable.

This hypothesis in the above model is that risk attributes of a firm lead to its inherent risk.

The target or output variable is the binary classification between High Risk versus Low Risk. The label can be assessed from identifying material restatement or fraud (any size) in a firm.

Management Risk

An alternative view of risk could be that as much as it is a factor of business model and industry dynamics, it is also driven by the management team. A management team may lack the sophistication to perform proper accounting or may intentionally change the accounting records. The input features of the artifact might include the following variables:

- **Management:** Management incentives, education, education type, previous roles, average experience, professional reputation, management style, years with firm, bonus plans, management buyout likelihood, management values, management conflict of interest, staff changes, pressure on management team, organizational structure, change in management turnover, and other such factors.
- **Target Variable:** The target variable is the restatements, errors, or fraud.

An alternative version of a supervised learning model could be treating the target variable as a continuous variable and using a ratio that measures the value of discrepancy (e.g., restatement) with the assets or revenues or profitability of the firm. Another target variable could be the severity or impact of misstatement. This could be calculated by the impact the discrepancy had on the shareholder wealth loss and can be estimated on a scale of 0 to 1. A number 1 would indicate the entire wealth was wiped out (bankruptcy) while a 0 would indicate no impact.

Industry Dynamics Risk

Industry risk is modeled based upon two drivers: the inherent characteristics of an industry may make it more prone to errors and fraud, and the change in the industry may increase the likelihood of fraud and errors. Both risks are manifested in terms of processes applied by a firm in business operations. In other words, just because an industry has risk, does not mean the risk is carried forward in all firms. Only those firms that participate in that industry and apply the processes related to the industry are exposed to that risk. The reason this point is important is because these days several companies are entering nonnative industries. For example, Apple's launch of a credit card places the firm in the financial services industry and therefore now exposes the firm to the risks attributable to the financial industry.

The objective of the audit agent that analyzes industry dynamics is twofold:

1. Evaluate the inherent risk in a firm based upon the industry it participates in.
2. Identify processes that could be more susceptible to fraud and errors.

To apply the first functionality, we have the input variables such as: industry, industry size, industry characteristics, technological change, regulatory change, sensitivity to technology changes, regulatory environment, industry structure, industry complexity, industry profitability, industry performance. Training data covers the industry.

The target variable in this case is to classify an industry based upon high risk and low risk. High risk signifies an industry with higher risk.

Within each industry (insurance, financial services, healthcare, etc.) there are activities and processes that are more susceptible to fraud and errors. Experienced auditors understand that these areas represent problem areas. The FBI keeps track of the processes and activities within industries that are more prone to fraud (Ngai et al., 2011).

Identifying processes and activities in industries can help in mapping accounts typically affected by these activities. This exercise requires identifying key processes within an industry. A data set of processes will be needed. The number of frauds, restatements, or errors identified in the process are distributed across the processes. Thus, the data set has the industry name, key processes, and risk factors as the input data. The output variable is the binary classification as fraud or no fraud. Such a process has been used in risk management literature. For instance, Christopher Culp details a process for developing the Risk ID of a firm (Culp, 2001). He specifies five types of risks, Market, Credit, Liquidity, Ops, and Legal, and links them to impacts on various functional (process) areas of a firm, including Treasury, Purchasing, Production, Marketing, Sales, Legal, and IT. Going through the iterations that add to the specificity, Culp builds a model that delineates detailed maps of risks. The risk analysis is exhaustive and systematic.

Developing these risk maps for industries is critical for audit firms.

ACCOUNT RISK

The inherent risk modeling consists of using various risk factors as input features. The input features include data sets with industry, company, industry risk factor, firm risk factor (calculated), and so on. However, the unique features of accounts themselves can help determine the inherent risk. The account-specific features include:

Account: account type, account size, account complexity, account volume, account activity, account usage (number of people), account history, transaction size (average), process complexity, accounting system sophistication

The target variable is to classify as high risk or low risk. The labeling can be performed by experienced auditors or from the history of the account. Much of the data can also be produced by using process mining tools.

Key Points

- In a fast changing and uncertain world, inherent risk needs to be dynamically identified and measured.
- Controls deployed in areas with immaterial inherent risk creates a waste of resources and controls not deployed in areas with high risks, and leaves those areas uncovered. That is why measuring and identifying inherent risks is critical.
- Artificial intelligence technologies allow us to develop inherent risk monitoring artifacts.
- Several models can be deployed to study firm, industry, management, business model, and account-specific risk.

REFERENCES

Calderon, T. G. and Cheh, J. J. (2002) A roadmap for future neural networks research in auditing and risk assessment. *International Journal of Accounting Information Systems*, 3 (4): 203–236.

Culp, C. L. (2001) *The Risk Management Process*. New York: Wiley.

Middleton, S. E., Middleton, L., & Modafferi, S. (2013). Real-time crisis mapping of natural disasters using social media. *IEEE Intelligent Systems*, 29(2), 9–17.

Ngai, E. W. T., Xiu, Li, Chau, D. C.K. (2011) The application of data mining techniques in financial fraud detection: A classification framework and an academic review of literature. *Decision Support Systems*, 50 (3): 559–569. Available from: http://dx.doi.org/10.1016/j.dss.2010.08.006.

Peters, J. M., Lewis, B. L., and Vasant, D. (1989) Assessing inherent risk during audit planning: The development of a knowledge based model. *Accounting, Organizations and Society*, 14 (4): 359–378.

Shailer, G., Wade, M., Willett, R. and Len Yap, K. (1998) Inherent risk and indicative factors: Senior auditors' perceptions. *Managerial Auditing Journal*, 13 (8): 455–464.

Vasarhelyi, M. A. and Kuenkaikaew, S. (2013) The Predictive Audit Framework. *The International Journal of Digital Accounting Research*, 13: 37–71.

Wu, D. D., Chen, S. H., and Olson, D. L. (2014) Business intelligence in risk management: Some recent progresses. *Information Sciences*, 256: 1–7.

CHAPTER NINE

Automating Internal Controls Assessment

RECENTLY, PRICEWATERHOUSECOOPERS (PWC) settled two major high-profile malpractice lawsuits in the UK. In the two cases (MF Global and Taylor Bean & Whitaker), the allegations against PwC indicated that the plaintiffs expected the audit firm to go beyond the management assertions and include management decision-making in the scope of the audit. Another firm, travel company Thomas Cook, was also audited by PwC between 2007 and 2016. Between 2017 and the collapse of Thomas Cook in 2019, Ernst & Young (EY) took over as the auditors. Upon investigation it was discovered that PwC provided remuneration advice to Thomas Cook, and that while both firms, PwC and EY, had information about the deep problems facing Thomas Cook, both gave clean audit reports to Thomas Cook. Commenting on audit failures, Bob Moritz, global chairman of PwC, said, "The expectations of the market is above the regulatory requirement. When big failures happen, it is not necessarily an audit failure. The controls might be appropriate, but the continuation of the business, its financial position and long-term sustainability can still be in question" (Kinder, 2019).

- Would it be possible for PwC and EY to gain deeper insights about their clients' material weaknesses in internal controls, even before an audit is launched?

- Is it possible for PwC to develop greater insights into the business operations of a firm?
- How can management, board, and the audit committee receive continuous evaluation of audit controls?
- How can new and emerging risks be identified and mitigated?
- Can audit expand its scope without incurring greater cost?

Answers to these and many other similar questions greatly depend upon the automation strategy of internal controls. In this chapter we develop a comprehensive strategic approach to automate internal controls assessment and audit.

AUTOMATING INTERNAL CONTROLS ASSESSMENT

Unlike the inherent risk, which is embedded in the strategic choices made by the firm due to its business model, industry, etc., the internal controls risk is a function of actions of management teams and boards. In 1993, the Committee of Sponsoring Organizations of the Treadway Commission (COSO) presented a framework, which has become the standard for internal controls. COSO defined internal control as (COSO, 2013):

> Internal control is a process, effected by an entity's board of directors, management and other personnel, designed to provide reasonable assurance regarding the achievement of objectives in the following three categories:
>
> - Reliability of financial reporting.
> - Effectiveness and efficiency of operations.
> - Compliance with applicable laws and regulations.

The COSO standard is based upon three objectives – effectiveness and efficiency of operations, reliable financial reporting, and compliance with laws and regulations. This means that the controls exist to achieve the three objectives. The first objective of effectiveness and efficiency of operations is based upon the corporate objectives as determined by the board and the senior leadership teams and constitute the primary goals that the firm must achieve to fulfill its strategy. The second objective of reliable financial reporting is based upon the assertions made by the firm and the numbers and disclosures reported about the financial performance of the firm. The third objective aims to ensure that the firm abides by the laws and regulations applicable to its business and industry.

For each objective, internal controls are built with the following five components: (1) control environment, (2) risk assessment, (3) control activities, (4) monitoring, and (5) information and communication. Each of the components is supported by principles and, as of 2013, 17 principles are part of the framework.

At this point it is important to note that audit automation can be viewed as a combination of tool-driven (where auditors don't rely upon any human-provided information) and human-based evidence collection. Auditees provide information in the form of data requests, access to systems and information, and responses to specific informational requests in the form of reports, questions and answers, forms, etc. Automated tools do not rely upon human-provided information and instead they directly access evidence from the source such as data, the databases, and the applications. Human-based evidence collection relies upon surveys and questionnaires. Artificial intelligence (AI) has a role to play in both areas and while this chapter primarily focuses upon the tools, the human-centric surveys and questionnaires automation involves the ability to generate and analyze surveys and questionnaires. We will cover human surveys and questionnaires in a following chapter.

Previous studies using AI methods of self-organizing maps (SOMs) based clustering techniques have suggested that internal controls form a complex nexus of capabilities where a firm may have one or more strong components (e.g., control activities and monitoring) but not all areas. Furthermore, firms may have strong components for one objective but not all three (Länsiluoto et al., 2016). Recall that there are three objectives: effectiveness and efficiency of operations, reliable financial reporting, and compliance with laws and regulations. To design an automated system, our strategy needs to cover all three COSO objectives and the related five components.

When designing an automated internal control system, our broad strategy is as follows:

- Approach the problem as an integrated interaction of various agents (both deterministic and stochastic).
- Use a variety of technologies, including process mining, machine learning, RPA, and expert systems.
- Check for internal control weaknesses that are embedded in the design of the client firm and hence create an environment ripe for errors and frauds, and to predict if a fraudulent activity is taking place.
- Use integrated internal controls system to perform continuous assessment.
- Apply integrated internal controls system to create an exhaustive assessment (i.e., the entire population is analyzed vs. a sample).
- Evolve and grow the system with business.

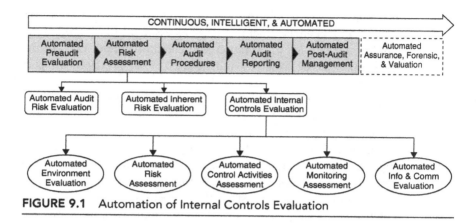

FIGURE 9.1 Automation of Internal Controls Evaluation

Automated risk assessment is composed of three areas: audit risk evaluation, inherent risk evaluation, and internal controls evaluation. Audit risk is a function of inherent risk, controls risk, and detection risk. In the previous chapter we covered the inherent risk. Inherent risk is the risk that exists in the absence of any internal controls. Internal controls risk happens when a firm does not have proper internal controls to manage and control the inherent risks. The lack of controls can be due to a firm's practices or design. It can happen intentionally or unintentionally. Internal controls can be evaded, overridden, or bypassed when management engages in fraud. Thus, while inherent risk is embedded in the nature of the business, internal controls risk is very much a product of how a firm is managed. When auditors observe gaps in internal controls, they are supposed to increase their substantive procedures to reduce or minimize the chances of misstatement.

As shown in Figure 9.1, to automate the internal controls evaluation, we follow the COSO model and break it down into five capability areas of automated environment evaluation, automated risk assessment, automated control activities assessment, automated monitoring assessment, and automated information and communications evaluation. Each of the areas is automated with various agents that work in a coordinated and collaborative manner to achieve total automation.

 AUTOMATED CONTROL ENVIRONMENT

The principles of control environment (Figure 9.2) are

■ The organization demonstrates a commitment to integrity and ethical values.

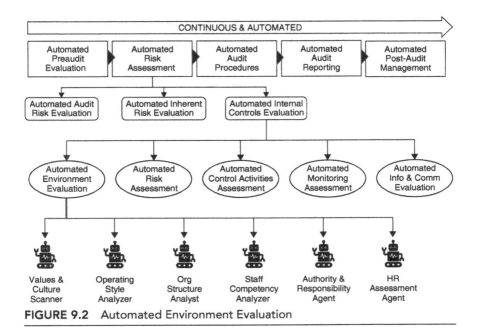

FIGURE 9.2 Automated Environment Evaluation

- The board of directors demonstrates independence from management and exercises oversight of the development and performance of internal control.
- Management establishes, with board oversight, structures, reporting lines, and appropriate authorities and responsibilities in the pursuit of objectives.
- The organization demonstrates a commitment to attract, develop, and retain competent individuals in alignment with objectives.
- The organization holds individuals accountable for their internal control responsibilities in the pursuit of objectives.

The assessment of control's environment is an inquiry about the patterns of human values and actions. For example, the word "organization" in the first principle implies there are one or more humans who demonstrate commitment to integrity and ethical values. Commitment is a cognitive construct and manifests via human communications and actions. At this time, we do not have reliable technology to observe what transpires in people's minds, but we can observe patterns about humans and human behavior that can provide us information about their mental or cognitive constructs. For example, speech, choice of words, gestures, and body language (including physiological information) can give us clues about the cognitive constructs. These could be general – or specific to a domain. For example, a general assessment can reveal the personality of a person and can be classified as aggressive versus passive. A specific assessment will search for speech (verbal, written) for values.

Thus, designing a system to assess the controls environment will be composed of:

- An agent that gauges the cognitive constructs of management teams (values, ethics, personalities, integrity, and others).
- An agent that gauges the cognitive constructs of management teams and boards specific to the task structure (e.g., values or personality types to function during a specific challenge for a firm or for the specific objective of financial reporting).
- An agent that determines if the board has undertaken the responsibility of the oversight, structures, responsibilities, and authorities.
- An agent that determines that Board separation with the management team, and exercises oversight over the development and performance of internal controls.
- An agent that measures and provides feedback on the firm's commitment to attract, develop, and retain competent individuals.
- An agent that evaluates accountability.

The above agents, once trained, form the integrated control environment system.

Integrity, Ethics, Personality, and Values

This system was explained in the audit preplanning chapter. We will reexamine it here from an internal (vs. external) system perspective. The auditor has access to significantly more documents internally than analyzing a company from the outside. In today's world, pictures, voice, and video data can also be requested and obtained. The core version of this system is natural language processing, which analyzes the written communications of the management team and the board members to search for words that signify integrity, ethics, values, and personality. As previously mentioned, this approach has been deployed to study the fraud risk from linguistic and vocal patterns of earnings calls (Throckmorton et al., 2015) as well as from documents (Management's Discussion and Analysis (MD&A) section of the Form 10-K) (Humpherys et al., 2011). The agent is expected to evaluate how much of management and board communication is applied to values and ethics. The input documents used for these analyses may include reports, messages, board meeting minutes, emails, and other communications. Using that as input, a classification engine is deployed that, based upon words, evaluates the presence, depth, and frequency of ethics and integrity-related discussions in the normal course of business operations.

Another, more complicated, way is to get data from communications of leaders of a firm that engaged in fraud and study the patterns of their expression versus the patterns of the firms that provided proper returns and met the fiduciary obligations.

Board of Directors

The board documents and emails, including the minutes from the audit committee meetings, are analyzed to determine the presence of discussions, guidance, directives, and references to ethics, values, and integrity. The same can be done to assess the references to internal controls. This reveals the instances where the references to the internal controls were made. The email analysis also reveals the communications flow, authority, and the nature of relationship in the organization.

The features used for email can be composed of metadata of emails, number of emails, headers, text, attachment or no attachment, signed emails, forwarded, replied to, cc'd, blind copied, and other features related to frequency of emails.

Management Philosophy and Operating Style

We briefly touched upon this area in a previous chapter where our model was based upon external data. Here we use the internal data to evaluate management philosophy and operating style. Once again natural language processing can give us an excellent start to understand the management philosophy and operating style.

Management philosophy and style can be observed by the language used by the management team, the social networks within the organization, and the company culture. HR files, court documents, and websites such as Glassdoor provide excellent data for modeling. Using machine learning, your goal is to train your algorithm to classify the culture of a firm in various classes. This can be viewed as a problem of classifying the management team into various buckets of operating styles, management philosophies, and management models. For instance, you can determine if the management style is authoritarian or collaborative, closed versus open, delegation centric versus empowerment based. Employee behavior in organizations can be predicted by deploying machine learning and data mining textual information such as emails (Straub et al., 2016).

Organizational Structure

The organizational structure assessment comes from multiple angles. The analytical capability is systematically built by layering the following capabilities:

- The analyzer for organizational structure: this utility looks at the organizational job descriptions and classifies employees into internal controls specific roles. The data mined are the job descriptions, departments names, people, titles, etc. A separate analysis of organization can also show power flows, influence, and informal social links (Fire and Puzis, 2016)
- The analyzer also looks at the chart versus actual authority structure. The chart authority structure is as represented in the organizational charts and subject to the reporting relationships. The actual authority structure is determined based upon analyzing the social networks from emails, texts, and other information. The social hierarchy can be determined from machine learning by analyzing the emails (Rowe et al., 2007).

Financial Reporting Competencies

The financial reporting competencies can be obtained by understating the educational background, experience, and type of education.

The training data set for competency includes the typical HR data, as well as data from resumes, LinkedIn, and other social media data. It also includes data from the number of publications by the person, involvement in various professional societies, trainings, and certifications.

This artifact can be designed two ways. The first approach is to use HR data from a larger data set (which might include data from multiple companies) and have a human apply labels to the data. The label in this case will be applied to learn the competence levels for a position. Factors such as years on the job, educational background, experience, etc., will be the input data set. Valuable information can be extracted from resumes (Reza and Zaman, 2017). The 'y' or output variable will be competent versus incompetent for a given job.

The second and more interesting artifact uses the data set of input variables including experience, years on the job, educational background from an actual data set of frauds and failure in that position. While interesting, it will be hard to reconstruct a data set for training purposes since it will be hard to pinpoint the blame for a failure.

Authority and Responsibility

Authority and responsibility are assessed by using various intelligent automation technologies. We are trying to assess whether management assigned the responsibility of internal controls appropriately and the employees were given the appropriate controls and authority to ensure that internal controls are in place and effective. There are several ways to assess that from the machine learning perspective.

The first is to have an agent that uses the human resources data to understand the job responsibilities. The data collection can also extend to the annual employee review and evaluation forms that typically contain more detailed accounts of actual work undertaken by employees. In addition, emails and communications can also be used as the data input. The model uses natural language processing to evaluate if, given the role of the individual, his or her responsibility structure includes references to position-specific internal controls. Notice that in this assessment, we are only evaluating the environment and not the activities. Therefore, our focus remains on studying the environment of the organization.

While responsibility is assessed using the above, analyzing authority is a whole different ballgame. Authority manifests in enabling a manager or employee to conduct themselves in the proper manner, not enforcing improper or unnecessary constraints, assuring employees that there will no negative consequences when employees file a complaint or become a whistleblower.

Authority is a function of being able to act upon what a person has been made responsible for. In corporate systems, access is provided to individuals by a workflow that records the person who authorized the access. Logs from that system can show if the authorization is being done at the right level and being done by the person who has the authority to do it, or by someone higher up in the organization, or by more than one person. The culture can provide an indirect proxy for authority assessment. More authoritative leaders will be less inclined to allow people to function independently, even when it comes to such an important role as internal controls. Finally, internal emails, meeting notes, and communications provide excellent data for assessing the level of authority key employees have. In advanced settings both video and speech can be used to study the cultural dynamics of a firm. To accomplish that level of automation, process mining and machine learning are used, and their applications are explained later in this chapter.

Human Resource Policies and Practices

Large data sets are available and can be mined in human resources (Jia et al., 2018). The objective of control environment assessment with respect to HR is to determine whether the department is aware of the underlying concepts of separation of duties, internal controls, and hiring the right talent to mitigate the risks. The policies and practices of HR can be analyzed using natural language processing and the usage of key terms (separation of duties, etc.) can be assessed to develop insights into HR capabilities. Similar concepts, as discussed above, are applied to determine the capability and contribution of the HR department in supporting stronger internal controls.

 ## AUTOMATED RISK ASSESSMENT

Automated risk assessment was extensively covered in the previous chapter from an inherent risk perspective. We recognized that there are at least four automated methods to explore risk in an organization. The first method focused on the account- and assertion-specific risk identification and management. The three remaining methods, shadow/parallel accounting, strategic objectives, and deep learning, can be used for any type of risk management capability development. In fact, in our case, COSO framework requires management to understand risks from the perspective of achieving company's objectives. The COSO 2013 framework outlines the four principles of risk assessment:

1. The organization specifies objectives with sufficient clarity to enable the identification and assessment of risks relating to objectives.
2. The organization identifies risks to the achievement of its objectives across the entity and analyzes the risks as a basis for determining how the risks should be managed.
3. The organization considers the potential for fraud in assessing risks to the achievement of objectives.
4. The organization identifies and assesses changes that could significantly impact the system of internal control.

In this chapter we will expand on the model presented in inherent risk evaluation and include risk assessment from an internal control perspective, and also introduce the concept of event-based risk assessment.

The process is composed of four levels of automation:

Level 1: Outside-in – Get a general idea about potential material weakness in internal controls (MWIC) by using publicly available information. This gives auditors a sense of how risky a client situation might turn out to be.
Level 2: Process centric – Understand the risk relationship between processes and controls.

Level 3: Enterprise – Develop greater insights into the value chain and business processes of the organization. This is similar to enterprise-based risk analysis frameworks.

Level 4: Business decisions – Auditors do not consider this to be part of their jobs; however, as the opening case study of PwC settling two lawsuits shows, there is a growing movement to place that responsibility on auditors. The reasoning behind that is clear. The economic consequences of management decisions and objectives flow through the financial systems and the stakeholders expect auditors to understand and evaluate such realities of business. The consequences of management business decisions can also become the motivation factors to conduct fraud. In other cases, management decisions impact the future cash flows and the cost of capital of a firm and therefore impact the valuation of many current assets.

Level 1: Outside-In Analysis

A group of researchers wanted to explore if it is possible to identify material weaknesses in internal controls from using publicly available external data (Simsek et al., 2018). Looking at various companies that announced material weakness in internal controls, the group identified financial data from historical financial statements one year prior to the disclosure. Using that data – data that included financial ratios such as total asset turnover, profitability, capital intensity, size, current ratio, and operating performance – the research team tried to predict the internal control weaknesses. After applying various methods, the team was able to obtain 70 to 80% accuracy in results. This means that the team was able to predict, with reasonable accuracy, that material weakness exists in internal controls only by using the historical financial data. A similar artifact can be deployed to identify such weaknesses in companies.

In fact, given today's technology advances, the predictive power of such an artifact can be significantly enhanced by adding features and using a deep learning environment.

Level 2: Process Centric

As we move beyond our Level 1 analysis, we can go a level deeper to determine if the primary processes in a firm carry greater risk. This evaluation is a function of feature data obtained from historical records of internal control problems. For instance, a data set that contains the examples of prior misstatements or disclosures of internal control weaknesses can be used to identify the presence of MWIC by industries, companies, and process types. At least two types of machine learning methods can be deployed to develop insights into process-centric MWIC.

The first approach is similar to the one by Simsek et al., discussed in the previous section, except that instead of using financial and operational performance data as feature inputs, we use industries, company types, business model descriptions, and processes to understand the likelihood of MWIC.

The second approach borrows from methods developed in studying human errors in accidents. The study of human errors in accidents has significant literature. In 1998, Hollnagel authored a book titled *Cognitive Reliability and Error Analysis Method* (Hollnagel, 1998). In that book he developed three taxonomies. The first was the taxonomy of technology, in which he pointed out the problems that can afflict machines (e.g., equipment failure, procedure failure, interface failure). The second taxonomy was of "man," implying the cognitive problems that can afflict a human (e.g., planning, execution, memory, interpretation, observation). The third taxonomy was of the organization, including the failure points in an organization (e.g., training, working conditions). Hollnagel presented a Cognitive Reliability and Error Analysis Method (CREAM), which shifted the focus from the task characteristics and on a hypothetical inherent human error probability, to the principle that context is the driving force behind Human Reliability (R. Moura et al., 2015). Moura, Beer, Patelli, Lewis, and Knoll identified the importance of the principle and expanded upon that to use a major accidents data set, applying a clustering technique (unsupervised) to classify the data to discover various causes of accidents. They used self-organizing maps (SOMs) to cluster and classify data (Moura et al., 2015; Moura et al., 2017). The SOM technique also enables multidimensional data to be viewed in a two-dimensional representation (Kohonen, 2013). Similar to what Moura, Beer, Patelli, Lewis, and Knoll (2015) did, SOM/Clustering can be applied to understand the drivers of MWIC.

Level 3: Value Chain and Enterprise Risk Relationships

We covered a risk management process in Chapter 7. By understanding the value chain relationships and enterprise-centric risk, we develop insights into potential problems that may arise in situations where external parties are involved (e.g., sales and procurement). Developing those insights helps give auditors an idea about potential deterioration in value of assets (e.g., knowledge about a major customer going bankrupt will impact the AR held by the client firm).

The enterprise risk management process is composed of the following processes: identify risks, develop assessment criteria, assess risks, assess risk interactions, prioritize risks, and respond to risks (Curtis and Carey, 2012).

The use of AI in the risk management process automates the process flow of risk management.

Level 4: Business Decisions Analysis

This area of risk analysis is critical to improve audit quality and to help develop a deeper, more insightful perspective for auditors. The automation in this case follows the standard approach of understanding the enterprise risk. There are established methods and approaches for identifying, measuring, and managing enterprise risks.

Technology Design

Before presenting the methodology to accomplish that goal, it is important to understand the two types of data critical for performing the control activity analysis. The first is the transactional data. This is the regular data we use to perform analysis and includes data from databases such as sales, accounting, and procurement. The second type of data, known as metadata, is the data about the data – for example, computer's log data about transactions. Metadata captures things like who accessed the system, when an entry was made, or what changes took place.

Control activities review is based upon three types of analysis: data-centric and metadata-centric and data + metadata-centric. To appreciate the power of automation, it is important to recognize that automated evaluation of control activities ties directly to the risk review done in the previous section, as well as actual audit procedures. Even though we presented the total audit automation model as a linear model, a machine, unlike humans, doesn't need the process transition nodes and can instead perform all processes simultaneously.

Metadata-Centric Analysis

Process-specific analysis is a growing area of audit automation. The advent of process-mining technology was a transformational step for conducting risk evaluation using event log data. Analytical methods are applied to extract insights from the log data to understand audit-related patterns. The data extracted from event logs includes information about which system was accessed, when, and by whom. This is known as the activity, routing, and resource information. Process mining is rules-based extraction of data. This information is used to capture the audit evidence to determine factors such as

- Was the system accessed by the people who are authorized to do so?
- Was the system accessed at odd times or near the closing period?

- Was the system accessed with higher frequency at some time intervals?
- Were two or more systems being accessed by a person whose responsibilities do not allow him or her to do so due to separation of duties?
- Were systems accessed by a group of people whose hours of accessing the system matched, however, they typically don't access systems at the same time?

In their impressive work, Jans et al. (2013) made a strong case for using process mining in audit and argued the value creation potential of using process mining. They presented the following four key attributes of process mining:

1. Process mining analyzes the entire population of data and not just a sample.
2. Critically that data consists of meta-data – data entered independently of the actions of auditee – and not just data entered by the auditee.
3. Process mining allows the auditor to have a more effective way of implementing the audit risk model by providing effective ways of conducting the required walk throughs of processes and conducting analytic procedures.
4. Process mining allows the auditor to conduct analyses not possible with existing audit tools, such as discovering the ways in which business processes are actually being carried out in practice, and to identify social relationships between individuals.

Process mining can be used to identify processes from beginning to end – giving a comprehensive view of how a process moves through the company's systems and laying out the audit trail. Van der Aalst et al. (2010) outline the capabilities of process mining as being able to provide business provenance by ensuring traceability, process discovery by identifying frequent patterns, and being able to compare an a priori model with the event logs and vice versa.

Data-Centric Analysis

Data-centric internal control analysis refers to analyzing the transactional data to assess internal controls and to performing actual substantive procedures and testing. This data includes that which resides in accounting systems and that becomes the source of information used to construct the financial statements supplied by the management. These are the general analysis, such as budgets, reports, business intelligence, business analytics, and other management information reporting. In human-led control structures, these reports are the life-blood of decision-making.

In an automated world, some of that decision-making will no longer be performed by humans. Much of this will be discussed in the next chapter. However, for this chapter it is important to consider that a computerized financial system is made up of transactional data, the underlying processes and structures, and the human who enters data or makes decisions outside of the system. These decisions could be about how to treat a transaction, or what/how to reconcile, or how to record an entry. But while the human decision-making can be considered as outside the system, since it happens in the human mind, those decisions impact what transpires in the computerized financial system. We, the humans, are both part of the system and exist outside of it. As we move ahead with the AI revolution, we may need to think differently about viewing what goes on in the human mind as external to the system and instead include those thoughts, decisions, and cognitive frameworks as part of the system. This broadening of the system concept happens as cognitive frameworks and decision-making is transferred from human mind and embedded in the financial system.

Data + Metadata

The addition of machine learning to process mining is a great innovation for audit. When combined, both can produce continuous, automated, and integrated audit. Six years after proposing the use of process mining, Jans, with another author, proposed the use of machine learning with process mining (Jans and Hosseinpour, 2019). The idea of machine learning comes from the fact the process mining creates an extremely large number of exceptions. These exceptions are then interpreted by humans and marked as "of interest" and "not of interest." The exceptions provide a huge source of learning data, such that the machine can learn how to classify the output of process mining data. In fact, human-classified data provides a perfect set of examples needed to teach machines how to identify good versus unacceptable patterns. Using the classification algorithms, the machine can identify patterns and generalize its learning to recognize previously unknown anomalous patterns.

 ## CONTROL ACTIVITIES

Unlike the control environment assessment, which focused on the passive factors of internal controls, control activities focus on actions and activities related to ensuring that internal controls are implemented, and that board and management directives are followed about internal controls. The goal of evaluation of control activities (McNally, 2013) is to ensure that the organization

- Selects and develops control activities
- Selects and develops general controls over technology
- Deploys policies and procedures

The goal of intelligent automation is to automate the evaluation of the achievement of the above three goals automatically.

Selects and Develops Control Activities

The selection and development of control activities is a function of the risks identified. Every significant risk requires controls so that the overall goal of ensuring that risk of material misstatement for all relevant assertions is effectively managed. In some ways, controls serve the preventative role. Frauds and errors should be detected and corrected before they enter the financial system.

The selection and development of controls can be viewed as establishing a link between each significant risk and the preventative process designed to block fraud and error entering the financial system. This preventative process is composed of activities that are embedded in the workflows and business processes. For example, hiring the right people, establishing separation of duties, developing limits on transaction sizes, implementing approvals in the workflow, and limiting access to systems are some of the key activities undertaken.

In the context of modernization of audit, there are two ways to determine whether management is actively selecting and developing controls and therefore actively engaging in control activities.

- The first is the direct evidence obtained in response to the known risks evaluation. This evidence is not based upon questionnaires but is acquired directly (as discussed in the previous section) and it shows whether the management has done a good job in preparing the organization to prevent material errors and fraud finding their way into the accounting systems.
- The second is to understand the management's ability and preparation for unknown or unanticipated emergent risks that can arise rapidly and lead to a material event. Since the auditor's focus is primarily on the historical information, one can question the need for including this in the assessment. The reason for that is simple. Even if we ignore the direct benefits for assessing the potential versus known risk-centric evaluation, the fact

that management is engaging in understanding potential risks is on its own an indication of management being responsible and active in preventative response.

The model implies establishing a context-sensitive model that offers a relationship between risks and preventative response processes. In many cases there will be similarities between various approaches and risks. An assertion risk may call for a specific functional separation of duties – for instance, in accounts payable, purchasing, and receiving – regardless of the company. In other cases, risks may require new, customized, or creative preventative responses. Most auditing operates with existing models, what van der Aalst et al. calls de jure models that "describe a desired or required way of working," in contrast to de facto models that "aim to describe reality with potential violations of the boundaries defined in de jure models" (van der Aalst et al., 2011, 2010). Hence, we can assume that the de jure model results from the knowledge of what works and what doesn't work. In this case, they come from auditor's knowledge of a certain preventative control being an effective mitigation to a certain specific risk. This implies that an ontology of risks and preventative measures can be created, which essentially can be transformed into a set of rules that can be invoked or checked against for an audit.

The machine learning – centric automation for control activities automation refers to two applications:

1. The application that studies new risk patterns and suggests mitigation strategies. This can be a combination of both unsupervised (clustering) and supervised (classification) approaches. The job of this application is to update the existing de jure models. Whether that update happens via learning or updating existing rules, risk-response patterns recognition is the core capability needed to propose and develop effective control activities in response to emerging risk patterns.

2. The application that incorporates the above learning and compares it to de facto situations. This is done from a combination of "metadata + data" analysis, as discussed in the previous section. Van der Aalst et al. clarified that concept when they said, "It is possible to promote a de facto model to a de jure one. A comparison showing that the actual process execution is inconsistent with the standard preexisting model may motivate an update of the de jure model" (van der Aalst et al., 2010). What machine learning does is to explore the inconsistency between the de jure model and the de facto model and then if it finds the de facto model more effective, it updates

the de jure model. The learning can happen from at least three sources: (1) historical data from previous audits; (2) auditor (human)-provided knowledge base where the auditor provides examples of an effective response; and (3) the system is designed with a critic that can simulate the risk scenarios and critique the strategies used to prevent and counter the risks in terms of a goal structure. This design will generally require the use of reinforcement learning.

Selects and Develops Controls Over Technology

Control activities related to technology were addressed by van der Aalst et al. (2011) in which they proposed the concept of an oversight system being created to monitor another system. They clarified that a control is "an automated task in the information system aimed at the prevention of violations of certain business rules. These controls are strongly related to the functions of the information system" and then cautioned that "often business rules are generic (i.e., not bound to a specific business context)." The process of management deploying controls over information technology is being achieved by continuous controls monitoring (CCM). CCM is a collection of tools that extract data from databases and scans for separation of duties, authorizations, breaches, errors, anomalies, size limits of transactions, etc. These controls are embedded within the technology.

Technology access controls are also important considerations. Separation of duties can be ascertained from the reports about who logged into systems. Ensuring that only those people who are authorized to access the systems do so is essential for establishing a better controls environment.

The advent of AI will have three important impacts on this area. First, two types of analysis – predictive and prescriptive – are added to the deterministic, rule-based anomaly detection of CCM. This means that the system not only analyzes data from databases, it uses the data to learn about breaches and hence predicts them and offers prescriptive remedies to counter the threats. The second impact is that significantly larger amounts of data can be processed and deployed in deep learning – centric architecture. This enables detecting frauds and errors that are not easily detectable. Third, AI's introduction will lead to control redesign and weakening of existing controls. Intelligent systems are deployed not only by those who are trying to protect a firm, but also by those who don't mean well. This means that intelligent controls will be needed.

Consider the fact that our transactional (deterministic) systems have a source of concern for us from a controls perspective – imagine the arrival of intelligent machines in our organization. How will we manage and control them? The advent of AI will further exacerbate the problem of controls. This topic is covered in Chapter 18 of this book.

Deploys Policies and Procedures

The policies and procedures are scanned and using natural language processing analyzed to determine if they comply with the risk types identified for the client firm. For instance, frequency of key words can classify documents into various areas of controls and determine if there was proper coverage of each area of controls. For instance, using the Term Frequency – Inverse Document Frequency (TF-IDF) method, documents can be analyzed and classified based upon importance and coverage.

example: What Is TF-IDF? Term Frequency – Inverse Document Frequency

TF-IDF is a natural language processing method that is based upon calculating the frequency of words. It has two parts, the TF part and the IDF part. In the TF part, the algorithm calculates the number of times a term is used in a document. For example, if you are analyzing a document pertaining to policies and procedures, you can learn that the words "Separation" and "Duties" were used 34 and 28 times respectively. If the document is a total of 1000 words long, the word frequency will be calculated as 34 divided by 1000 for Separation and 28 divided by 1000 for Duties. This gives an estimate of how many times each term was used in a document and can provide a sense of importance of that term in a document. In the IDF part, we calculate the inverse document frequency by taking the whole corpus (all documents) and identifying how many documents used the term overall. It is calculated by taking a base 2 log of the number of documents divided by the number of documents in which the term was used. Let us say that there are 50 documents that make up the policy and procedures and the terms "Separation" and "Duties" appear in 12 and 32 documents, then log of 50/12 and 50/32 respectively will give us the inverse document frequency. The TF-IDF is then calculated by multiplying TF by IDF. By using this method, we can determine the relevance of documents to various topics. Once TF-IDF values are determined, we can also calculate the similarities among documents. For example, we can estimate which documents focus on Separation of Duties – related internal controls.

Physical Controls and Machine-Generated Data

Physical controls are necessary to protect certain types of assets. In the past, the controls for physical access were limited to installing cameras and locks. With the advances in AI we now have the opportunity to make significant improvements in the physical controls. The opportunities exist in automated evaluation of video input to assess whether that usage of the asset is in accordance with the expected use. The video feed can be analyzed for misuse, theft, and intentional asset destruction. In addition to video, other Internet of Things (IoT) data can be analyzed to determine controls over production, inventory, warehouses, etc. Similarly, data from trucks can be analyzed regarding travel miles, maintenance, and fleet usage patterns.

AUTOMATED MONITORING

Monitoring refers to the management monitoring the internal control activities on an ongoing basis. The standards require the management team to

- Conduct ongoing and/or separate evaluations.
- Evaluate and communicate deficiencies: The goal of evaluation is to ensure that management actively leads, manages, and participates in reporting. In an automated system, the function of automated monitoring is embedded within the machines. In the initial stages of automation, it is expected that humans and machines will share the monitoring responsibility but as technology moves forward, the responsibility will shift to the machines.
- Automated controls providing information about machines: The auditors would want to see evidence that automated controls are providing evidence about monitoring activities.
- Risk simulation: Auditors should be able to simulate risk in an environment and observe the performance of controls.
- Critic: Determine if a critic exists that automatically critiques the performance of the monitoring controls.
- Business process gap analysis: Automated checks are performed for business process gap analysis.
- Budgets, variance, and scorecards.

INFORMATION AND COMMUNICATIONS

The guiding principles of COSO about information and communications emphasize that an organization must

- Obtain or generate and use relevant quality information to support the functioning of internal controls.
- Internally communicate information, including objectives and responsibilities for internal controls, necessary to support internal controls.
- Communicate with external parties regarding internal controls.

The goal of the automated internal control information and communications systems is to constantly collect and compile actionable information about internal controls and then disseminate it to both internal and external parties.

The previous sections addressed several artifacts that can be deployed to automate internal controls. These artifacts will provide information about their own state as well as about their activities. For instance, self-governance can be built into the artifact and can report on factors such as

- Business process
- Transaction details
- Other events
- Data lineage

Reports generated from these can be sent to all relevant parties and an escalation workflow can be designed.

 ## CONTROL RISK AND NEXT STEPS

Our audit planning began with using extensive information about the firm from external sources to develop a good analysis for risk. In some cases, the external (outside-in) analysis will expose the risk areas as clearly as a flashlight exposing a point of interest in a dark room. In other cases, they will develop our instincts and make us more aware of what lies ahead in an engagement.

From outside-in we moved to the internal data and systems of a firm. Our approach became more invasive and deeper. We penetrated the shields of obscurity and gained direct access to data. It was from that point where we began gaining confidence in our ability to monitor and assess controls intelligently and constantly.

With a good understanding of inherent risks and control risks, auditors can assess the focus and extent of substantive procedures. We discuss direct evidence collection from accounts and substantive procedures in the next chapter.

Key Points

* Internal controls testing is one of the most important objectives of an audit. While inherent risk is usually unmanageable and is a function of a company's business model among other things, control risk can and should be managed.
* Control risk is composed of five types of automations including automated controls environment, automated risk assessment, automated control activities assessment, automated monitoring assessment, and automation information and communications evaluation.
* An audit automation plan must address all of these areas.

▪ REFERENCES

COSO (2013) *Internal Control – Integrated Framework.* [online]. Available from: https://www.coso.org/Documents/990025P-Executive-Summary-final-may20.pdf.

Curtis, P. and Carey, M. (2012) Risk assessment in practice. *COSO*. coso.org.

Fire, M. and Puzis, R. (2016) Organization mining using online social networks. *Networks and Spatial Economics*, 16 (2): 545–578.

Hollnagel, E. (1998) *Cognitive Reliability and Error Analysis Method*. Oxford: Elsevier Science.

Humpherys, S. L., Moffitt, K. C., Burns, M. B., Burgoon, J. K., and Felix, W. F. (2011) Identification of fraudulent financial statements using linguistic credibility analysis. *Decision Support Systems*, 50 (3): 585–594.

Jans, M., Alles, M., and Vasarhelyi, M. (2013) The case for process mining in auditing: Sources of value added and areas of application. *International Journal of Accounting Information Systems*, 14 (1): 1–20. Available from: http://dx.doi.org/10.1016/j.accinf.2012.06.015.

Jans, M. and Hosseinpour, M. (2019) How active learning and process mining can act as Continuous Auditing catalyst. *International Journal of Accounting Information Systems*, 32 (November 2018): 44–58. Available from: https://doi.org/10.1016/j.accinf.2018.11.002.

Jia, Q., Guo, Y., Li, R., Li, Y., and Chen, Y. (2018) A conceptual artificial intelligence application framework in human resource management. Proceedings of the International Conference on Electronic Business (ICEB), December, 106–114.

Kinder, T. (2019) Thomas Cook collapse will intensify UK audit debate, PwC says. *Financial Times*.

Kohonen, T. (2013) Essentials of the self-organizing map. *Neural Networks*, 37: 52–65. Available from: http://dx.doi.org/10.1016/j.neunet.2012.09.018.

Länsiluoto, A., Jokipii, A., and Eklund, T. (2016) Internal control effectiveness – a clustering approach. *Managerial Auditing Journal*, 31 (1): 5–34.

McNally, J. S. (2013) The 2013 COSO Framework & SOX Compliance: One approach to an effective transition. *Strategic Finance. June (The Committee of Sponsoring Organizations of the Treadway Commission (COSO)).* Available from: https://www.coso.org/documents/COSO McNallyTransition Article-Final COSO Version Proof_5-31-13.pdf.

Moura, Raphael, Beer, M., Lewis, J., and Patelli, E. (2015) Learning from accidents: Analysis and representation of human errors in multi-attribute events. *12th International Conference on Applications of Statistics and Probability in Civil Engineering, ICASP 2015* (July).

Moura, R., Beer, M., Patelli, E., Lewis, J., and Knoll, F. (2015) Human error analysis: Review of past accidents and implications for improving robustness of system design. Safety and Reliability: Methodology and Applications - Proceedings of the European Safety and Reliability Conference, ESREL 2014. [Online] (September), 1037–1046.

Moura, R., Beer, M., Patelli, E., Lewis, J., and Knoll, F. (2017) Learning from accidents: Interactions between human factors, technology and organisations as a central element to validate risk studies. *Safety Science*, 99: 196–214. Available from: http://dx.doi.org/10.1016/j.ssci.2017.05.001.

Reza, T. and Zaman, S. (2017) *Analyzing CV/resume using natural language processing and machine learning.* BRAC University. Available from: http://dspace.bracu.ac.bd/xmlui/bitstream/handle/10361/9480/14101061™ percnt;2C14101171_CSE.pdf?sequence=1™isAllowed=y.

Rowe, R., Creamer, G., Hershkop, S., and Stolfo, S. J. (2007) Automated social hierarchy detection through email network analysis. *Joint Ninth WebKDD and*

First SNA-KDD 2007 Workshop on Web Mining and Social Network Analysis. [Online] 109–117.

Simsek, S., Bayraktar, E., Ragothaman, S., and Dag, A. (2018) A Bayesian approach to detect the firms with material weakness in internal control. *IISE Annual Conference and Expo 2018.* 971–976.

Straub, K. M., (2016) *Data mining academic emails to model employee behaviors and analyze organizational structure.* Available from: https://vtechworks .lib.vt.edu/bitstream/handle/10919/71320/Straub_KM_T_2016.pdf; sequence=1.

Throckmorton, C. S., Mayew, W. J., Venkatachalam, M., and Collins, L. M. (2015) Financial fraud detection using vocal, linguistic and financial cues. *Decision Support Systems,* 74: 78–87. Available from: http://dx.doi.org/10 .1016/j.dss.2015.04.006.

van der Aalst, W. M. P., Van Hee, K. M., Van Der Werf, J. M., and Verdonk, M. (2010) Auditing 2.0: Using process mining to support tomorrow's auditor. *Computer,* 43 (3): 90–93.

van der Aalst, W., Van Hee, K., Van Der Werf, J. M., Kumar, A., and Verdonk, M. (2011) Conceptual model for online auditing. *Decision Support Systems,* 50 (3): 636–647. Available from: http://dx.doi.org/10.1016/j.dss.2010.08 .014.

CHAPTER TEN

Automated Procedures

A UDIT PROBLEMS ARE NOT confined to the United Kingdom and the United States. Recently, India saw its share of audit issues when Deloitte (Deloitte Haskins and Sells LLP) stepped down from the audit of Dewan Housing Finance Corporation, as the firm raised concerns about intercorporate deposits and problems with transparency. Deloitte's resignation was seen as a response to systemic problems that existed in the banking sector. Covering that development, the *Financial Times* reported that both Deloitte and KPMG affiliate BSR were facing criminal charges and a five-year ban after a major finance group, Infrastructure Leasing & Financial Services, nearly collapsed (Findlay, 2019). Indian prosecutors alleged that the firms were complicit in conducting the fraud, but the firms have rejected such allegations. PricewaterhouseCoopers (PwC) was banned from auditing for two years when it failed to spot the $1.7 billion accounting fraud at Satyam Computer Services. In 2019, PwC resigned from Reliance Capital audit engagement and claimed that it was abiding by a regulation in India that requires an auditing firm to report reasonable suspicion of fraud to relevant authorities.

On June 13, 2019, in Mumbai, a spokesperson from Reliance Capital came out strong against PwC's resignation as statutory auditor and stated (taken from the media release of Reliance Capital (Reliance, 2019)):

- PwC's observations are completely baseless and unjustified.
- PwC has acted prematurely without even statutory discussions with the Audit Committee.

- Reliance Capital's continuing auditor has been mandated by the Audit Committee to submit its independent report on PwC's observations within 15 days.
- There is no question of "diversion"; zero loans and/or liquidity have been provided by any lender in the PwC audit period.
- Reliance Capital is by law required to fund only group entities, being a Core Investment Company (CIC).
- All resources have been utilized purely to support group debt servicing of Rs 35,000 crore in past 14 months.
- Reliance Capital is confident the independent report of the continuing auditor will establish that there are no irregularities.

The following is Reliance Capital's statement on the matter, which was intimated to the stock exchanges on June 11, 2019:

> The Company does not agree with the reasons given by PwC for the resignation. The Company has duly responded to the various queries and letters of PwC and has also duly and validly convened a meeting of the Audit Committee on June 12, 2019 to further respond to the letter dated May 14, 2019 from PwC. The Company expected PwC to have participated in the meeting of the Audit Committee and not resigned on the eve thereof. The Company has also duly furnished all requisite and satisfactory details as required by PwC, especially including certification and confirmations of the transactions in question on multiple occasions by PwC themselves. As regards legal proceedings, the Company had clearly stated that the same would be initiated only if so legally advised, that too if required to protect the interests of all stakeholders, and it is hard to see how PwC has taken exception to this approach. (Reliance, 2019)

Nearly two months after the resignation, Reliance Capital conducted its own investigation and claimed that it had conducted no fraud and the allegations made by PwC were untrue and that PwC failed to provide even a single example of irregularity. The jury is still out on this matter, but it indicates that the problems with the quality of audit are universal and there seems to be a problem with evidence accumulation. Clearly, either PwC failed to provide enough evidence and jumped the gun on Reliance Capital or the evidence was provided but rejected by the management team.

Here are some questions to consider:

- How can audit firms use artificial intelligence (AI) to provide unchallengeable evidence to clients?
- How can evidence accumulation be automated?
- What automation is possible in inquiry, observation, document inspection, and reperformance?
- What is reconciliation automation?
- What is journal entry-based automated inquiry?
- What other ways automation can enable audit (e.g., drones, physical robots, etc.)?

These areas are covered in this chapter.

ACCUMULATING EVIDENCE

Up until this point in the book, we have focused on the preventative measures and planning. In this chapter we will introduce the application of AI in various tests. Tests provide us the evidence we need for verification and assurance. We can think of two broad categories of tests: tests of internal controls and tests related to the transactions and accounts. The former focuses on ensuring that misstatements do not enter the financial reports/system and the second tests the presence of error and fraud. If material weaknesses are identified in internal controls, auditors apply more tests and then, depending upon the control weakness, proceed to testing transactions and accounts. The good news for audit automation using AI is that in many cases internal controls tests can also perform substantive procedures.

BEYOND INTERNAL CONTROLS

In addition to the The Committee of Sponsoring Organizations of the Treadway Commission (COSO) standards, Public Company Accounting Oversight Board (PCAOB) standards require a broader review of controls. The assessment requires various approaches and includes controls related to control environment, management's risk assessment, reporting process, and policies. We discussed the automation of entity-level controls in the previous chapter. This automation focused on top-down assessment that begins with the management, culture, management styles, people, and company strategy – and then systematically moves down to the level of processes and policies. The controls risk is assessed first in areas where higher inherent risk exists and also in areas where material weaknesses have been discovered.

We have already touched upon the transaction and account level controls. Testing these controls requires accessing client systems and applying machine learning and process mining technologies. Disclosures and management discussion, as well as earnings calls, can be analyzed using various technologies including natural language processing and deep learning.

Design effectiveness is assessed not by looking at a single or a few factors but the overall approach of a firm to design its internal controls. Information obtained from the agents deployed to conduct audit provides a nexus and network of activities. In the last chapter we recognized that a combination of natural language processing, support vector machines, Bayesian approaches, clustering, classification, regression, self-organizing maps, neural networks, and deep learning are used in various types of audit automations. The use of these methods implies that no single method can automate the entire audit function. In fact, we recognized that for audit automation to be successful, we need a mix of technologies. We can visualize the audit function automation as a three-dimensional map between intelligent automation technologies (the toolset we have), the audit areas that we are automating, and the various audit applications (such as drones, robots, software bots) (Figure 10.1).

This approach of mixing technologies continues beyond the controls and inherent risk functions and into the transaction and account level assessments via substantive procedures.

Before moving to the procedures, it is helpful to recognize the importance of assessing transactions, accounts, and balances, etc. Clearly, in cases where we find material weaknesses in internal controls, we need to deploy substantive procedures to develop a better understanding of the risk. But even if we do not discover obvious violations of internal controls, we need to keep in mind that the presence of written policies and procedures does not imply that they are being followed. Additionally, management leadership can decide to override the policies. This can happen with the collusion of other team members, or employees can be bullied into accepting leadership's directives.

To identify such matters, it is critical that the audit teams deploy tools that can perform and report constant assessment of internal controls. The other option, which must be simultaneously pursued, is to assess the actual transactions and account balances with procedures (Figure 10.2).

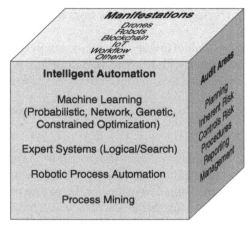

FIGURE 10.1 The Audit Automation Map

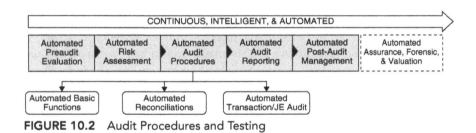

FIGURE 10.2 Audit Procedures and Testing

AUTOMATING BASIC FUNCTIONS

The development of the audit plan for account and transaction testing can be divided into the following: inquiry, observation, document testing, reperformance. We will cover each one of them below.

Tools of Inquiry

The standard tools of inquiry are interviews and questionnaires. Audit firms have developed questionnaires that can help understand both control and account issues. As the evidence collection moves toward direct access to systems and the underlying processes, and as processes and transactions are managed by machines, posing questions to humans may not seem all that necessary. However, we are still a bit far from full automation and even if we had full automation, factors such as having the ability to override systems would require us to receive direct responses from the management team and other stakeholders.

One of the primary tools of inquiry is a questionnaire. A questionnaire has two work streams associated with it: generating a questionnaire and analyzing the responses. AI can be used to generate context-sensitive questionnaires and also to analyze the responses.

Generating Questions

While audit firms do have questionnaires that can be deployed to meet the audit requirements, having the ability to generate context-sensitive questionnaires implies that machines are trained to recognize the nature of the question that needs to be asked in response to a certain development. That development could be identifying the potential for fraud, or observing a weak internal control, or learning about a new risk. These factors create specific situations that require a custom response. The generation of audit questions to meet the needs of the specific audit situations can be attempted by following similar approaches to those used in other areas by using machine learning for question generation. Automated question generation (AQG) from a given text has been around since 1970s. Several approaches have been used with mixed results. The technology has improved considerably but generating questions from sophisticated text still requires more work. When a human generates questions from text, the process consists of reading the text, identifying some answer phrase or important concept about which a question can be asked, and creating the question based upon the text. From a machine perspective, the general approach followed is to simplify the text, select answer phrase, transform sentence, and evaluate and rank question (Divate and Salgaonkar, 2017). A topic of interest composed of a body of text provides a fertile ground for generating questions by extracting named entity information and the predicate argument structures of sentences (Chali and Hasan, 2015).

Analyzing the Responses

Response analysis consists of evaluating the answers provided to open-ended text-based or choice-based responses. Typically, classification algorithms are used to analyze responses to classify into different buckets. As previously mentioned, language contains clues to people's personalities and intentions and can also reveal fraudulent behavior.

Interviews

AI is used in interviews. Video-recorded interviews provide significantly rich information since they contain both spoken language and other features such as emotions, gestures, expressions, and body language.

Observation

Auditors obtain evidence by observing various processes, functions, and job performance of employees. AI is deployed to understand processes and to evaluate human interaction and roles in processes. For instance, process mining and machine learning are used to evaluate and identify segregation of duties, and learn about at what time systems were accessed and what are access patterns to the systems. Given that these types of insights are enabled by millions, even billions, of machine-readable data, it is not possible for humans to conduct such analysis without machines. Machines allow us to evaluate things that are not possible for humans to observe naturally. That is why machines will be able to extract and show us patterns that we don't know and may not even be able to know without deploying AI-centric machines.

Document Testing

Document examination is about inspecting actual documents related to transactions. These documents are often traced in accordance with the processes and provide the audit trail. Computer vision is one of the most promising technologies. It focuses on giving computers the ability to analyze digital images and videos. Document examination can be conducted like a human auditor would do. Computer vision research involves various ways by which high-dimensional data can be extracted by processing and analyzing images and hence a view of the real world is established in the machine's mind. Just as an autonomous vehicle can see things and understand what they are, data observed in computer vision is classified in a way where real-world objects can be named, their relationships and actions identified, and decisions can be made about them.

Optical character recognition is one type of computer vision. The goal of OCR is to analyze text from images and documents. For instance, pdf files and pictures can be scanned, and the content can be categorized in accordance with our interest. Consider the diversity of documents we encounter in business. At the highest level, extracting data from different types of files (e.g., pdf or picture) is the first challenge. Once extracted, the data could have different structure, fonts, concentration, types, and position in a document. Imagine the variety of invoices that a business can receive. Some can have the supplier's name and logo on the top left while others can have it on top right. Some may use Arial font while others may use Times New Roman. Some may have darker background and colors, others may have just white background. The sheer variety and diversity of documents makes OCR a challenging field. In general, however, the methodology used in OCR is as follows:

- Take the document under consideration and apply filters such that the text (characters) stand out and are differentiated from the background.
- Use contour detection methods so that each character (or parts of image) can be recognized. Contour is the outline that defines the shape or boundary of something. Contour detection is segmented into three approaches – pixel-based, edge-based, and region-based. This can be viewed as extracting features that are used for classification (Gong et al., 2018).
- Apply image classification.

Edge detection detects important properties of objects in an image identified by studying discontinuities in the photometrical, geometrical, and physical characteristics of objects (Ziou and Tabbone, 1998). Boundary detection uses characteristic changes in brightness, color, and texture associated with natural boundaries (Martin et al., 2003). Recently, deep learning is being used for image recognition.

Automating the document reading and inspection will allow auditors to check for important details that a human auditor checks in the documents. The classification can identify patterns that are of interest. From balances to descriptions, and from numbers to text, the information is extracted and classified in accordance with predetermined criteria. The examples of documents can be sales orders, vouchers, invoices, checks, etc. The use cases can be observing the signatures, authorizations, stamps, and other impressions on documents to determine who approved the document and when. While digital data does not require such treatment and data transfer protocols enable seamless transfer of data, data from paper documents can now be easily extracted and classified without human intervention.

Reperformance

Performance or reperformance is the reconstruction of a process such that the auditor performs the steps done by the client staff to arrive at a certain account balance, number, or estimate. This is the manual process to compute and compare to the numbers as reported by the management or provided by the staff. Automation of reperformance testing is achieved by using process mining technology to understand the underlying processes, mapping the process steps, and then conducting the testing. A broad corporate data model can be created that includes metadata. With provenance, data relationships, lineage and transformations, structure, and data ownership designations, such data can be an invaluable source of value for audit. The testing can be based upon preconfigured routines based upon ranges of values for transactions or account balances. The threshold or range-centric testing can be achieved with robotic process automation or an expert system. The obvious limitation of this model is that it can only work with known test areas and under known conditions. New patterns, new transactions, or any creative accounting may go undetected in this setup. Automating the patterns of testing is covered below in journal entries. A similar concept can be applied for reperformance.

AUTOMATED RECONCILIATION

One of the most important functions performed in accounting and auditing is reconciliations. They are performed for bank accounts, currencies, inventories, goods receipt invoice, payroll, intercompany, suspense accounts, etc. While it is possible to develop specialized and deterministic reconciliation solutions for specific problems where the variables and their values are known, there remained a need to develop reconciliation solution where machine learning can be used and the solution can be generalized for different types of data. The deterministic solution works based upon preestablished rules applied to known data sets such that rules are created for known matches. Data-set–specific configuration of a solution was too expensive and too slow to implement, and that's when researchers began thinking about using machine learning solutions. When machine learning solutions were introduced, they focused on using labeled data for various data sets and then support-vector machines, or Naïve Bayesian approaches were applied for classifying based upon learned patterns of data. In 2012 Chew and Robinson observed that even the deployment of the machine learning classification technique took significant manual effort to label the data, and proposed a more efficient approach. In their proposed approach they used several fields from the typical accounting data that is available these days, and applied natural language processing to words used in the description fields as features to classify (Chew and Robinson, 2012).

AUTOMATED JOURNAL ENTRIES

As we concentrate on the actual account balances, going to the transaction level becomes inevitable. In fact, to achieve the goal of automated, integrated, and continuous audit, that is not a terrible thing to have. It can give us assurance at the lowest level. The accounting process shown in Figure 10.3 clarifies that business events and transactions produce source documents. Accountants determine what classifies as a recordable transaction and what doesn't. For instance, if your salesperson meets with a prospective client for dinner, and the prospective client assures your salesperson that she will buy from your firm, you will not record that purchase intention as new revenue. However, if your salesperson paid for the dinner, that payment will require some accounting treatment. Source documents become the basis for recording in journals as journal entries. Journal balances are posted in the general ledger. In addition to transactions based upon transactional source documents, many entries require accruals, non-cash, and other adjusting entries. Adjusted trial balance is developed, and statements are generated along with disclosures, explanations, and commentary.

Many of the above steps are being automated. From an auditor's perspective, going at the lowest level to collect evidence, especially if done cost effectively and efficiently, is a valuable option. Bay et al. (2006) demonstrated that by extracting attributes from journal entries they were able to identify suspicious journal entry activity. Since pure anomaly detection can yield a significantly large volume of results with many false positives, they used a two-step approach where they first extracted unusual transactions in accordance with a firm's own history and its peers and then used a classifier that was trained on previously known misstatements. Using the general ledger as a feature vector the researchers identified over 50 features which they changed into numbers and ratios before feeding into the Naïve Bayes classifier.

A different method was used by another research team where they considered the links between accounts to determine the account pairs (e.g., cash-A/P, cash-AR, etc.) and then analyzed the anomalies that resulted from G/L (McGlohon et al., 2009). Each account in the G/L is viewed as a node, and edges between a pair results from exceeding a threshold for debit or credit. Neighboring nodes are used to classify the target node. The neighboring nodes pass a message which serves as a belief about a given node. As the procedure starts, domain knowledge is used to initialize the system.

FIGURE 10.3 The Accounting Process

Schreyer et al. (2017) provide an excellent example of using deep learning for identifying anomalies in journal entries. As explained above, one way to identify anomaly is to use handcrafted rules. Schreyer et al. explain that these rules are defined by accountants and auditors and they are designed to perform "red-flag" tests; they include factors such as timing of posting, backdated account adjustments, or statistical analysis such as Benford's Law and time series evaluation. These rules-based solutions can only solve known problems for which the rules are known and configured in the system. Beyond that, they do not generalize or pick up unexpected or unknown patterns. To solve that problem, they created a powerful deep learning model that uses various attributes of journal entries and identifies anomalies using a deep learning autoencoder neural network. The anomalies were defined as irregular or unusual values of attributes or an unusual or rare pattern of combination of attribute values.

PUTTING IT ALL TOGETHER

As you will have observed in this chapter, intelligent automation requires use of different technologies, approaches, and focus areas. To plan our journey, we need to start with the basic functions first. This means to bring in technologies that help with inquiry, observation, document testing, and reperformance. Context-sensitive question generation is helpful but in many cases your firm will already have an elaborate set of questionnaires. Hence, resources can be better spent on first deploying machine learning solutions that automate analysis of answers obtained from client staff. Observation consists of many different technologies and as the name suggests is a function of how many and what kind of sensors are being used by a client. It will be a worthy exercise to study the business model of a client and to suggest to the client the use of sensors that can help make the client's internal controls stronger. OCR technologies can help tremendously with reading documents. From invoices or contracts, OCR helps in extracting data. This is a must-have and will be an important addition to corporate systems. Finally, reperformance will not be easy to do without a combination of process mining and other technologies. That type of automation has been going on for more than a decade. Adding machine learning to process mining can do wonders for testing.

Key Points

- The lower level audit testing is an expensive part of audit. Internal control weakness results guide auditors to develop the further testing plan.
- It involves three areas of basic functions, reconciliation, and journal entries analogy detection.
- Many of the current technologies are used to perform these analyses; however, most are rules-based. While rules-based technologies can work for known patterns, they do not generalize to new instances of problems or to unseen problems.
- Three types of solutions are being used for testing: (1) the rules-based systems that may include expert systems or robotic process automation; (2) statistical systems that focus on detecting anomalies using Benford's law or time series analysis; and (3) machine learning-based. Machine learning-based systems try to identify unusual, rare, or irregular patterns. These patterns result in identifying fraud and errors. Deep learning appears to be a promising solution for anomaly detection in journal entries.

 REFERENCES

Bay, S., Kumaraswamy, K., Anderle, M. G., Kumar, R., and Steier, D. M. (2006) Large scale detection of irregularities in accounting data. *Proceedings – IEEE International Conference on Data Mining, ICDM.* [Online] (99): 75–86.

Chali, Y. and Hasan, S. A. (2015) Towards topic-to-question generation. Computational Linguistics, 41 (1): 1–17.

Chew, P. A. and Robinson, D. G. (2012) Automated account reconciliation using probabilistic and statistical techniques. *International Journal of Accounting & Information Management,* 20 (4): 322–334.

Divate, M. and Salgaonkar, A. (2017) Automatic question generation approaches and evaluation techniques. *Current Science,* 113 (9): 1683–1691.

Findlay, S. (2019) Deloitte resigns from Indian non-bank lender. *Financial Times,* 6 August.

Gong, X. Y., Su, H., Xu, D., Zhang, Z. T., Shen, F., and Yang, H. Bin (2018) An overview of contour detection approaches. *International Journal of Automation and Computing,* 15 (6): 656–672.

Martin, D. R., Fowlkes, C. C., and Malik, J. (2003) Learning to detect natural image boundaries using brightness and texture. *Advances in Neural Information Processing Systems*, 1–20.

McGlohon, M., Bay, S., Anderle, M. G., Steier, D. M., and Faloutsos, C. (2009) SNARE: A link analytic system for graph labeling and risk detection. *Proceedings of the ACM SIGKDD International Conference on Knowledge Discovery and Data Mining*. [Online] 1265–1273.

Reliance (2019) *Reliance Media Release*. Available from: https://www .reliancecapital.co.in/pdf/MEDIA-RELEASE-13062019.pdf (Accessed 20 November 2019).

Schreyer, M., Sattarov, T., Borth, D., Dengel, A., and Reimer, B. (2017) *Detection of Anomalies in Large Scale Accounting Data using Deep Autoencoder Networks*. Available from: http://arxiv.org/abs/1709.05254.

Ziou, D. and Tabbone, S., 1998. Edge detection techniques–an overview. *Pattern Recognition & Image Analysis*, vol. 8, no. 4, pp. 537–559.

CHAPTER ELEVEN

Reporting and Post-Audit Management

W E WILL CLOSE THE AUDIT AUTOMATION part with a brief discussion on audit opinion detection and prediction and then a deeper coverage of post-audit value management (Figure 11.1). When auditors obtain and test their evidence, the last step of the traditional audit is to issue an opinion. This opinion summarizes the findings related to the likelihood of a material misstatement in the financial statements. The opinion issued typically depends upon several factors and includes the results of activities related to the internal controls and substantive testing. Even when the audit opinion is clean (unqualified), critical audit matters and information about the audit team might be disclosed. Critical audit matters may include areas where auditors had to use subjective or complex judgment in areas of accounts or disclosures that are material to the company (AS 3101).

Some of the key questions to consider are:

- Is it possible to predict what the audit opinion should/could be without even going through the entire evidence collection process?
- If yes, what are some ways in which we can use artificial intelligence (AI) to do that?
- Can that information help in adjusting the audit plan?

AUDIT OPINION DETECTION

Being able to determine if an audit opinion was qualified (adverse opinion) or unqualified from the historical financial and other data is a powerful predictor for forecasting future opinions. Opinion detection is an ongoing area of research. The general concept behind audit opinion detection is that because the history of similar companies as the *client company X* with similar conditions received adverse or qualified opinions, therefore based upon the conditions of *client company X*, there is a greater likelihood of a qualified or adverse opinion. The approach or model is clearly to use some numerical values or measures of the "conditions" and then try to predict the opinion as classified between adverse or qualified and unqualified. This classification exercise therefore takes the input features and tries to output the target variable qualified or unqualified opinion. The challenge, of course, from an AI perspective raises the following questions:

- What "conditions" (input features) should be included?
- What models should be used?
- What is the target variable?
- How do we use this information?

In 2007, researchers took data from a UK and Irish database known as FAME (Financial Analysis Made Easy) Database and attempted to predict the audit opinion (Kirkos et al., 2007). The database contained audit opinions but did not elaborate the reasons why adverse/unqualified opinions were issued. They made adjustments in the data to ensure that macroeconomic factors or multiple occurrences of same companies do not introduce bias. Using 26 input variables that were primarily financial ratios, they used three methods for opinion detection. Kirkos et al. (2007) used Decision Trees, Bayesian belief networks, and neural networks to predict the outputs. The results obtained were promising as they were able to obtain medium to high accuracy across all three methods.

Notice that while they used financial ratios as inputs, it is possible to use additional structured and unstructured data (e.g., textual data from 10k filings) to evaluate the prediction outcomes. Using a combination of financial and non-financial data (e.g., credit ratings, whether a big audit firm was involved or not), researchers have successfully predicted audit opinions (Gaganis et al.,

2007) using probabilistic neural networks. Opinion detection has also been applied in the public sector, and other methods have been used (e.g., k nearest neighbor); see Arianto et al. (2017).

Finally, how do we use opinion prediction information? This is highly valuable information for audit planning. It can introduce an extra layer of caution but also a new way to assess risk. It gives an intuition that something may not be right. However, it is important for the human auditor to understand that many factors can impact a business, and the audit opinion forecast can contain significant bias. Use it with caution, but it's a good idea to start an audit with it.

The important insight, however, is that once auditors have accumulated the internal evidence, using that data to predict the audit opinion can be a worthy exercise.

POST-AUDIT MANAGEMENT

Unlike in legacy audits, where the audit team walks away from the day-to-day analysis of a client at the conclusion of an audit, the continuous and intelligent automated audit requires ongoing management. This ongoing management comes from the following:

- Use of the deployed tools to constantly assess and monitor the inherent risks
- Use of the deployed tools to constantly assess and monitor the controls risks
- Use of the deployed tools to perform audit in various areas (e.g., cash, accounts receivable)

Throughout this book, we have not separated the capability deployment at clients versus at the audit firm. However, as we discuss the post-audit management, distinguishing between the two is important.

Audit Firm Systems

The deployment of the intelligent automation tools and systems requires development of tools on both sides of audit. Audit firms will have their own intelligent automation systems infrastructure and clients will have their own. Let us first divide the capability areas and then understand the issues and maturity of intelligent automation on both sides of audit.

The audit firm will need to have a clear strategy and build four types of capabilities:

1. Data management capabilities
2. Latent scanning capabilities
3. Client-specific capabilities
4. Data preprocessing

Data Management Capabilities

The traditional data management programs include data governance, data quality, metadata management, and master data management. These capabilities are critical foundational elements for architecting an intelligent automation program. Data governance includes developing a thorough understanding of the data that the enterprise has, identifying data movement across systems, knowing data lineage, and classifying the data. Data quality assures that reliable and quality data is used across the enterprise. Factors included in data quality are completeness, timeliness, reliability, relevance, usability, and cleanliness. Metadata is data about data and is critical for process mining. Master data provide a single point of reference for data.

Data capabilities implies that the audit firm should have data of interest to develop automation capabilities. Data of interest include financial data but also unstructured data including graphics, images, videos, sound files, etc. As audit firms begin developing their intelligent automation tools, they will have to make sure that they develop a clear strategy to source and organize data. It is helpful to approach the data sourcing as composed of five different classes (Figure 11.2).

1. The first data class is of data type and it is simply classification between structured and unstructured data. Structured data is what you see neatly lined up in columns and rows (e.g., tables) and unstructured data is data that lacks structure and includes videos, pictures, sounds, text files etc.
2. The second is data availability and it has three subclasses of available, dark, and null data. Available data is usable, relevant, and accessible. Dark data is data that the firm knows it possesses and needs but that is not easily accessible. The third data subclass is null data and it represents the data that the firm needs or will need in the future but that it doesn't possess. The audit firm will need the capability to identify and extract dark data. More importantly an audit firm will need to develop a strategy for sourcing the data

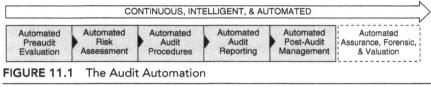

FIGURE 11.1 The Audit Automation

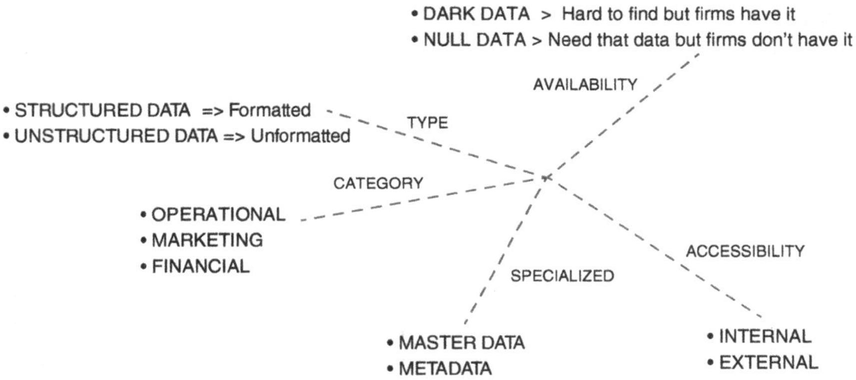

• DARK DATA > Hard to find but firms have it
• NULL DATA > Need that data but firms don't have it

AVAILABILITY

• STRUCTURED DATA => Formatted
• UNSTRUCTURED DATA => Unformatted

TYPE

CATEGORY

• OPERATIONAL
• MARKETING
• FINANCIAL

ACCESSIBILITY

SPECIALIZED

• MASTER DATA
• METADATA

• INTERNAL
• EXTERNAL

FIGURE 11.2 Data Classes

that it needs but doesn't have. This could mean either purchasing such data from external sources or to install sensors so that the firm can start collecting this data.

3. The third class of data is based upon accessibility and is divided into internally accessible versus externally accessible data. It is important to identify the sources of external data and assess the reliability and quality of both internally and externally sourced data.

4. The fourth class of data is the master data and metadata. This data needs to be organized, structured, and classified.

5. The fifth class of data is the functional split of data, such as marketing data, finance data, and operational data.

Latent Scanning Capabilities

Latent scanning capabilities refers to the tools that are deployed to scan the market, industry, and firms to develop keen insights about the business, management, competitive factors, and other strategic issues. Latent scanning capabilities are used to plan audits but also used in sales and customer relationship management.

Client-Specific Capabilities

Client-specific capabilities (CSC) refers to the capabilities that relate to the audit engagements and are deployed when an engagement begins. Typically, these capabilities can be viewed as linking a conceptual hose with the client systems where data can flow into the audit firm's systems. The audit firm's systems become active as soon as they receive client data. The infrastructure that enables such linkages is extremely valuable. The deployment of this can be temporary or permanent. In a temporary setup the client will disconnect the hose when the audit is finalized. In a permanent setup, the hose link stays and provides constant data flow into the audit firm.

Data Preprocessing

As we covered in Chapter 5, data preprocessing is a critical step for machine learning, and this is the area that takes significant time. Many steps are involved in getting the data ready to be fed into an algorithm. This area needs to be deployed as a capability area and the data processing needs to be undertaken by experts. Processes and IT infrastructure would be needed for both inbound and outbound parts of the data. The data would come in from different sources – including client, audit firm, or external sources – and is received in the data preprocessing area. Once it is feed ready, it is fed into the algorithm.

Client Systems

As AI-centric systems become more common, significant changes will be needed on the client side. Your client will have to be far more transparent and open with the auditors. The audit will become invasive and client systems will become hard linked with the audit firm's systems through the data hose. Notice that since the audit scope now involves automation related to the entire audit process, tremendous amounts of data sharing will be needed. Would a data lake or big data environment be necessary? Most likely yes, but it doesn't mean that every single data element would need to be tagged before it is usable. The important thing is that automation must begin even if a data repository is under construction or does not exist. In those situations, automation can be deployed the old way (i.e., via file transfer). With the amounts of data sharing that will take place, it will be best if auditors have direct access to both data and metadata.

The invasive approach would certainly lead to some reaction in certain companies, but it is the responsibility of the auditor to explain to the client about the benefits of intelligent audit automation. Some clients would prefer to have all audit tools in their own environment. Instead of sending data to the audit firm, those clients will prefer to only send the outputs of audit automation to the auditor. In that case, the audit firm would have to understand how to improve the performance of the intelligent tools deployed for a specific function. If a client is unwilling to share data that can land in the auditor's environment, each instance of the intelligent solution will only receive its learning from the client data. In other words, the client will train the algorithm using only their own data versus an intelligent audit artifact deployed centrally at the audit firm that can receive data from multiple firms for its learning. In some ways, it is not a bad thing to have a client-specific solution. In particular, if the underlying distributions of the data are significantly different across companies, then the prediction capability of a certain artifact may not be optimum for a firm if it is trained on different data. Similarly, some clients may be able to provide more features (input data) than others. As an analogy, if an autonomous vehicle is trained on a certain terrain x while it will be used in terrain y, and x and y are very different terrains, it will not be wise to deploy the car in terrain y.

Business Models of Audit Firms

With the advent of AI, the service delivery model of audit firms is changing rapidly. Two variables impact the business models of audit firms. The first is connectivity and it measures how embedded the audit firm is into the client. Connectivity is described by a spectrum of Limited (analogy *in vitro*) to Deep (analogy *in vivo*). Borrowed from biology, *in vitro* refers to performing a given procedure in a controlled environment outside of a living organism. *In vitro* is Latin for within or enclosed in the glass. We call it Limited Connectivity where an audit firm treats the client as inside a glass box. In contrast, *in vivo* in Latin means "within the living" and refers to experimentation inside the whole living organism. We call it "Deep" where Deep implies having continuous and unrestricted access to data. Note that the concept of "embedded" does not mean political or social embedding which may constitute a violation of independence. Again, it refers to having continuous and unrestricted access to the client data.

The second variable is intelligent automation and it measures three things: how much of the audit process has been automated by a firm, the quality of automation, and the number of successful implementations. We can identify at least four models on the basis of these two capabilities (Figure 11.3):

1. **Legacy Manual Audits:** The audit firm is neither deeply embedded in a client nor uses advanced technologies.

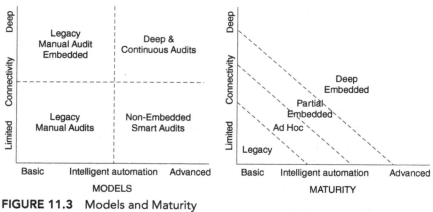

FIGURE 11.3 Models and Maturity

2. **Legacy Embedded:** The audit firm is deeply embedded and has access to data but does not actively use intelligent automation.

3. **Non-Embedded Smart Audit Firm:** The audit firm uses intelligent automation but conducts audit by using data as an on-demand model where data is provided to the audit firm in response to specific requests and that data flows in in the form of file transfers.

4. **Deep and Continuous Audits:** This audit firm actively uses intelligent automation in audit and has established unrestricted access to client data such that it can apply intelligent automation on an ongoing basis.

Based on the above classifications of models, a maturity model can be established for audit firms. This is composed of the following four maturity levels:

1. **Legacy Auditor:** The legacy auditor uses basic technologies (e.g., spreadsheets, basic audit tools) to perform audits. Many audit firms today fall into the legacy auditor model. Audit firms in this category have not made significant investment in audit technologies. Their client connectivity is limited to the scope of the audit.

2. **Ad Hoc Enabler:** The ad hoc enabler uses more advanced technologies – for instance, predictive analytics – but uses them on an ad hoc and selective basis. Typical use of technology is in risk analysis and that part is usually composed of using premade or editable questionnaires. An ad hoc enabler does not enable or prepare clients for a continuous audit setup. The sporadic and selective use of technology becomes part of the service

delivery model and while it uses technology, it does not bring forth the innovation in intelligent innovation.

3. **Temporary Connector Model:** An audit firm with a temporary connector model uses all significant audit automation technologies but does so within the temporal scope of the audit. Once the audit of a period is finalized, the firm disconnects the hose and turns off the audit systems.

4. **Permanent Embedding Model:** In the permanent embedding model an audit firm provides audit services while being permanently connected to the client data hose. From a model perspective, the audit firm performs and enables continuous audit and monitors the risk environment of the client. This is the highest level of maturity for an audit firm.

In summary, the maturity of audit firms can be evaluated based upon the two dimensions of connectivity and intelligent automation. This implies that to achieve maturity, an audit firm must pursue both: improve access and management of data, and develop intelligent automation products. Intelligent automation products are of no use if usable client data is not available.

CHALLENGES IN ACHIEVING THE MATURITY

The legacy IT infrastructure in many companies will be the greatest barrier to achieving the highest level of maturity. The legacy IT infrastructures will exist on both sides – audit firms and client companies. Here are some of the symptoms of such problems:

- Layers of expensive technology, which are extremely hard to access from a data perspective.
- IT uses a large number of tools and several vendors. Many systems have no way of communicating with each other.
- Data residing in spreadsheets or little-known point solutions.
- Company has several off-the-shelf packaged software systems, which are heavily customized.
- There are significant points of failure.
- Many outdated and obsolete legacy applications.
- Multiple, often conflicting, standards.
- A cocktail of point solutions.
- Significant debris of back office tools.

- Significant cost burden due to legacy infrastructure.
- Lack of data governance, data quality, data management.

As intelligent technologies are being introduced in the jungle of existing technologies, it can lead to even bigger problems:

- Disjointed and haphazard development of AI artifacts, causing proliferation, overcomplexity, and gridlock.
- AI professionals and IT professionals have separate mindsets and skills levels.
- Design constraints makes scalability impossible.
- Slow and expensive development cycles. Likely rip-out scenarios.
- Companies marketing robotic process automation (RPA) as AI and telling clients that RPA does not require any development, and that every employee will be able to develop their own solutions (essentially adding another point of failure).
- Perpetual trialing mindset versus taking deliberate strategic change – happens when companies perpetually experiment but don't adopt a technology, and hence create islands of isolated and siloed capabilities.
- Significant points of failure emerging.

BUILDING AN IN-HOUSE ARCHITECTURE FOR AN AUDIT FIRM (OR INTERNAL AUDIT)

Building and managing the integrated capabilities for AI will require a comprehensive capability design and development. The basic conceptual architecture requires an integrated technology design that includes machine learning, expert systems, robotic process automation, and process mining. The key difference between regular digital systems and machine learning-based systems is that the former are made for data while the latter are made from data. Hence, data management becomes critical for deploying critical audit automation capabilities.

As enterprises move to intelligent automation, four layers of integrated capability building are critical for efficient deployment (Figure 11.4). The first capability is of data management and includes areas such as data governance, data quality management, master data management, and metadata management. The second capability is of data preprocessing. Data preprocessing includes activities related to preparing the data for feeding to the algorithms.

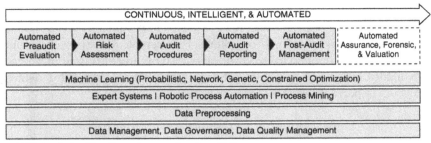

FIGURE 11.4 The Four Layers for the AI Era

These activities include normalization, scaling, converting to machine readable formats, transferring into vectors, and understanding the most relevant or critical features. The third layer of capability is composed of deterministic or low variability process automation using expert systems and RPA as well as deploying process mining tools. The highest level is of machine learning, which uses different types of methods to automate more complex processes.

 ## A FEW IMPORTANT THINGS TO CONSIDER

As you deploy the above intelligent automation framework, you must track three important issues on an ongoing basis.

The first issue is of giving identity to your digital workers and keeping track of them. At this point companies are rushing into intelligent or even not-so-intelligent (e.g., RPA) automation and developing hundreds, even thousands, of these smart tools. Many firms are now running into scalability issues and they are facing tremendous difficulty in making the intelligent systems work with each other. Treating these systems as digital workers, giving them a unique identity, documenting their processes, functions, and work goals, and viewing them as agents will help a lot in reducing total costs of ownership.

The second issue is of keeping track of the underlying distributions of features and always looking to see if new features would improve the performance of an AI artifact. The features used to train machine learning artifacts have their underlying distributions. If those distributions change significantly, the learning may not be relevant to the new realities. Therefore, it is important to check the quality and performance of AI artifacts on an ongoing basis.

The third issue is about the IT infrastructure. Once a machine learning artifact is trained and tested, it needs to be deployed in production. At that time, it may have to interact with other systems. For example, it may receive input related to its core function from one or more systems and its output may need to be loaded in to another system. Managing these IT infrastructure–related tasks is an important milestone for project success.

Key Points

- This chapter addressed many different issues in building audit capabilities in audit and client firms, and in audit opinion automation and post-audit management.
- Post-audit automation management challenges us to explore different audit models available to a firm.
- Audit models also signify competitive advantage and maturity model for an audit firm.
- To meet the requirements of the AI era, an audit firm would need to build capabilities in four areas: data management, data preprocessing, low-variability automation, and complex task automation.

 REFERENCES

Arianto, A. D., Affandi, A., and Nugroho, S. M. S. (2017) Opinion detection of public sector financial statements using k-nearest neighbors. *International Conference on Electrical Engineering, Computer Science and Informatics (EECSI).* [Online] 4 (September): 498–502.

Gaganis, C., Pasiouras, F., and Doumpos, M. (2007) Probabilistic neural networks for the identification of qualified audit opinions. *Expert Systems with Applications*, 32 (1): 114–124.

Kirkos, E., Spathis, C., Nanopoulos, A., and Manolopoulos, Y. (2007) Identifying qualified auditors' opinions: A data mining approach. *Journal of Emerging Technologies in Accounting*, 4 (1): 183–197.

Forensic Accounting Automation

N PART TWO WE FOCUSED on audit and emphasized the automation of planning, inherent risk automation, internal controls automation, reporting, and post-audit management. Audit helps in providing assurance and gives a sense of confidence to investors. The emphasis on internal controls also helps in developing a fraud prevention mindset. In contrast to fraud prevention, in Part Three we will concentrate on fraud detection. We approach fraud detection from the angle of forensic accounting and expand it to include value destruction from strategic decision-making. Part Three is divided into Intelligent Automation of Fraud Detection, Forensic Accounting, Managing for Value and Valuation, and a summary chapter, which also introduces robotics.

CHAPTER TWELVE

Intelligent Automation of Fraud Detection

W E COVER AUDIT RELATED ERRORS AND FRAUD throughout this book; however, this chapter is dedicated to intelligent financial fraud detection and investigation (IFFDI) using artificial intelligence (AI). The internal controls environment serves as the firewall to protect against fraud. Prevention is different than detection and detection is different than investigation. Detection implies active search to discover, find, uncover, or expose fraud. Investigation begins once a reasonable degree of suspicion develops about the likelihood that a fraud is taking place. In this chapter we will cover both detection and investigation.

When deploying your fraud detection capabilities, you will address questions such as

- How to allocate capabilities between prevention, detection, and investigation? What technologies to deploy for each?
- When and for what to use deterministic versus stochastic technologies?
- What methods, models, or techniques should you use?
- How do you design and architect your IFFDI system?
- How to protect your firm from AI-centric fraud?

DETECTING FRAUD

Fraud happens when material misrepresentations of facts are made intentionally and they lead to loss for one or more victims. The Association of Certified Fraud Examiners (ACFE) classifies fraud against a firm into two types: internal and external (ACFE, n.d.). Internal fraud, also known as occupational fraud, is defined by ACFE as "the use of one's occupation for personal enrichment through the deliberate misuse or misappropriation of the employing organization's resources or assets." Internal fraud is committed by the managers, employees, owners, or board members of a firm. External fraud, in contrast, is conducted by parties external to the firm, for example, customers, suppliers, partners.

ACFE classifies internal fraud into three areas: corruption, asset misappropriation, and financial statement fraud. ACFE has developed a powerful and comprehensive representation of internal fraud. Known as the Fraud Tree (Figure 12.1), it covers the various subcategories and subclasses of internal fraud.

Fraud can happen at any point in an organization. For example, it can happen at the employee level, at the board level, or across the value chain via collaboration between partners and even competitors. Detecting fraud is one of the most complex undertakings. Protecting a firm from any possible fraud can be expensive and therefore costs of IFFDI need to be considered.

Let's not forget that in many cases savvy managers operate on the borderline of law and while technically statements and disclosures may not qualify as misrepresentations from a legal perspective, the underlying motivation for business decisions could be self-serving. For instance, the management team of a nonprofit deploys a CEO friendly board and with the board approval starts making investments in a manner that the CEO intends to personally benefit from in the future. Such situations make fraud detection extremely hard.

 ## ELEMENTS OF FRAUD

In the 1950s, Donald Cressey presented the fraud triangle theory that identified the three fraud elements as pressure, opportunity, and rationalization (Cressey, 1953). A fourth element of capability was later added and the model transformed from a triangle to a diamond (Wolfe and Hermanson, 2004; Mansor, 2015). As we think about intelligent automation, our design elements must first begin by analyzing the elements of fraud and building capabilities around them.

THE FRAUD TREE

OCCUPATIONAL FRAUD ABUSE CLASSIFICATION SYSTEM

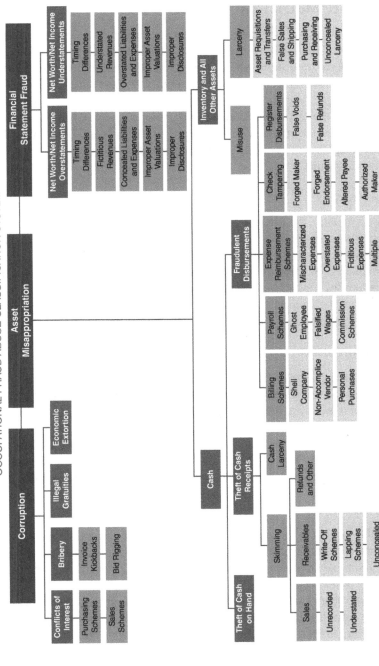

FIGURE 12.1 The Fraud Tree

Pressure or Motivation

Preemptive detection of motivation can go a long way to detect and prevent fraud. Motivation can be anything from personal to business situations. At an individual level it could be when a person is facing financial difficulties and hence decides to engage in a fraud. On a management team level, it could be pressure to report certain earnings numbers for which guidance has been provided. Motivation determination technologies are deployed to evaluate the situations that can motivate a person or management team to commit a fraud. They typically involve understanding the situational dynamics to predict the likelihood of fraud.

Opportunity

The opportunity for fraud is based upon the internal controls weaknesses. An environment that lacks controls or that has a culture that promotes recklessness can be a fertile ground for fraud. The opportunities are identified and exploited by individuals and management teams. Fraud opportunity assessment technology is deployed to assess the control weaknesses as well as cultural and behavioral modeling to assess the seriousness and desire of the management team and boards to deploy internal controls.

Rationalization

Rationalization is the justification that a person or team gives to the conduct of fraud. This is a self-deceiving factor where teams and individuals say to themselves that it is okay to engage in a fraudulent behavior for such-and-such reasons. The justification could be that it is a one-time thing or that they are only borrowing money or that they were denied proper compensation and therefore it is their right to steal. Rationalization detection technology is composed of systems deployed to perform behavioral analysis of individuals and teams.

Capability

Capability is when a person or team believes that they have the capability to get away with doing the fraud, to not get caught, and to pull it off. Capability detection technology is also used to assess the materiality of the impact a person, machine, or team can have.

AI has been used to combat fraud by building capabilities in accordance with the fraud triangle in practice. For instance, Lin et al. (2015) employed Logistic Regression, Decision Trees, Classification and Regression Trees

(CART), and Artificial Neural Networks (ANNs) to study the three aspects of the fraud triangle.

 ## DOMAIN-SPECIFIC FRAUD DETECTION

The FBI classifies financial frauds into various areas such as securities fraud, credit card fraud, financial statement fraud, insurance fraud, and corporate other fraud. One way to approach your design is to consider each specific domain area in which you have material exposure. This means that specialized solutions need to be developed in those specific domains. Significant research exists in the use of intelligent automation for domain-specific fraud detection (Ngai et al., 2011; West and Bhattacharya, 2016).

 ## STOPSCAM

The American Institute of Artificial Intelligence has developed a model known as STOPSCAM. This model expands upon the domain-specific model and fraud elements to develop broad classification of fraud by capability areas or detectors that focus on building and deploying intelligent capabilities. STOPSCAM is an acronym for Strategy, Transactions, Operations, Processes, Statements, Culture, Attitudes, and Model.

Strategy

The strategy tool analyzes a company's strategy to obtain key insights to capture signals of significant changes or persistence in a company's strategy. A sudden or abrupt change in strategy, a reluctance to change strategy when it is evident that the strategy is not working, rise of a new competitor, a change in technology, bankruptcy risk, and other strategy concepts are captured and analyzed. Strategy changes also include mergers and acquisitions and major financing events. Automated strategy analysis is performed from analyzing analyst reports, company press releases, and other news and opinions about a firm.

Transactions

Transaction-level analysis is achieved by deploying systems that scan transaction-level details. For example, journal entries, G/L, supporting documents inspection, and other similar applications of technology in automated audit forms the baseline for transaction-level continuous audit with the explicit focus on fraud-centric anomaly detection. The primary goal in transaction analysis is anomaly detection.

Operations

Operational-level fraud assessment is done by assessing the operational footprint of a firm and including the value chain of a firm in both directions. This means including the suppliers and partners (e.g., channel partners) and customers to analyze the potential of fraud. In many cases the interaction or structures among partners, subsidiaries, customers, and suppliers shows the presence of fraud.

Processes

Process-centric evaluation of fraud focuses on understanding anomalous process patterns. These patterns could be based upon transaction patterns, or people accessing systems abnormally, or awkward timings of accessing systems. Process mining technologies, along with machine learning, are used to evaluate this.

Statements

Statement analysis is performed by external parties where publicly available financial statements are analyzed to determine the presence of fraud. This can be based upon analyzing the text or other unstructured data from annual reports, or financial ratio analyses, or by analyzing other company communications, such as earnings call.

Culture

Organizational-level automated analysis focuses on understanding the culture, management, reporting relationships, social networks, board, and other such factors. Many such factors provide information about potential fraud. For instance, a forceful or overly aggressive CEO with a submissive board can create an environment ripe for fraud.

Attitude

The attitude is the behavioral analysis of the management team and board members. This is a critical part of analysis. Using pictures, videos, text, and other combinations and available data, intelligent automation is used to create a profile of individuals and of social networks. Social networks can exist inside or outside the firm. They can exist between management team members or board members and certain executives. They are formed by shared interests and in terms of structural dynamics, the influence patterns could be completely different than that shown on corporate organizational charts. Understanding those patterns can shed light on how fraud can take shape and who could be involved in that.

Model

A firm's business model is at the heart of its strategies and processes. Changes in the business model can signify several things – including opening up of opportunities for fraud. Technologies used to analyze business models include business process mapping using machine learning (Evermann et al., 2017). The rise of AI in business will also enable businesses to launch new business models (Ehret and Wirtz, 2017).

 TECHNOLOGIES AND MODELS

Ngai et al. (2011) performed literature research and showed that a wide variety of approaches are being used in fraud detection. They developed a model where they first outlined the broad categories of frauds such as insurance fraud, securities and commodities fraud, bank fraud, and other financial fraud. Then they further categorized based upon fraudulent activities such as money laundering. And from a solution side they divided the data mining solutions into classification, clustering, outlier detection, prediction, regression, and visualization.

More recently, another group of researchers also performed an extensive survey of fraud detection (West and Bhattacharya, 2016). They, too, first categorized by fraud classes (e.g., insurance, financial statements, etc.). However, they investigated several methods, including neural network, logistic, support-vector machine, decision trees, genetic algorithms, Bayesian belief network, process mining, artificial immune system, and hybrid methods. Their extensive survey revealed that a diversity of methods are used in intelligent automation.

A third survey of literature used a similar approach to others; however, these researchers divided the machine learning techniques into broad groupings of supervised, unsupervised, and semi-supervised. They also provide examples of challenges in implementing some of the solutions and techniques of addressing those problems (Abdallah et al., 2016).

The above research is very helpful to learn about various AI approaches being used in different types of business areas. As we have discussed throughout this book, a point solution approach is not enough if you want to build a modern-era audit or forensic accounting firm. Tools must work together to form an ecosystem within which various agents can work together to get work accomplished.

OUR APPROACH

We have approached fraud detection not only from the angle of problem area (i.e., fraud category > fraud activity > solution) but also by introducing a class layer for solution deployment in practical business areas (i.e., STOPSCAM agents). The STOPSCAM agents can be deployed in various areas for comprehensive fraud detection. Building a comprehensive fraud detection system requires blending the four key technologies of process mining, robotic process automation, expert systems, and machine learning. Within machine learning various types of models exist and some are better than others for certain types of models.

Strategy, organization, culture, attitude, and business model are automated by algorithms modeling social, behavioral, game theory – centric processes. Transaction and financial statement fraud detection is automated by using anomaly detection, behavioral, and process mining.

Supervised Models in Fraud Detection

Supervised learning techniques are deployed in anomaly detection, social, and behavioral models. Both regression and classification can help in fraud detection. Since supervised techniques are based upon known examples, they are easier to interpret. The main issue with using supervised learning is that we usually (and thankfully) have many more examples of fraud-free transactions than fraudulent transactions. Therefore, teaching the algorithm becomes harder when, say, for every thousand examples of clean transactions, one example of a fraudulent transaction is provided. There are techniques that can be applied to balance out the examples. For example, one way is to introduce synthetic (made-up) examples of anomalous behavior. The second limitation is that data requires labeling and unless data is being pulled out of systems where both input and target output values are present for the specific problem being addressed, we may have to rely upon human-centric labeling of the data. Recall that labeling means providing the target output value for each input vector. That can become quite a laborious project.

Naïve Bayes, support-vector machines, k-nearest neighbors, decision trees, logistic regression, deep learning, and artificial neural networks are used to create intelligent artifacts for the various fraud detection applications outlined in the STOPSCAM model.

Unsupervised Techniques

Unsupervised techniques are used in anomaly detection, including in transactions, statements, and processes. They include clustering methods like k-means, dimensionality reduction methods, subspace based, and classifier based (Goldstein and Uchida, 2016). The goal here is to identify patterns that we don't know exist. As data being analyzed clusters in various segments, it reveals the presence of different patterns. One example of that will be using unsupervised techniques to identify fraud detection in credit card frauds.

Key Points

- Fraud detection and fraud prevention are different.
- Financial fraud detection automation is performed by intelligent financial fraud detection and investigation.
- The general approach for designing fraud detection intelligent automation includes understanding the broad categories of fraud (banking, insurance, healthcare, etc.), identifying the activities within the categories, and then deploying machine learning-based solutions that include supervised, unsupervised, semi-supervised, and other methods.
- From a solution category perspective, we propose to develop solutions around the STOPSCAM method.

 REFERENCES

Abdallah, A., Maarof, M. A., and Zainal, A. (2016) Fraud detection system: A survey. *Journal of Network and Computer Applications*, 68 (C): 90–113.

ACFE (n.d.) *Association of Certified Fraud Examiners*. Available from: https://www.acfe.com/fraud-101.aspx.

Cressey, D. R. (1953) *Other People's Money: A Study of the Social Psychology of Embezzlement*. Glencoe, IL: Free press.

Ehret, M. and Wirtz, J. (2017) Unlocking value from machines: Business models and the industrial internet of things. *Journal of Marketing Management*, 33 (1–2): 111–130. Available from: http://dx.doi.org/10.1080/0267257X.2016.1248041.

Evermann, J., Rehse, J. R., and Fettke, P. (2017) Predicting process behaviour using deep learning. *Decision Support Systems*, 100: 129–140. Available from: http://dx.doi.org/10.1016/j.dss.2017.04.003.

Goldstein, M. & Uchida, S. (2016) A comparative evaluation of unsupervised anomaly detection algorithms for multivariate data. *PLoS ONE*, 11 (4): 1–31.

Lin, C., Chiu, A., Yan, S, and Yen, D. C. (2015) Detecting the financial statement fraud: The analysis of the differences between data mining techniques and experts' judgments. *Knowledge-Based Systems*, 89: 459–470. Available from: http://dx.doi.org/10.1016/j.knosys.2015.08.011.

Mansor, R. A. N. (2015) Forensic accounting and fraud risk factors: The influence of fraud diamond theory. *The American Journal of Innovative Research and Applied Sciences*, 7 (28), 186–192. Available from: http://citeseerx.ist.psu.edu/viewdoc/download?doi=10.1.1.695.8486&rep=rep1&type=pdf.

Ngai, E. W. T., Hu, Y., Wong, Y. H., Chen, Y., and Sun, X. (2011) The application of data mining techniques in financial fraud detection: A classification framework and an academic review of literature. *Decision Support Systems*, 50 (3): 559–569. Available from: http://dx.doi.org/10.1016/j.dss.2010.08.006.

West, J. and Bhattacharya, M. (2016) Intelligent financial fraud detection: A comprehensive review. *Computers and Security*, 57: 47–66. Available from: http://dx.doi.org/10.1016/j.cose.2015.09.005.

Wolfe, D. T. and Hermanson, D. R. (2004) The Fraud diamond: Considering the four elements of fraud: Certified public accountant. *The CPA Journal*, 74 (12): 38–42.

CHAPTER THIRTEEN

Forensic Accounting

H ORRIFIED BY THE INSENSITIVITY and deceit, the business world was left with deep scars from the Bernie Madoff scandal. Harry Markopolos, the analyst who caught and reported Madoff's fraud, observed and calculated the numbers and realized that it was mathematically impossible for Madoff to deliver the numbers that he was reporting. Nearly 20 years later, Markopolos analyzed the financial statements and other publicly available information of GE and GE's value chain partners and peers, and then in mid-August of 2019 issued a report accusing GE of falsifying financial statements. According to Markopolos, GE was hiding $29 billion in long-term care insurance liabilities, and it will turn out to be "a bigger fraud than Enron." A forensic accounting firm named Forensic Decisions PR LLC drafted the report. Markopolos's claims shook the markets. GE's stock plunged more than 10%. As time passed, jittery and nervous investors slowly began regaining confidence in GE. At the time of the accusation, GE board and audit committee were packed with senior executives in finance, governance, and audit. The company handled the onslaught with elegance and survived by showing that Markopolos's analyses were not based upon facts.

The whole GE saga was strange for many reasons. First, the accuser, one accountant, challenged a legendary Fortune 100 company, an American icon. Second, GE stood its ground and eventually prevailed. Third, within a matter of a few weeks, it was as if nothing had happened, and everything was back to normal. But despite its awkwardness, it offered an interesting example of using public information to catch alleged wrongdoing, and also of the risk of being wrong, since you operate with limited information.

FORENSIC ACCOUNTING

Unlike auditing that focuses on risk that impacts a business in recent, current, and future times, forensic accounting generally deals with events that have already happened. In audit we look for control weaknesses, apply procedures, and evaluate various risks so we can determine whether material errors or frauds can enter the financial systems. In forensic accounting, we usually operate with the knowledge that some unfavorable event has happened and that our goal is to assess its root cause or evaluate its real impact.

However, lately the role of forensic accounting is changing. Forensic accounting is becoming proactive and is being applied to protect the interests of shareholders. Known as positive activism, forensic accounting firms are proactively investigating suspicious activities in companies. When investigating shareholder value destruction, and before an official investigation is launched, they rely upon publicly available information to make their case and claims. We covered shadow and counter-accounting in previous chapters. Forensic accounting offers powerful ways to protect the interests of the investors.

The GE example is unique. In the GE case, Mr. Markopolos claimed that he would financially benefit from the decline in the GE stock value. Clearly, we can assume that Mr. Markopolos understood that issuing his report on GE while being able to benefit from the stock decline could have exposed him to liability if his claims turned out to be bogus. This implies that he was willing to take the chance and probably had a strong belief in his report. Forensic accounting, therefore, is enabling a new type of shareholder activism known as negative activism. Negative activists take a short position from declining stock prices as they reveal negative information about a firm and provide evidence to back it up (Bliss et al., 2019).

Forensic accountants are also asked to help in litigation. They support litigation by providing expert opinion, performing analysis, and helping in evaluating valuation or discovery of assets. Forensic accountants aid in government or regulator investigations. Finally, they provide help in risk management and fraud prevention.

Financial Reporting Fraud

Amiram et al. (2018) clarified that financial fraud is often addressed by different terms – "fraud, misconduct, irregularities, misreporting, and misrepresentation" – and attribute that to the inability to clearly define it under US law:

The securities laws that define fraud – in particular, Section 17(a) of the 1933 Securities Act, Section 10(b) of the 1934 Securities Exchange Act, SEC Rule 10b-5, and case law (e.g., *United States v. Simon*) – are situational and define fraud variously.

Nevertheless, relevant laws and rulings share a common feature when defining fraud, namely, that fraud is a combination of multiple elements. The most basic of these are that (i) there must be a misrepresentation in the form of a misstatement, misreporting, or omission; (ii) that misrepresentation must be material; (iii) the person making the misrepresentation must have done so with some fault in the sense that the material misrepresentation was committed negligently, recklessly, or with knowledge of its falsity; and, (iv) in private suits, the misrepresentation is causally related to a loss suffered by the plaintiff. While additional elements can be considered, the elements vary depending on the particular type of transaction.

The above clarification by Amriam et al. is integral for designing a cognitive automation approach for forensic accounting automation. The legal versus financial approach to define financial fraud could be different. Not every financial fraud (e.g., some cases of earnings management) may qualify as the legal definition of fraud as approached by Securities and Exchange Commission or Department of Justice.

 ## CAPABILITY BUILDING IN FORENSIC ACCOUNTING

Intelligent automation of forensic accounting is about building automated capabilities in a forensic accounting firm. The intelligent capability development comes in two forms:

1. **Latent Capabilities:** Latent capabilities are structural capabilities that a forensic accounting firm must develop. These capabilities are general in nature and refer to the automation that needs to become part of a firm's infrastructure. These are the capabilities that are essential to the survival and competitive advantage of the firm. They are generally applicable, and they enable a firm to stay competitive. These capabilities can be considered as scanning capabilities as they scan the business environments (e.g. markets) to search for inconsistencies, fraud, and anomalies. They also perform risk assessment to analyze the risk factors that are based upon a sector, industry, or a firm. The structural capabilities are built in accordance

with the continuous and intelligent characteristics. As they scan markets, industries, and businesses, they try to detect anomalies that suggest the presence of fraud or material misrepresentation.

2. **Assignment-Centric Capabilities:** Assignment-Centric Automation deals with agents that are invoked in relation to a project. This happens when a specific project is outlined and pursued. As previously stated, a project can come from a client where a client requests a specific investigation, or it can be a self-assigned project based upon the analysis performed by the forensic accounting firm (typically based upon the analysis revealed by the latent capabilities or discovered as a lead from another project). The assignment-centric capability development is more domain and project specific. In contrast, latent capabilities are more general in nature.

Latent Capability Building

Typical latent capabilities automation are composed of using learning agents that learn to spot anomalies, fraud, and inconsistencies. As shown in previous examples in the book, these agents are typically composed of neural networks, deep learning systems that take in the publicly available structured and unstructured data and classify into high likelihood of fraud versus low likelihood of fraud. You can also use clustering (unsupervised) where the agents will scan the markets and industry and discover interesting patterns. The design of agents can accommodate a two-step process where one agent can scan the unstructured information to look for patterns (linguistic, speech, vocal etc.) that indicate deception and then based upon the findings a second agent can apply the learned model composed by looking at financial ratios. The latent capabilities must extend across the value chain and specific agents should be deployed that can explore relationship patterns between a target firm and its partners/suppliers and customers.

This automation is enabled by a set of agents that work together to scope, analyze, and scan the business environment to search for anomalies, inconstancies, and fraud in the financial and business reporting and representation of a firm.

There are six latent scanning agents:

1. Industry Assessment: This agent looks at a sector or industry risk patterns and extracts actionable information from various material economic developments in the industry. Its job is to learn and recognize patterns that are applicable to an industry. The sources of features could be news, press releases, government reports, and other industry reports. The output variables could be risk classifications and sentiments. Besides classification, clustering can help identify emerging patterns.

2. Value Chain: Analyzing the value chain is done to establish transparency about the nature of relationships that exist in the ecosystem of a company. An audit opinion analyzing agent, for instance, will not be able to draw attention to a potential fraud taking place in two more firms, or to use an example of firms in the sector and to apply that to study another member of the sector. For example, announcements of collaboration, adverse news about a supplier or customer, regulatory changes in a sector, and abrupt management changes can indicate problems. To identify such changes, we can either approach the problem as based upon multiple classifiers – implying that classification will be made about different aspects – or a larger classifier with several input variables that will internally pick the most relevant attributes. These agents will look for cross-industry patterns and relationships across the value chain. Process mining has been applied to understand the supply chains (Lau et al., 2009; Gerke et al., 2009; Hofman, 2013) but for that internal firm data is needed. In many cases, supplier data is released by firms and it is possible to map the supply chain from that data.

This class of agents identify the partners, suppliers, customers, and other stakeholders – and then attempt to understand the nature of relationship and/or business interaction between the firms. They track and classify news and stories that provide information about the value chain of a target firm. An agent like that can also try to understand the collusion in the industry. For instance, the US Department of Justice indicted a firm and its owner for sharing price information (DOJ, 2015) and it became one of the first cases in e-commerce collusion charges.

Artificial intelligence (AI) is used to develop insights into the business model of a firm, as well as to assess the changes in the business model. For example, Lee and Hong used text mining (TD-IDF and Linear Regression – both explained in previous chapters) to analyze business models of firms along the lines of weak versus strong growth signals as measured by emerging and disappearing trends (Lee and Hong, 2014).

3. Audit Opinion Prediction: Since the 1980s there have been several attempts to automate the audit opinion prediction. The desired core functionality is to be able to provide data to an algorithm and for the algorithm to predict whether the audit opinion was qualified or unqualified. The focus of most of the studies has been on using the financial data. A recent study showed that the success with methods such as neural networks, support-vector machines, and data tree methods was marginal. To improve the reliability of the model, some research studies added other nonfinancial features and were able to improve the performance. For example, researchers added the governance information and were able to improve the prediction considerably (Fernández-Gámez et al., 2016). The structural deployment of the model is to increase awareness about the relationship of the audit opinions and the data. One way to gain insights is to use midyear data to evaluate the likelihood of adverse audit opinion.

4. Fraud Detection: This class of agents explicitly focus upon fraud detection and their role is to use public information to identify fraud. Many recent studies have demonstrated the use of financial information to predict fraud. Machine learning has enabled capabilities to detect fraud by using publicly available information. For instance, support-vector machines were used to predict fraud in public companies by looking at the quantitative elements of financial statements (Cecchini et al., 2010). Ravisankar et al. (2011) applied multilayer feedforward neural networks, support-vector machines, genetic programming, logistic regression, and probabilistic neural networks on over 200 Chinese companies, and used financial ratios as input features.

Since fraud can transpire from many angles, it is better to build a model that focuses not only on financial ratios but also on other features such as governance, management, competitive situation, regulatory conditions, and other business domains. The advances in processing power and the application of deep learning methods provide an excellent platform for searching for patterns that may indicate fraud.

Autoencoders, by design, push for features to converge and hence can show anomalies that will be missed by general scanning of the market.

5. Management: The management agent focuses on management of a firm and develops management profiles for fraud detection. We have seen several examples of where intelligent artifacts were applied to study the speech patterns, vocabulary, text, and other such features of leaders during earnings calls and from authored documents. Add to that the background, experience, and other data and we can have extremely powerful insights about people's likelihood of engaging in fraud.

6. Organization: Scanning the organizations for culture is an important exercise. As MIT research showed, culture can be measured (Sull et al., 2019). The process used by Sull et al. can be enhanced by adding other features and using different algorithms. Using ant colony clustering, a study clustered documents based upon the cognitive situation dimensions of temporality, spatiality, protagonist, and activity (Guo et al., 2015). AI application in organizational studies is an emerging area of analysis (Kobayashi et al., 2018).

Assignment-Centric Capabilities

A forensic-focused project either starts with a client requesting an investigation or is launched by a forensic accounting itself to study a particular target or case. Whether client-initiated or self-initiated, the focus is usually on fraud, material misstatement, or misrepresentation. In some cases, the focus can be about demonstrating strategic weakness or leadership lapses leading to value destruction.

The project-specific automation is based upon the specific demands of the project. Generally, the project-specific automation is related to legal issues and hence the agents developed for project-specific automation are as follows.

Background Check on Clients

If project is launched on a client request, then it makes sense to learn and know about the client. The agent collects information about the client and classifies the client based upon different criteria. For example, we may want to know if the client we are dealing with is reputable, trustworthy, and credible. We may want to understand the personality of the client. In that regard, natural language processing is used to classify into various personality characteristics based upon speech patterns.

Meeting with the client to understand and capture his view of the dispute can be enabled by the following:

- Client notes can be analyzed for consistency. In many cases details presented by a client are sketchy, fabricated, opinionized, or speculative. Text mining can extract important details about the case and separate fact from fiction.
- Client conversations can be analyzed for their personality (Sewwandi et al., 2017; Ma and Liu, 2017; Mehta et al., 2019).
- Text analysis can also reveal social patterns (e.g., who influences whom, or who has authority over whom).
- The state of client's feelings or sentiments can be assessed from the conversation.
- For video-recorded conversations, body language and facial expressions can provide additional rich data for further analysis.

Background Check on the Case

This involves gathering preliminary information on the target. While a firm that has already implemented the latent capabilities will already have some understanding of the target company, it is possible that the scanner technologies either did not cover the specific client or the client could be a small firm, a foreign firm, or an individual. It is possible that the scanner technologies will not have much detail available on the specialized domain areas. For those situations, or to improve upon the data gathered by latent capabilities scanners, we perform target-specific analysis. To conduct target-specific analysis, we need to understand the nature of the problem that we are trying to assess. However, in most cases, the inquiry will be focused on first finding the relevant information and then using that information to determine the likelihood of client success or the complexity of the overall case. For example, a forensic investigation is focused upon the allegations of defrauding the shareholders by not disclosing certain risks when they should have been disclosed. The scope of the investigation is on a certain specific period, and a certain specific assessment of issues at that time. However, the surrounding, more specific, information about the specific business unit, its management team, its marketing, customers, and other such factors can now be analyzed with AI.

Solvability and Case Success Analysis

In cases that involve lawsuits or legal charges, it may be worthwhile to check for the success potential and solvability of a case. Conrad and Al-Kofahi (2017) analyzed jury verdicts to develop case outcomes. Significant data exists on case outcomes and jury verdicts. Conrad and Al-Kofani show that their company (Thomson Reuters) captures over 25 fields of case-related information in its JVS (Jury Verdict and Settlements) database and a section included in the record contains seminal facts of the events. These facts are authored by their company employees who are trained to write such summaries in a standard, semi-closed vocabulary. All of that provides rich data for mining. Different AI techniques are applied to evaluate the likelihood for case success.

Know the Party Being Investigated

If your assignment is investigating a certain case, begin by using AI to develop insights about the management team, culture, organizational dynamics, communication styles, personalities, and social networks of the people involved. In many cases, motivations can be assessed once the other factors are clarified.

Clarify the Goals

With the case success analysis and motivations of various parties analyzed, you can now be in a position to assess what winning really means. This implies developing a clear picture of attainable results and satisfactory outcomes of the case. From a financial viewpoint, regression can be used to develop a financial estimate for the cost and expected winning from the case.

Assess the Capability and Independence

If the case is client initiated, it helps to understand the capabilities and test for independence for the investigators. Automation in capability assessment and independence testing has been described in Part Two. The solution for forensic accounting will not be much different. While conflict-of-interest screening for investigators is an important consideration in client-initiated investigations, in self-initiated investigations, it is both beneficial and ethical to understand your own biases.

Document Organizing

Forensic investigations require discipline and structure. In the absence of discipline, investigations can go out of control quickly. Since investigators deal with many types of documents, it is very helpful to use mining technologies for classifying documents. The great news is that AI allows you to classify documents in many different ways, including cognitive components. For instance, Conrad et al. (2005) detail classifying documents on the basis of multiple legal criteria. Classification can help classify documents where representative labeled data is available. However, in cases where we don't have the target variable, clustering algorithms can help find patterns across documents.

About the Occurrence in an Investigation

Documents about the incident can verify the occurrence of the allegations. Text classification can reveal the use of language that is objective versus subjective. Subjective language may indicate more speculation or rumors instead of an actual occurrence. Early stage evidence review can be done by extracting such information from documents.

The contents of the reports can also be analyzed to corroborate if the facts and reported circumstances are consistent with the offense or allegation claimed.

Violations

Natural language processing can be extremely useful in extracting important elements about the violations. It can classify contents of documents to expose the procedural, policy, managerial, administrative, or other types of violations.

Confidentiality

From the inception of an investigation, it is essential that the confidentiality of the investigation is maintained. Metadata about the systems on which the investigation documents are stored becomes a powerful source of assurance that documents were not tampered with. It can show who accessed the systems, when, and what were they interested in. This also helps in maintaining the integrity of the investigation.

Case Execution

As the planning process ends, the execution of an investigation requires accumulating evidence on behavioral, legal, business, and financial bases.

Understanding personalities and behaviors can give important clues about motivations. In addition to several clustering and classification-centric models identified previously, researchers have used a broad range of lexical variables such as aggregate word categories and individual English words to suggest lower order traits, such as anxiety, anger, vulnerability, or openness (Yarkoni, 2010). In fraud-related investigations, we covered the fraud triangle and fraud diamond in a previous chapter. Revisiting the concept of "capability" from (Wolfe and Hermanson, 2004), they explained that capability is composed of position, smart/intelligence, ego, coercion, deceit, and stress.

Legal research includes search in legal documents related to case law and the case itself. As Lu et al. (2011) point out, legal documents are "often multi-topical, contain carefully crafted, professional, domain-specific language, and possess a broad and unevenly distributed coverage of legal issues." They presented a model for classifying legal documents based upon a classification-based recursive soft clustering algorithm with built-in topic segmentation.

Industry and business model research is part of the latent capability development (see above in the chapter).

Financial analysis related to the investigation is covered in earlier and later chapters.

Interview

Interviewing witnesses is a critical element of forensic investigation. Automation in this area is composed of four processes. First, automation is about identifying whom to interview. Based upon the documents analyzed, named entities (such as people and places) can be identified. Key people who were directly or indirectly involved or had some role in the incident can be revealed. Second, automation is about interview preparation. This can help in formulating the right questions. Third, automation analyzes the video, responses, or sound files to determine the veracity, personality, or other case-related details about a witness. Fourth, AI can be used to perform background checks on the witnesses.

Discovery

Discovery is one of the hottest areas in automation. It involves being able to scan thousands or millions of documents to find patterns. It also includes scanning videos, audio files, and other unstructured data. A firm reported that it was able to identify that two employees were collaborating on a claim when in fact they were denying having any collaboration at all. Data mining was able to find a pattern where the data showed that both individuals happened to be at the same restaurant at the same time rather frequently. Transactional documents, emails, contracts, and metadata – all provide a rich source for mining. Automation also helps in organizing the documents. Finally, the evidence development can benefit significantly from automation.

Conclusion

As shown in the opening GE case, forensic accounting is a powerful discipline. Markopolos and Forensic Decisions PR LLC were able to develop the allegations by looking at publicly available information. As intelligent automation starts to come mainstream, it offers tremendous opportunity for advanced forensic accounting. The development and deployment of these agents needs to be done in a manner that the forensic accounting firm can systematically add new features, new agents, and scale accordingly.

Key Points

- The field of forensic accounting can benefit tremendously from intelligent automation.
- Intelligent automation in forensic accounting can be divided between latent capabilities and assignment-centric capabilities.
- Latent capabilities are intelligence collection capabilities that are conducted on an ongoing basis. They tend to be general in nature.
- Assignment-centric capabilities are built to support particular assignments. They tend to be specific and customized to a self-initiated or client-initiated project.

REFERENCES

Amiram, D., Bozanic, Z., Cox, J. D., Dupont, Q., Karpoff, J. M., and Sloan, R. (2018) Financial reporting fraud and other forms of misconduct: A multidisciplinary review of the literature. *Review of Accounting Studies*, 23 (2): 732–783.

Bliss, B. A., Molk, P., and Partnoy, F. (2019) Negative activism. *Washington University Law Review*, 97: 19.

Cecchini, M., Aytug, H., Koehler, G. J., and Pathak, P. (2010) Detecting management fraud in public companies. *Management Science*, 56 (7): 1146–1160.

Conrad, J. G. and Al-Kofahi, K. (2017) Scenario analytics analyzing jury verdicts to evaluate legal case outcomes. *Proceedings of the International Conference on Artificial Intelligence and Law*, 29–38.

Conrad, J. G., Al-Kofahi, K., Zhao, Y., and Karypis, G. (2005) Effective document clustering for large heterogeneous law firm collections. *Proceedings of the International Conference on Artificial Intelligence and Law*, 177–187.

DOJ (2015) *E-Commerce Exec and Online Retailer Charged with Price Fixing Wall Posters*. Available from: https://www.justice.gov/opa/pr/e-commerce-exec-and-online-retailer-charged-price-fixing-wall-posters.

Fernández-Gámez, M. A., García-Lagos, F., and Sánchez-Serrano, J. R. (2016) Integrating corporate governance and financial variables for the identification of qualified audit opinions with neural networks. *Neural Computing and Applications*, 27 (5): 1427–1444.

Gerke, K., Mendling, J., and Tarmyshov, K. (2009) Case construction for mining supply chain processes. *Lecture Notes in Business Information Processing*, 21 LNBIP 181–192.

Guo, Y., Yan, L., and Shao, Z. (2015) An ant colony-based text clustering system with cognitive situation dimensions. *International Journal of Computational Intelligence Systems*, 8 (1): 138–157.

Hofman, W. (2013) Compliance management by business event mining in supply chain networks. *Vmbo* (February 2013).

Kobayashi, V. B., Mol, S. T., Berkers, H. A., Kismihók, G., and Den Hartog, D. N. (2018) *Text Mining in Organizational Research*. Vol. 21. [Online].

Lau, H. C. W., Ho, G. T. S., Zhao, Y., and Chung, N. S. H. (2009) Development of a process mining system for supporting knowledge discovery in a supply chain network. *International Journal of Production Economics*, 122 (1): 176–187. Available from: http://dx.doi.org/10.1016/j.ijpe.2009.05.014.

Lee, J. and Hong, Y. S. (2014) Business model mining: Analyzing a firm's business model with text mining of annual report. *Industrial Engineering and Management Systems*, 13 (4): 432–441.

Lu, Q., Keenan, W., Conrad, J. G., and Al-kofahi, K. (2011) Legal document clustering with built-in topic segmentation categories and subject descriptors. *Proceedings of the 11th ACM International Conference on Information and Knowledge Management*, 383–392.

Ma, A. and Liu, G. (2017) *Neural Networks in Predicting Myers Brigg Personality Type From Writing Style*, 1–9.

Mehta, Y., Majumder, N., Gelbukh, A., and Cambria, E. (2019) *Recent Trends in Deep Learning Based Personality Detection*. Available from: http://arxiv.org/abs/1908.03628.

Ravisankar, P., Ravi, V., Raghava Rao, G., and Bose, I. (2011) Detection of financial statement fraud and feature selection using data mining techniques. *Decision Support Systems*, 50 (2): 491–500. Available from: http://dx.doi.org/10.1016/j.dss.2010.11.006.

Sewwandi, D., Nugaliyadde, A., and Thelijjagoda, S. (2017) Linguistic features based personality recognition using social media data. *Proceedings of the 2017 6th National Conference on Technology and Management: Excel in Research and Build the Nation, NCTM 2017*. [Online] (January), 63–68.

Sull, D., Sull, C., and Chamberlain, A. (2019) *Measuring culture in leading companies*. Available from: https://sloanreview.mit.edu/projects/measuring-culture-in-leading-companies/.

Wolfe, D. T. and Hermanson, D. R. (2004) The fraud diamond: Considering the four elements of fraud: Certified public accountant. *The CPA Journal*, 74 (12): 38–42.

Yarkoni, T. (2010) Personality in 100,000 words: A large-scale analysis of personality and word use among bloggers. *Journal of Research in Personality*, 44 (3): 363–373. Available from: http://dx.doi.org/10.1016/j.jrp.2010.04.001.

CHAPTER FOURTEEN

Managing for Value and Valuation

T HE ACCURACY, SPEED, AND TIMELINESS of valuation are important considerations in modern business. In 2019 Kraft Heinz company took a $1.2 billion impairment charge to account for the decline in value of its brands. Of the $1.2 billion, over $740 million was attributed to the reduction in value and about $474 million to the market perceived risk in its valuation. Taking the impairment charge shows that the existing and prevailing conditions in the marketplace and the investor expectations are driving the accounting adjustments. Valuation is becoming dynamic. From a machine learning perspective, we can ask the following questions:

- How is the value created in companies?
- How is value creation related to valuation?
- How does fraud impact value creation?
- How do we improve the accuracy, speed, and timeliness of valuation?
- Can machine learning be deployed to determine dynamic and accurate valuation of assets that do not provide active market (trading) information?

In this chapter we will first develop a general framework of business as a value creation entity. Using that framework, we will develop a conceptual model of how value gets destroyed in companies. The first part of the chapter will focus on areas where forensic accountants can develop new capabilities to identify shareholder value losses. The second part will focus on valuation.

INFINITY CYCLE

In this book we take the position that value destruction via intentional or negligent management decision-making is equally harmful as fraud. In such cases, management discloses scanty details about their strategies, reports in compliance with the established standards (e.g., GAAP), walks close to the boundary of the law, and destroys shareholder value. Thus, while there may not be any legal violations in accordance with the established laws, management decisions or self-dealing lead to stakeholder value destruction.

The Infinity Cycle framework (Figure 14.1) is the value creation cycle in a company and is composed of two integrated and interdependent loops. The left loop of Operational Excellence is where a business conducts its operational activities, including marketing, production, supply chain, sales, and others. This represents a set of integrated activities that make the business create profits from sales to customers. The right loop, Investment Excellence, is where a company is connected to its shareholders. In this loop the firm communicates with its shareholders, finds investment, and delivers returns to the shareholders (via dividends and stock value increase). Finance, investor relations, and treasury-related activities are performed in the right loop.

The central part, where the two loops meet, is composed of activities related to governance, capital allocation to projects, and strategy. This point, known as the Control Room, can be viewed as the transfer point where investment cash

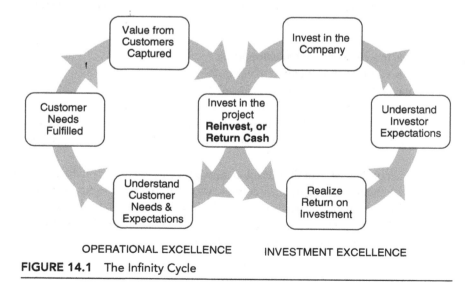

FIGURE 14.1 The Infinity Cycle

handoff happens from investors to the management, and management gets to decide how to invest the cash and run the strategy of the firm. Notice that in addition to cash from investors, the cash generated from operations (i.e., profits) also gets added to the pool. The collective cash can be invested back into the operations, kept as cash reserve, or returned back to the shareholders.

For as long as the company continues to produce good results – which are a function of making the right investments and being able to conduct strong operations – the Infinity Cycle works great. When any of the points in the two loops break down, problems start for a company.

For instance, the left loop is composed of understanding customer needs and expectations, producing products and services, selling and capturing cash, and creating profits. A breakdown in these activities would lead to investor disappointment and fresh investment in the business would dry out. In the right loop, failure of the leadership team or the investor relations department to effectively manage investor expectations also leads to value loss. When the management team invests in value destroying value-destroying projects, that, too, leads to value destruction.

The left loop is led and managed by Chief Operating Officer and VPs of departments such as research and development, marketing, sales, operations, supply chain, manufacturing, CIO, etc. The right loop is led and managed by VP of treasury, VP of investor relations. The Control Room in the center is led by the board, the CEO, and the CFO. In this book we suggest that a new position titled Chief AI Officer should be added to the control room.

Figure 14.2 shows the problems that materialize in the two loops of infinity cycle. The first set of problems transpire in the left loop and they are related to the operational decision-making and excellence. This is not an exhaustive set of issues, but only examples of some of the major problems that lead to shareholder value loss.

For instance, starting from the lower-left side of the loop, marketing and product planning departments' failure to understand customer needs leads to suboptimal products and marketing campaigns. Failure to fulfill customer needs is a function of suboptimized production, quality, distribution, supply chain, and other operational lapses. Being unable to price products effectively, or to collect cash, impacts the profitability potential of a firm.

Similarly, as we move to the right loop, not being able to track investor expectations can result in the company making investments inconsistent with the return expectations of the shareholders. Having an inefficient capital structure, or having too little or too much capital also creates problems in firms.

Many problems are created via misappropriation of funds or misallocation of capital from the Control Room. When CEOs invest in bad business deals, often

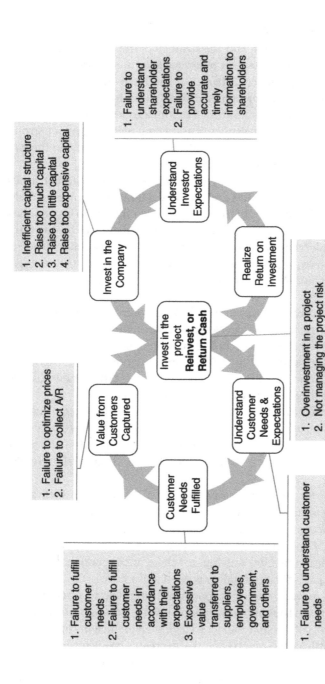

FIGURE 14.2 Value Destruction

due to their ego or self-interest, it offers an example of value destruction from the Control Room. Notice that the strategy of the entire firm is driven by the Control Room and therefore ultimately the Control Room is responsible for all performance, governance, and compliance.

Machine learning can help explain why businesses failed (Muñoz-izquierdo, Segovia-vargas, et al., 2019) and also predict bankruptcy (Muñoz-Izquierdo, Camacho-Miñano, et al., 2019) from using data from financial reports.

 ## INFINITY CYCLE AND FINANCIAL FRAUD

The Infinity Cycle can also be viewed from a fraud perspective (see Figure 14.3). Fraud can happen at any point in the two loops. In fact, by understanding the two loops of value creation we can analyze the various ways how companies try to deceive the stakeholders by playing with numbers or by conducting fraud.

Fooling the investors happens at various nodes of value creation. For example, in the bottom node of the left loop, revenues can be increased by selling customers defective products or products based upon bogus research. This happened when Elizabeth Holmes, CEO of Theranos, cheated customers by making claims that her firm can run blood tests with only a few drops of blood. Theranos, which once commanded a $9 billion valuation, was eventually dissolved.

When customer needs are fulfilled (operations, distribution, sales, etc.) companies commit fraud when they overstate earnings or revenues, hide costs, or move revenues and costs in periods where they don't belong.

Companies can also misstate inventories and accounts receivable, or pass value captured from the firm to the management team via self-dealing.

On the right side of the loop, firms distort numbers or metrics when raising money or communicating with investors. In some cases, companies make up or invent metrics to deceive investors or provide misleading or noisy metrics. Burford Capital, a firm that provides specialized finance to the legal market, was accused by a short seller, Muddy Waters, of providing "misleading metrics" and that allegation wiped out over 50% of the market value of Burford stock (Patrick, 2019).

Machine learning can help detect fraud (Cecchini et al., 2010) and identify irregularities (Humpherys et al., 2011; Bay et al., 2006). The idea is that in addition to the accounting information disclosed in financial reports, these days significant unstructured data provides a source of tremendous value. Learning algorithms can use all that information to develop deep insights about earnings

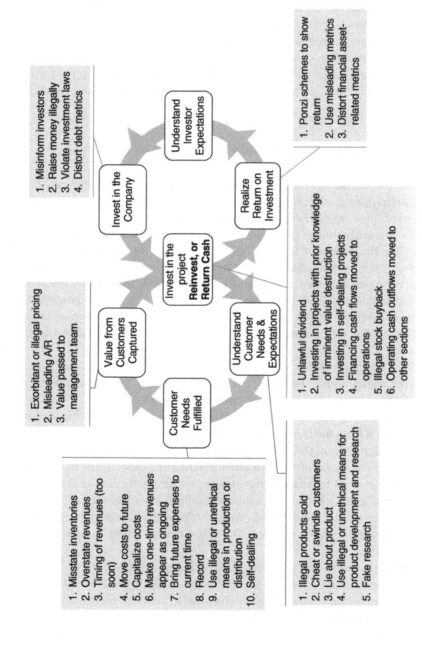

FIGURE 14.3 Fraud in the Value Creation Cycle

management, fraud, or deception. The art of building a fraud detection system is to deploy tools at the nodes of the Infinity Cycle.

VALUATION

The valuation – as based upon the fundamentals – also depends upon the Infinity Cycle. The left side of the loop creates the cash flows and the growth, and the right side of the loop brings in the cost of capital. The cost of capital from the right loop comes from investor expectations for the risk and reward relationship in a particular investment and the capital structure of a firm. A basic model of valuation (Gordon and Shapiro, 1956) based upon the present value of future dividends of stocks (aka Gordon growth model) can also be viewed as representing the above two loops.

As shown in Figure 14.4, the value of a firm equals the free cash flows divided by weighted average cost of capital (WACC) less growth. Growth is calculated by Return on Invested Capital times the investment rate where investment rate is Net Investment divided by Net Operating Profit less adjusted taxes. Economic profits are equal to ROIC less WACC divided by the Investment Capital and ROIC equals NOPLAT divided by Invested Capital.

What makes intelligent automation powerful is not only the ability to accurately and efficiently calculate the values of the variables that go into the calculations of the valuation but also, most importantly, to know that the valuation is current and dynamic. If an asset value has moved, we know instantly that it has.

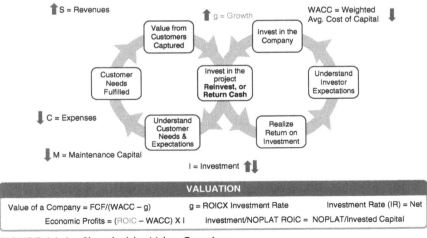

FIGURE 14.4 Shareholder Value Creation

To increase the value of a firm, management must increase revenues, lower costs, lower maintenance capital, and lower the weighted average cost of capital. From an intelligent automation perspective, the problems of valuation can be divided into the following:

- Valuation of stocks and financial products
- Valuation of alternative and other assets
- Historical valuation of an asset

Valuing of Stocks and Financial Products

The primary input going into the valuation of a firm is often limited to the data reported in the financial statements and the forecasts made by financial analysts based upon normal course of business. Most importantly, it assumes that the information reported is accurate and reliable. A forensic perspective introduces the element of the potential for numbers to be inaccurate and unreliable. The combination of governance and accounting information provides a good predictor for both downside signals and stock upside prediction. Using neural networks, Ophir Gottlieb (2014) showed that stock value can be predicted with governance and accounting information. To give the analysis the predictive power, Gottlieb used quarterly stock returns rather than the SEC's AAER data.

Thus, machine learning allows us to develop current and dynamic valuation models that incorporate the most recent information from the business, markets, and economy on one hand and information about governance on the other hand. Valuation becomes a living and dynamic number that gives us more accurate information by actively incorporating and updating most recent data. Machine learning is an effective application for asset pricing. Specifically, viewed as a prediction problem, machine learning offers a powerful way to improve risk premium measurement (Gu et al., 2019).

Valuation of Alternative and Other Assets

Machine learning is being applied to value many other types of assets. For example, text mining, social network analysis, technology clustering, and descriptive statistics are used to value technology (Jun et al., 2015).

Clustering has been used to estimate variable annuities (Gan, 2013) and several machine learning methods are currently deployed for estimating real estate valuations (Kok, 2017).

One of the complex areas of valuation where timing is critical is the valuation of derivatives. Ferguson and Green trained a neural network to value derivatives (Ferguson and Green, 2018). They generated the training sets by using Monte Carlo simulation. As they clarify that a simple derivative can take five inputs and a more complex derivative product can take in hundreds and even thousands of inputs, however, a deep learning environment can handle such inputs. From their application they observed that neural networks performed better than the legacy methods and had both accuracy and speed.

Historical Valuation

Many forensic investigations involve providing valuation estimates from the past. Some forensic experts use comps to calculate those valuations. In doing so, many times we end up using bad comparisons. One comp may indicate one value and another may give a materially different value. Also, it is often hard to find which are the closest peers of a firm. Machine learning offers a better way to determine valuations. Instead of using SIC codes, machine learning – based clustering methods are used to identify peers (Ding et al., 2019). Using the historical data, forensic accountants can first determine which are the most relevant variables and then estimate significantly more accurate estimates of valuation.

Key Points

- Valuation is one of the most promising areas of introducing artificial intelligence. Valuation analysis can be viewed from two different perspectives: current and past. The current scope of valuation is to understand the valuation of assets in the present time. This is usually based upon the expected future cash flows and risks. The past valuation problems usually arise from forensic pursuits of trying to determine the valuation of one or more assets at some time in the past. Both of these problems require different approaches and both can benefit from intelligent automation.
- The value creation cycle of a firm, known as the Infinity Cycle, is composed of two loops. The left loop is the operational loop. The right loop is the investment loop. The central point of the two loops, known as Control Room, is where capital allocation decisions are made.
- Intelligent automation is being applied to increase overall value of firms and to understand why value destruction happened in companies.
- The Infinity Cycle also provides an easy-to-visualize detector of deception tactics employed by management teams. Intelligent automation uses both internal and external data to scan various operational and investment areas of a firm to detect deceptive tactics.
- The Infinity Cycle also provides the foundation for a valuation model. Intelligent automation is used to determine valuation of a firm and other types of assets, including technology, patents, real estate, alternative assets, and derivative products.

REFERENCES

Bay, S., Kumaraswamy, K., Anderle, M. G., Kumar, R., and Steier, D. M. (2006) Large scale detection of irregularities in accounting data. *Proceedings – IEEE International Conference on Data Mining, ICDM*, (99), 75–86.

Cecchini, M., Aytug, H., Koehler, G. J., and Pathak, P. (2010) Detecting management fraud in public companies. *Management Science*, 56 (7), 1146–1160.

Ding, K., Peng, X., and Wang, Y. (2019) A machine learning-based peer selection method with financial ratios. *Accounting Horizons*, 33 (3), 75–87.

Ferguson, R. and Green, A. (2018) Deeply learning derivatives, *arXiv preprint arXiv:1809.02233*, 1–14. arXiv.org.

Gan, G. (2013) Application of data clustering and machine learning in variable annuity valuation. *Insurance: Mathematics and Economics*, 53 (3), 795–801. Available from: http://dx.doi.org/10.1016/j.insmatheco.2013.09.021.

Gordon, M. J., and Eli Shapiro (1956) "Capital Equipment Analysis: The Required Rate of Profit," Management Science, 3 (1) (October) 102–110. Reprinted in Management of Corporate Capital, Glencoe, Ill.: Free Press of, 1959.

Gottlieb, O. (2014) Can governance and forensic accounting metrics predict stock returns? *Rotman International Journal of Pension Management*, 7 (1).

Gu, S., Kelly, B. and Xiu, D. (2019) Empirical asset pricing via machine learning. *The Review of Financial Studies*, 33(5), 2223–2273.

Humpherys, S. L., Moffitt, K. C., Burns, M. B., Burgoon, J. K., and Felix, W. F. (2011) Identification of fraudulent financial statements using linguistic credibility analysis. *Decision Support Systems*, 50 (3), 585–594.

Jun, S., Park, S. and Jang, D. (2015) A technology valuation model using quantitative patent analysis: A case study of technology transfer in big data marketing analysis. *Emerging Markets Finance & Trade*, 51 (5), 963–974. Available from: http://dx.doi.org/10.1080/1540496X.2015.1061387.

Kok, N. (2017) Big data in real estate? From manual appraisal to automated valuation. *The Journal of Portfolio Management*, 43 (6), 202–211.

Muñoz-Izquierdo, N., Camacho-Miñano, M. D. M., Segovia-Vargas, M. J., and Pascual-Ezama, D. (2019) Is the external audit report useful for bankruptcy prediction? Evidence using artificial intelligence. *International Journal of Financial Studies*, 7 (2), 1–23.

Muñoz-Izquierdo, N., Segovia-Vargas, M. J., and Pascual-Ezama, D. (2019) Explaining the causes of business failure using audit report disclosures. *Journal of Business Research*, 98, 403–414. Available from: https://doi.org/10.1016/j.jbusres.2018.07.024.

Patrick, M. (2019) Short seller accuses litigation finance firm Burford Capital of "meaningless metrics". *The Wall Street Journal*, August 7.

CHAPTER FIFTEEN

Tying It Together and Robots

T HIS IS THE LAST CHAPTER of Part Three, and in this I wanted to bring various concepts together to enable you to approach your audit automation needs from the perspective of a combination of various capabilities. In addition, I will provide a short introduction to robots.

 ## CYCLES OF AUDIT

Both audit and forensic inquiry often require digging deeper into various accounts. Machine learning improves accounting estimates (Ding et al., 2019). Accounting estimates are a critical part of financial statement generation. However, estimation errors impact financial reports. Ding et al. found that machine learning techniques can improve estimates and enhance the usefulness of financial information. Estimation includes accruals and other adjustments (Chen and Li, 2013). In this chapter we will take a look at various automations of processes in accordance with different cycles.

We approach it through the lens of the Infinity Cycle. In Figure 15.1, the left loop, that is, the operations loop has three cycles: Revenue Cycle, Production Cycle, and Procurement/SC Cycle. The Investment Loop has three cycles: Financing, M&A, and Capital Structure Management. The Control Loop has Planning, Strategy, Governance, Incentives and Compensation, and Capital Allocation.

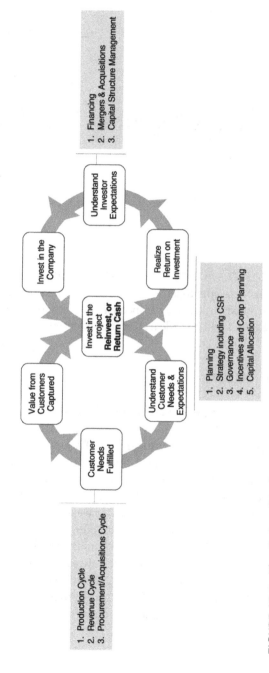

FIGURE 15.1 The Cycles of Audit

PRMIT Model

For each of the cycles in the Infinity Cycle, we can identify the automation strategy by defining the scope of automation with five integrated design elements. The five integrated design elements are known as the PRMIT model and they include predictors, risk, motivators, internal controls, and tests (see Figure 15.2).

- **Predictors** include ratios, metrics, discovered relationships, and unspecified clusters as proxies to evaluate risk and strategy.
- **Risk** involves assessing inherent risk for the cycle and developing a deeper understanding of assertions. Both risk assessment and assertion identification become dynamic (i.e., based upon the business conditions and the strategy of the firm, they are constantly updated).
- **Motivators** are the behavioral elements and they include evaluating human behaviors related to the specific cycle. Human behavior analyses

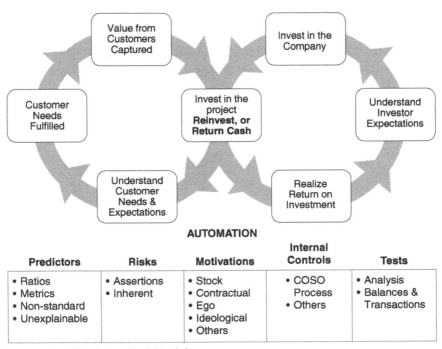

Predictors	Risks	Motivations	Internal Controls	Tests
• Ratios	• Assertions	• Stock	• COSO Process	• Analysis
• Metrics	• Inherent	• Contractual	• Others	• Balances & Transactions
• Non-standard		• Ego		
• Unexplainable		• Ideological		
		• Others		

FIGURE 15.2   The PRMIT Model

include using various data to predict and estimate the risk of errors and fraud. Motivations can be related to stock (capital markets) or contracts (i.e., anticipated benefits from misstating earnings like bonuses, avoiding triggers of debt covenants) (Amiram et al., 2018).

- **Internal Controls** implies observing and analyzing the internal controls within each cycle. This includes understanding the structural elements of the environment that may give rise to risk of error or fraud.
- **Tests** are the procedures employed by audit or forensic firms and include analytical procedures and transactional/balance/entries-level procedures.

For each cycle we recognize that our goal is twofold: first from a classic audit automation perspective where we can automate typical audit processes, and second from the business value protection perspective. The second is about value destruction as a consequence of activities that will be classified as border-line illegal or operating at the edge of standards and law.

Using the PRMIT methodology we can now form a comprehensive plan of total audit and forensic automation for the various business management cycles.

Some of those cycles and their PRMIT analysis are discussed below. I will provide examples of Cash and Revenue cycles. Readers are encouraged to develop the PRMIT analysis for all cycles. (See Table 15.1.)

TABLE 15.1 The PRMIT Table

	Predictors	Risks	Motivators	Int. Controls	Tests
Cash					
Revenue					
Production					
Procure/SC					
Financing					
M&A					
Cap Structure					
Planning					
Strategy					
Governance					
Incentives					
Capital					

Example of Cash Cycle

In 2019, PwC launched a product, Cash.ai, an intelligent automation model that automates the audit of the entire cash cycle of a firm. The company claims the following on its website (PwC, 2019):

> PwC's Cash.ai uses AI to automatically read, understand and test client documents, including reported cash balances, bank reconciliations, bank confirmation letters, foreign exchange and financial condition of the bank – in essence, the complete audit of cash.

Cash-related evidence includes documents such as bank statements, checks, cash receipt journal, cash disbursement journal, and others.

Cash-related audit processes ensure proper internal controls and substantive testing of cash includes bank reconciliations, account balance assessments, inspection of checks, foreign currency implications, and other legal obligations associated with cash (e.g., endowments or financing-related minimum cash balance that must be maintained). See Table 15.2 for a simple PRMIT analysis of Cash. As mentioned before the machine learning solution has both evidence reading and collection, as well as testing done to assess cash-related internal controls. Other forensic-centric tests may include counting cash, determining the net assets of the management team, and looking at how much money they spend on a monthly basis.

Example Revenue Cycle

The Revenue Cycle includes key Infinity Cycle processes, including customer orders, credit authorization, delivering products and services, billing, and collection. Customer master data, sales systems (Customer Relations Management

TABLE 15.2 Cash PRMIT Analysis

	Predictors	Risks	Motivators	Internal Controls	Tests
Cash	▪ Revenues ▪ Capex ▪ Inventories ▪ AR ▪ Ratios	▪ Existence ▪ Presence ▪ Disclosures ▪ Presentation ▪ Value ▪ Constraints	▪ Self-enriching ▪ Stealing	▪ Access ▪ Responsibility ▪ Structure ▪ Others	▪ Reconciliation ▪ Documents

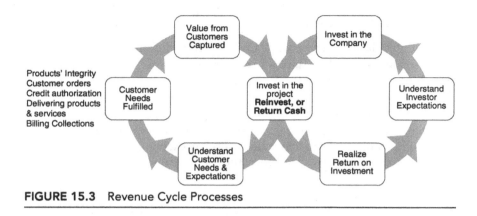

FIGURE 15.3 Revenue Cycle Processes

CRM), billing system, pending orders, and inventories are all part of the revenue audit. See Figure 15.3.

In general, the assurance interests are to evaluate that revenues did happen, they happened with the right parties, their quality was good, they were based upon actual products and services sale, they were recorded in the right time period, they were not stated under or over, and they were recorded in the appropriate accounts. The revenue cycle is at the heart of a company's operations and the survival of the entity depends upon that.

There are several key processes in the revenue cycle.

- **Product Integrity:** Product Integrity refers to the firm selling legitimate products and services, that it is not a Ponzi scheme, or that it is not based upon known product deficiency. For example, VW continued to sell cars while knowing that its cars were not compliant with the environmental standards. Legitimacy of what is being sold and marketed is often not evaluated in the audits. It is a critical element of quality of revenues and quality of earnings. The evaluation includes the assessment that the product or service is one-time, growing, or dying. Both social media and financial statements of a firm can help evaluate if the firm is offering legitimate products and services. Complaints lodged with the regulatory agencies, whistleblower cases, and even rumors provide important source of data to evaluate.
- **Customer Orders:** Customer orders data can show inconsistencies, trends, and relationships about the authenticity of customers. It can also reveal information about returns or sustainability of revenues. Knowledge of who the customers are is key to this inquiry. In financial industry, the

regulatory requirement and best practice of Know Your Customer can be applied in other sectors as well. From a forensic and auditing perspective, this knowledge is critical to identify and uncover schemes where fake customers are used to manipulate revenues or where sales are made in a manner that the sales do not involve permanent value transfer from both sides. Fake sales and fake customers are discoverable by applying the PRMIT model.

▪ **Credit Authorization:** Authorizing credit is critical to evaluate if the company will be able to collect cash from sales. It also indicates if proper authorizations were obtained to grant credit. This is closely related to how well we know our customers. Machine learning is widely used for credit risk management. A dynamic system will constantly update information about customers in a manner that provides greater insights to manage credit risk (Khandani et al., 2010; Su et al., 2019).

▪ **Delivering Products and Services:** The various PRMIT-based design concepts for products (and services) are related to proper transfer of value where the value gets transferred based upon legitimate products and services, without misleading marketing to the customers, with proper custody transfer, going to legitimate customers, and without anyone in the value chain stealing or diminishing value during the transfer. This process is managed by various documents, including shipping orders, bills of lading, various contracts, packing slips, and other shipment documents.

▪ **Billing:** At the center of billing is the invoicing process. From a PRMIT perspective, several predictors of revenues and accounts receivable can be deployed to assess invoicing problems. The risk of changing the invoice or manipulating accounts receivable or inventories exists. The motivations, among others, can be to overcharge a client or hide money received. The automation of motivation can reveal how much motivation exists in the management and related parties to conduct billing fraud. The AR record itself is a source of value for the firm. Automation of billing audit and forensic analysis includes automated analysis of internal controls, automated incorporation of predictors and motivators in developing an understanding of billing-related misconduct, developing an ongoing risk profile, and automating the procedures and tests.

▪ **Collections:** Being able to convert a sale into cash received by a firm is an important element to ongoing concern status of a firm. Automation of this process involves predicting the collections efficiency, timeliness, and accuracy. Motivators may include the assessment of hiding money, inflating AR, giving write-offs to related parties, and others.

ROBOTS: A REVIEW

Most of our discussion has been about machine learning's applications as a software. The modern AI field in business applications includes several technologies, such as autonomous vehicles, robots, and drones. While each one of them is very different from the others, most of the artifacts that have a physical component and mobility can be viewed as a form of robot.

Retailers (for example, Walmart) have started to use robots for performing inventories in stores. Drones are also used to perform physical counts or estimate valuation of assets. For example, by flying a drone over properties, it could be possible to estimate the value of the properties by looking at the state of their property (lawn maintenance, roof, etc.).

Robots in movies are often shown as hominoid robots. The word *robot* comes from the Czech language, where it means "servant." It can be defined as a machine that can sense, think, and act in its environment and pursue its goals. A normal non-autonomous car is not considered a robot because it does not have any autonomy. This means that to be considered a robot, a machine must have at least some level of autonomy. Being able to perform work autonomously, that is, without human help, is an important part of being a robot.

Robots can be electromechanical or virtual. They can also be biological. In business we use electromechanical robots to conduct operations such as production, warehouse management, and autonomous cars. Robots can be classified by their use or mode of locomotion. Based upon that criteria, the following are some types of robots:

- **Stationary:** These robots perform their work from a single point where they stay at a fixed position. They can move their arms or along rails.
- **Wheeled:** Wheeled robots can move around. They are mounted on motor-powered wheels that enable them to move on surfaces. Walmart's robot is of this type. They can also have tracks or belts (such as in construction equipment or tanks) to move them.
- **Legged:** Robots can have legs. They can mimic bipedal humanlike movement or have multiple legs like a dog or a spider.
- **Swimming:** This robot type can move on the surface or underneath water. They can be viewed as autonomous boats, ships, or submarines.
- **Flying:** Flying robots are drones. They can fly like an airplane and perform the tasks given to them. They use propulsion wings or propeller blades to fly.

- **Swarm:** Swarm robots can be any of the above, except they function in a collaborative manner. They can be viewed as an ant or bee colony. They communicate with each other, function as a single entity, accomplish their tasks jointly, and cooperate and collaborate with each other,
- **Small, Mini, Micro, Milli, and Nano robots:** These are tiny robots. A nanorobot is at or below 1 micrometer. A microrobot is less than 1 millimeter. A millirobot is at or below 1 cm. A minirobot is at or below 10 cm. A small robot is at or less than 100 cm. These robots can be useful in many types of business and other applications. For example, a swarm of microrobots can be used to explore areas that are dangerous for humans to explore.

Robots have several parts, including:

- **Sensors:** Sensors are like the eyes, ears, and nose in humans. They bring in information from the environment. This information is used by a robot to understand its environment and to react to the sensor information received in accordance with its goals. Some examples of sensors are speed sensors, temperature sensors, light sensors, pressure sensors, sound sensors, and ultrasonic sensors.
- **Effectors:** Effectors create an effect on the environment in which a robot operates. The legs, arms, wheels, and fingers are the effectors. In a physical robot, the movements or effects are obtained by motors and hydraulic cylinders.
- **Actuators:** Actuators are the motors and hydraulic cylinders – the parts that make effectors do things. These parts convert energy so the robot can perform work.
- **Manipulators:** Manipulators are like joints and links in human arms.
- **End Effectors:** They are at the ends or tips of effectors. They can be viewed as fingertips or a palm in a human hand.
- **Locomotion:** It refers to the parts that work together to make a robot move from one point to another. It may involve bipedal walking, running, rolling, swimming, hopping, etc. Locomotion parts achieve integrated response to the mode of movement in a robot. They can include electric, hydraulic, or pneumatic motors.
- **Controller:** Analogous to the human brain, controller is the brain of the robot. It receives information from sensors, processes it, and decides what actions to take in accordance with its goals.
- **Power supply:** Robots use a power supply such as batteries.

Notice that learning algorithms are being applied in all of the above parts. For example, they are applied in various areas to improve or optimize performance (e.g., computer vision to make better sensors or in robotic navigation) (Li, 2018).

Key Points

- The operations loop has three cycles: Revenue Cycle, Production Cycle, and Procurement/SC Cycle. The Investment Loop has three cycles: Financing, M&A, and Capital Structure Management. The Control Loop has Planning, Strategy, Governance, Incentives and Compensation, and Capital Allocation. PRMIT analysis has Predictors, Risks, Motivations, Internal Controls, and Tests to enable an organization to develop automation strategy.

REFERENCES

Amiram, D., Bozanic, Z., Cox, J. D., Dupont, Q., Karpoff, J. M., and Sloan, R. (2018) Financial reporting fraud and other forms of misconduct: A multidisciplinary review of the literature. *Review of Accounting Studies*, 23 (2): 732–783.

Chen, J. V. and Li, F. 2013. *Estimating the amount of estimation in accruals.* Working paper. Available from: https://www.fox.temple.edu/cms/wp-content/uploads/2013/03/Estimating-Estimation-v49-Feb-2013.pdf.

Ding, K., Lev, B., Peng, X., Sun, T., and Vasarhelyi, M. A. (2019) Machine learning improves accounting estimates, [online]. Available from: https://ssrn.com/abstract=3253220.

Khandani, A. E., Kim, A. J., and Lo, A. W. (2010) Consumer credit-risk models via machine-learning algorithms. *Journal of Banking and Finance*, 34 (11): 2767–2787. Available from: http://dx.doi.org/10.1016/j.jbankfin .2010.06.001.

Li, Y. (2018) Deep reinforcement learning: An overview. *Lecture Notes in Networks and Systems*, (16): 426–440.

PwC (2019) *Harnessing AI to pioneer new approaches to the audit* [online]. Available from: https://www.pwc.com/gx/en/about/stories-from-across-the-world/harnessing-ai-to-pioneer-new-approaches-to-the-audit.html (accessed 11 April 2019).

Su, C., Tu, F., Zhang, X., Shia, B., and Lee, T. (2019) A Ensemble machine learning based system for merchant credit risk detection in merchant MCC misuse. *Journal of Data Science*, 17 (1): 81–106.

PART FOUR

Management, Organization, and Governance for AI in Audit

B UILDING AN AUTOMATED AUDIT FIRM is not just about audit automation. As the world economy shifts to an artificial intelligence (AI) economy, AI must also be applied in sales and support roles including customer relationship management. Additionally, other aspects of business management such as organizational design, project management, and governance will also change. As the digital workplace empowers companies, new types of organizational capabilities and skillsets will be needed. As machines make decisions interdepedently, a new framework for ethics and AI governance will be required. The next three chapters introduce the audit firm to incorporate these extremely critical capabilities.

16

CHAPTER SIXTEEN

Client Management

A N AUDIT OR FORENSIC ACCOUNTING firm must pay close attention to sales and client satisfaction. AI technologies allow for tremendous capabilities in customer relationship management (CRM). This chapter provides a general introduction to the CRM and sales management capabilities. Since regulatory requirements vary by country, readers are expected to understand which of the capabilities discussed are approved in the areas where the firm operates.

Note that the advent of intelligent automation may change the business models of the audit firm and may impact the regulatory environment. We discussed the four business models of legacy auditor, ad hoc enabler, temporary connector model, and PC permanent embedding model. Each one of those models will introduce different sales paths. In a traditional audit, the sale to the audit committee and the board could be sufficient to qualify as an audit partner. As audit firms introduce new audit models and deploy technology in audit, new gatekeepers will be introduced in the sales process. These gate-keepers could be the IT departments, the data science departments, or other leaders who must provide information, access, and link to the internal systems and data. Deployment of new technology implies that the audit firm will move away from sample-based manual audits and move toward population-based continuous audit.

As mentioned before, technology-centric continuous audit introduces an element of invasiveness that has not been experienced by firms before. It implies that the audit firm's technology will link up with clients' technology directly and the communication between intelligent systems will take place just as humans connected and communicated with each other. This invasiveness requires deep presence in the firm, access to systems, and stepping into the well-protected fiefdoms.

Selling in this new world will require different and creative approaches. The proposed bills demanding to split large audit firms into smaller firms or performing joint audits with other firms also implies that the standard sales techniques may not work. The musical chairs game of a large audit firm taking over a client left by another large client may not last too long. As soon as the music stops, the supply – demand conditions might change dramatically.

The introduction of AI will also give rise to new types of audit firms. These audit firms will primarily rely on their technology expertise and will claim to improve audit quality significantly while reducing the cost. Traditional audit sales are usually based upon credibility, brand, experience, and human resources.

AI is not just the remedy; it is also an ailment. The introduction of AI will introduce new and unseen risks. It will increase the likelihood or magnitude of certain risks and may accelerate the impact of risks. Explaining these scenarios to clients will demand ongoing skill building among the employees.

3P MODEL

The client acquisition and relationship management are a function of the 3 Ps: People, Process, and Prospects. People are your employees and partners who are involved in the sales efforts, the rainmakers. Process implies your internal sales processes. Prospects are the firms you are pursuing as clients. As noted before, this is a general introduction to the AI-centric CRM capabilities; you must evaluate your respective regulations to formulate your firm's strategy.

People

As the new realities of modern times will transform the audit profession, a new type of salesperson will be needed who will possess a clear and deep understanding of the AI-centric intelligent automation in audit.

Modern Audit

The salesperson will be trained and equipped with the knowledge of automated audits. This means that he or she should be able to comprehend and communicate the various AI-centric models of audit that the audit firm is offering. As the audit becomes more technology centric the salesperson should be able to comprehend and evaluate which audit model will be suitable for a specific client. Many factors – such as size of the client, current technology state, and risks – will be considered to make that evaluation.

Artificial Intelligence

The salesperson should be knowledgeable about various methods of AI. The salesperson does not have to be an AI expert, but he or she must develop a business-centric understanding of various AI technologies that are deployed in audit. This book covers several of those technologies.

Risks

While AI will help evaluate and identify many risks, artificial intelligence will also create new types of risks. Adversaries and competitors can destroy the reputation of a firm, steal its innovative ideas or intellectual property, hack its systems, create a campaign to attract its key employees, and do things that can sabotage the operational and performance potential of a firm. AI can also accelerate the risk impact. For example, in financial markets flash-crash can destroy hundreds of billions of dollars in value within minutes. The manifestation of such risks doesn't have to be external, as an audit firm's own business strategy can lead to risk magnification due to AI. For example, a firm may launch a new type of credit card, a product, or a service with AI embedded in the product or the production platform of the service or the product. This can lead to an increase in the inherent or controls risk for a client. The salesperson should be able to explain to clients those risks and the relevant audit solutions needed to manage those risks.

Client Gatekeepers

Since the new audit environment would likely be invasive and require significant internal cooperation, the salesperson should be able to address client issues about the technology. This may require the presence and support of the technology and data science staff of the auditor who may have to serve in the presales capacity. The clients would want to know how the auditor's technology will work with the internal client technology, or how the data will get transferred on a continuous basis, or how the audit firm can ensure data security. These types of questions will require elaborate answers and the audit sales teams would have to be fully prepared to answer such questions.

Internal Systems

The traditional Enterprise Resource Planning (ERP) systems are also experiencing a powerful change. For decades audit automation has been built upon the traditional ERP implementations. Companies have realized that ERP systems are expensive to maintain, and they lack the flexibility to change as the business changes. Many businesses are now opting for microservices-centric architecture where large monolithic systems are being parted, simplified, and opened up. Microservices introduce flexibility and simplicity and can be viewed as a slow transition away from the traditional ERP solutions. The microservices movement is expected to get stronger as technology advances. Salespeople must recognize that ERP-centric audits will not be the only game in town.

Board/Audit Committee

Audit salespeople would need to reskill in terms of being able to communicate with the board and the audit committee. Even if the board or audit committees are not sophisticated to understand the implications of the introduction of AI, it is incumbent upon the sales team to make sure that board and audit committee fully understand the play and perils of the AI technology.

Industry Knowledge

A modern audit salesperson is not only well versed about the industry of the prospect client but also understands the latest developments, challenges, and competitive environment of the industry. This information is obtained by agents that collect, summarize, and report this to the sales teams on a daily basis. Your agents should be able to analyze the markets, competition, and developments in the industry. We discussed the role of a similar agent in audit planning.

Company Knowledge

Just as an intelligent agent will guide the sales teams about the industry, another agent will provide a deep dive into the client. This implies all the pertinent analysis (e.g., management team, strategy, risks, processes, financials, new announcements) should be analyzed. Such analysis needs to be deep and machine learning based such that special and never-before-seen insights can be obtained. The auditor's knowledge of such issues can become the greatest differentiator in a sales situation.

Approach

The sales approach may shift from a need-based sale to a value- and quality-based sale. In many cases audit is sold as the necessary evil that a firm must possess. This fear- and necessity-oriented sales approach sometimes ignores the important contribution that good auditors can make in the governance and reporting of a firm. Quality audits don't just protect investors, they also protect honest management teams and boards. The new sales approach will require emphasizing the value-centric benefits of conducting audits.

Incentives

Sales incentives need to be configured to deliver upon real value creation for a client. True value gets created with a high-quality audit. The incentives should be designed not only for signing up a new client but also for ensuring that the client and client's stakeholders derive maximum value from the audit.

Experience

Sales leaders may come from different personal and professional backgrounds. Tracking the experience and background is a valuable resource to develop better insights about their sales skills and skill development needs.

Process

Identifying the client: An advanced audit and forensic accounting firm will use machine learning to identify client opportunities. One of the jobs of the latent scanners discussed in the previous chapters could be to provide information about potential clients that can help from the firm's offerings. This includes not only the needs-based assessment but also an understanding about the probability of success in pursuing a certain client. That could be a function of previous experience, personality or chemistry match, relationships, audit committee style, and obviously the critical needs of the client. This can be viewed as a multidimensional segmentation exercise.

Prospecting

AI not only helps to identify best candidates for pursuing sales, but also for prospecting. In today's world, the prospecting part does not begin when the first client contact is made. Instead, it is built in as part of the automation to assess and respond to a client's areas of interest and other such credibility building activities. For example, if a target client makes a comment about a subject matter on LinkedIn or Twitter, the audit firm's systems should be able to automatically send the option to the person to download the firm's reports or research on the topic. Formal prospecting also involves understating the most natural styles and preferences of communications of a client.

Understanding Client Needs

The higher level of client needs assessment reveals the opportunity to pursue a client. The deeper needs assessment leads to winning the client. Audit committees expect the audit firms to have an in-depth understanding of the business, industry, and the special requirements of the client. An audit firm should be ready to respond to RFP (request for proposal) at all times. This means the latent scanning capabilities should be deployed to reveal significant competitive, industry, firm, strategy, management team, and special challenges information efficiently.

Burning Platform

The sales process should be able to identify the most important burning platform issues of a client. A true value-added audit firm will be proactive and will help the client identify problems and opportunities for improvement before the problems surface and impact the client.

Risks

Identifying risks related to the client's business – as well as risks related to the potential engagement – should be analyzed to determine a fact-based perspective of a client. This knowledge can be critical in discussions with the client, in planning the audit, and in pricing the engagement.

Audit Committee, Management Team, and Board Members

The sales process must include thorough research about the management team, audit committee, and board members of the prospect. The investigation should reveal the relationships between them, their backgrounds, incentives, independence, personalities, and other such areas. In some cases, friendly-to-CEO boards act as if it is their moral duty to protect the CEO from any inquiry. These boards, in such cases, are weak and composed of yes-men/women who sit around the table as cabinet members of the king or queen CEO. Knowing such relationships is critical to evaluating if the audit firm wants such firms as clients.

Pricing

The sales process also involves pricing the engagement. As the audit becomes more technology centric, audit firms will have to rethink their pricing strategies. The tools used and deployed at the client site would be priced separately versus the human services needed to conduct the audit or to implement the systems.

Prospect

While we have covered a significant number of ideas about prospect analysis in the previous chapter and in this chapter, it helps to repeat the key message: know thy client. This means that it is not enough to have cursory or superficial information about a client. You must develop an elaborate system that can identify not-so-observable areas of a client. Another way to think about this area is to ask the question: What do I know about this prospect that my competitors don't?

 ## MACHINE LEARNING IN SALES

The above changes in business models and functioning must be supported by intelligent automation. In a thought-provoking and comprehensive coverage article Syam and Sharma (2018) outlined the applications of machine learning in sales automation. They start by separating the sales process into seven steps of selling: Prospecting, Pre-approach, Approach, Presentation, Overcoming Objections, Close, and Follow-up. Then they outline the various applications (in terms of important research questions) where machine learning can be immensely powerful. For instance:

- For prospecting they suggest machine learning applications for customer sentiment analysis, forecasting and demand estimation, video and audio analyses of chat logs, text analysis of emails, text mining, and keyword analysis for lead qualifications.
- For pre-approach and approach, use ML to develop a recommendation system to cross-sell and upsell, enable smart and continuous customer targeting in real time, recommend customer engagement strategies based on

analysis of past engagements and their success/failure and depending on salesperson, industry, and customer characteristics.

- For presentation, design dynamic sales presentations by incorporating customer feedback (verbal and non-verbal) and the salesperson's goals even while conducting a presentation, provide dynamic financial valuation arguments or total cost of ownership analysis, incorporating "attribution modeling" that can attribute the relative contributions of various communication alternatives in achieving successful sales, using 3D printing technology to construct customized prototypes, and applying Collaborative Filtering to improve recommendation systems to optimize presentations.
- For overcoming objections and closing, using AI to conduct "lost order audit" and help sales organizations better anticipate objections; to recommend negotiation strategies; to identify sales anomalies such as "channel-stuffing"; audit product returns by customers; provide advanced warning of lost sales, based on analysis of history of objections and how they were handled.
- And for follow-up, using AI/ML for streamlining sales–marketing links and integrating upstream (inbound) supply chain with the downstream (outbound) supply chain.

The above examples show the importance of intelligent automation in sales. Sophisticated and explainable models can be built to predict sales (Bohanec et al., 2017).

Key Points

- An Audit and Forensic Accounting firm needs more than just audit automation. It also needs automation in the sales and customer relationship management.
- Prospecting, sales, onboarding, and managing clients offer great opportunities for automation.

REFERENCES

Bohanec, M., Kljajić Borštnar, M., and Robnik-Šikonja, M. (2017) Explaining machine learning models in sales predictions. *Expert Systems with Applications*, 71: 416–428.

Syam, N. and Sharma, A. (2018) Waiting for a sales renaissance in the fourth industrial revolution: Machine learning and artificial intelligence in sales research and practice. *Industrial Marketing Management*, 69: 135–146. Available from: https://doi.org/10.1016/j.indmarman.2017.12.019.

CHAPTER SEVENTEEN

AI Organization and Project Management

A I-CENTRIC TRANSFORMATION is not an extension of the traditional digital era. It is a revolution of its own. The processes, strategies, business models, competitive structures, and economics of AI-centric business are different than the digital era. The AI revolution is also changing the organization. In this chapter, we will discuss three areas of AI transformation. First, we will cover the unique requirements of modern-era AI-centric organizations. Second, we will cover the AI-related change management. Third, we will cover how to manage an AI project.

NEW CAPABILITY ASSESSMENT

Recently, a top-tier consulting firm laid off data science and AI people. Surprised, since data science and AI people are in high demand, I asked a person why the layoff. The person answered that the consulting firm was unable to figure out how to sell the services of the data science team and therefore due to the high cost associated with expensive consultants being on the bench, decided to lay off the AI/data science resources. This is an example of an organization that is not strategically ready to move into the AI era.

AI has introduced at least two broad categories of professionals. The first are the technology and machine learning – trained AI professionals. These people are at the center of the revolution. They are driving this innovation and technology forward. Note that these people are not necessarily from an IT background. It is a mistake to assume that people with an IT background will understand AI or will be able to develop or design AI systems. AI/data science is a unique skill that requires significant training and skill development in data science – related subject areas, such as data preprocessing, algorithms, learning techniques, and optimizing algorithms. They may come from backgrounds such as data science, cognitive science, neuroscience, statistics/mathematics, artificial intelligence (AI), or other engineering or science backgrounds. Typically, these professionals have doctorate-level education and are well published.

The second category of professionals for the new era are the business leaders who understand AI to drive change and innovation in their firms. They are the drivers and leaders of change. They conceptualize moving their businesses forward and become the project owners of solutions. These professionals can be in marketing, sales, finance, audit, accounting, supply chain, or any other functional area of a firm – but their specialization will be to combine their functional expertise with AI to innovate.

 ISSUES OF THE NEW ORGANIZATION

As innovation will become critical for competitive advantage, companies will have to make important decisions. There are two critical areas that will need to be addressed by the board, the CEO, and the HR departments, as follows.

Leadership Roles for the Legacy versus Traditional

As automation kicks in, the traditional functional roles may need major revisions. Machines don't need the bureaucratic structures that are needed to manage human organizations. Automation may eliminate the need for existing function-specific silos that exist in companies. Additionally, legacy leaders could be replaced with leaders with strong understanding of AI. Many organizations are starting by hiring a director or VP-level person who is responsible for innovation or future-of-work-type transformations. This is not the right way to transform. These people usually have no budget, no teams, no ability to influence traditional departments, and no ability to create an impact. At best, they can hire professors or consultants, make recommendations, and come up with some ideas. Experience from the 1980s with ERP systems, and from the late 1990s when the Internet changed the business world, shows that this is the wrong way to lead the transformation. Every person in the company must transform. Every leader must develop critical skills to understand the impact of the AI revolution. Every VP or functional head must have a comprehensive transformation plan. Every area of the organization must dare to imagine a world where the present state of technology and processes will become irrelevant – akin to buggies after the invention of automobiles – and the need for new technology will become crystal clear.

For such a transformation to happen, CEOs must lead their organizations with an AI-centric strategic transformation plan. AI should not be approached from the "use case" perspective. The hope that arbitrarily designed use cases will somehow blend to erect a barrier of competitive advantage around a firm is self-deceiving and delusional. Strategy must lead the use cases and not the other way around.

PhDs versus MBAs struggle

The new organization will need data scientists and AI people. Legacy (non-tech) companies have been designed around "business" graduates. In such firms, technology people are often stereotyped or labeled as lacking people skills, business acumen, and leadership traits. Such a categorization is completely misleading and problematic. One clear example of such a firm is where CIOs still struggle to find a seat at the boardroom/CEO table. Going forward, it will be the responsibility of CEOs and HR to ensure that science-oriented (PhDs) people can become part of the culture – and not just in the company's research labs but also in the boardrooms. This transformation will be critical to thrive in the modern era.

Science versus Pseudoscience

For the most part, business management has been a pseudoscience. We apply science in some areas (e.g., financial and operational) but also override what science and data suggest. In many other areas, we make decisions based upon what consultants inform us as results of executive surveys. Results of executive surveys are not the best way to plan your company's future. First, those results will contain bias of the consulting firm asking the questions; second, it contains the bias of the people responding; and third, it is limited to what your peers and competitors are thinking. Breakthrough thinking does not materialize from survey-think.

Enterprise-Based Thinking

CEOs and executives must develop an AI-centric enterprise-based strategy model. Today, companies think in terms of siloed use cases where Nancy from HR is implementing one use case and John from Finance is implementing another use case. Both are telling CEO and the board that their company is "going AI." First, Nancy and John are not talking to each other, so there is no way to leverage the design, structure, strategy, or future of work into such a setup. Second, one could be experimenting with a chatbot and another with robotic process automation but both are not transformational innovations by any means. Third, these projects do not represent enterprise-based transformation. Limited by their vision, CEOs are trapped in the whirlpool that gets created in changing times.

Investment into AI

AI technology development is not like regular IT development. It is stochastic and requires data. I call it developing systems from data versus for data. Many projects can take a long time to optimize. Some projects may fail despite best efforts. Companies need to have a plan and be ready to make significant investment in AI. The investment needed will easily bypass the investments made in the enterprise resource planning systems or Internet-based transformations.

Change Management

The second important topic for the new era is about change management. Specifically, there are three areas of concern from a change management perspective: unemployment, work planning, and reskilling.

Fear of Unemployment

To get your team excited about AI, you need to address the elephant in the room: if I automate a job, this will mean the end of my job. The concern of employees about cutting the branch on which they sit is not without merit. AI is transforming and automating processes and it is quite possible that many jobs will be eliminated. Several companies approach this issue in a deceptive way. They say to employees that AI will create more jobs – so people should not worry. At other times they change the words from "artificial intelligence" to "augmented intelligence" to reduce the fear of losing job to a robot. From their perspective, *augmented* means that AI will help automate routine or non-value-added tasks and give more time to people to spend on value-added work. While this may be true in some cases, in others AI will wipe out the entire job category. In my lectures, consulting, and conferences, I advise companies to be honest and truthful about what type of jobs will be eliminated; however, inform employees that they will need to be part of reskilling.

Work Planning

Work planning involves understanding how various roles in a firm will emerge and what will be automated and what will not. It involves function-by-function and job-by-job detailed planning about what work processes, tasks, and jobs will be eliminated. As companies prepare for a digital workforce, they need to identify what work processes will be covered by machines and which ones will require human involvement.

Reskilling

The most critical element, and the one that companies are not paying attention to, is reskilling. Reskilling means to introduce new skills and train employees for the new world. This is an area in dire need of rapid and deep attention. Companies need to reskill their employee base from three angles and two conceptual points.

The first angle is to train business employees to understand the power of intelligent automation and how to apply it to innovate their companies. The second is to train IT people to learn how to develop AI technologies. The third is to train executives to understand how to lead in the AI economy.

The two conceptual points are to train and incentivize employees to automate the existing processes but also to innovate and think in terms of what is possible. AI has opened up tremendous opportunities to develop new business models.

MANAGING AI PROJECTS

I will discuss this at two levels. The first discussion is about the conceptual structure of AI-centric project leadership and management. The second is the AI project planning.

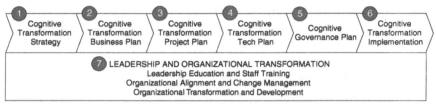

FIGURE 17.1   AI Organizational Planning

AI project leadership is composed of seven steps, as shown in Figure 17.1.

1. **Cognitive Transformation Strategy:** This part of the plan defines the transformation mission, approach, and vision for the future.
2. **Cognitive Business Plan:** This is built to incorporate the strategy into plan by business units and functions.
3. **Cognitive Transformation Plan:** This is based upon use cases. In this plan, use cases are prioritized and developed.
4. **Cognitive Transformation Tech Plan:** This is where firms develop their technology or tech stack plan.
5. **Cognitive Governance Plan:** AI has introduced new and profound challenges in governance. They are covered in detail in the next chapter. In this step, firms develop a comprehensive AI governance plan.
6. **Cognitive Transformation Implementation:** This is where AI artifacts are developed and implemented.
7. **Leadership and Organizational Transformation:** In this step, firms develop plans for leadership and staff education, organizational alignment, change management, and reskilling and organizational development.

In step 3 projects are prioritized based upon experience, value, complexity, and customer need.

AI project planning is performed in Step 6. The AI project-specific plan is composed of the following steps:

1. **Understand business problem or business transformation opportunity:** Begin by scoping out a problem or simply inventing a new business model by applying innovation and business model transformation techniques.

2. **Understand the data:** Figure out where the data exists in the enterprise or where you can source the data from. Develop a detailed understanding of data, including assessing the quality of data.
3. **Preprocess the data:** Preprocess the data needed in your machine learning.
4. **Learn:** Apply the machine learning techniques to help the algorithm learn from the data.
5. **Test:** Ensure that the learning is optimized.
6. **Implement:** Take the system live in the production environment and integrate it with the IT infrastructure.

The above six steps constitute the project-specific implementation steps.

Application to Audit and Forensic Accounting

How can we apply the above concepts and learning to audit and forensic accounting? Large audit firms have announced that they will be automating audit with AI. With the exception of PwC's Cash.ai, other firms have not demonstrated or shown working solutions. While many have presented the high-level vision, that is analogous to presenting a plan for a mission to a distant planet. It could be all in-the-works, or worse, only on paper.

That is why it is critical for audit firms of all sizes to take this transformation very seriously. In fact, technology transformational times are great times to launch and build major companies or to reinvent yourself as a new firm. For instance, the rise of the Internet enabled several Indian firms (e.g., Tata, Infosys) to effectively compete with large consulting firms and win major contracts. Midsized firms have a bigger opportunity to transform than the large firms. By automating, they can emerge as powerful players to take significant market share away from the top four firms and make the audit industry more competitive and less oligopolistic.

To make that transformation, audit firms will need to have solid and clear plans for transformation. This book can be used as a reference to design all the areas of innovation and transformation. These plans must be actionable, time and goal oriented, and with a clear path to success. Most importantly, audit firms must recognize that AI has the potential to improve the audit quality and that with AI they can truly create tremendous value for their clients and for the world in general.

Key Points

- The advent of AI in the global economy requires new types of organizational planning, skill development, and management approaches.
- Specifically, leaders are now responsible for both digital and human workers.
- AI project management has seven steps. All must be followed to achieve good results.

CHAPTER EIGHTEEN

Governance and Ethics

THE QUESTIONS OF GOVERNANCE and ethics require two types of inquiries:

1. How will AI impact the existing governance and ethics in a firm?
2. How will AI technology be governed?

These two questions form the basis of fundamental analysis on these topics and are some of the most important considerations for the new era. While the prospects and the promise of new technologies and the AI era are certainly the most exciting part of the transformation, from an audit perspective we are confronted with the following issues:

- We must ask what specific artificial intelligence (AI) technology we will use to conduct audits. Given the variety and speed of innovation in the AI (machine learning) field, this question does not have easy answers.
- We need to understand how to audit intelligent systems. Audit has barely caught up to have the ability to audit non-intelligent accounting systems; having the ability to audit intelligent systems will require a lot more effort. As clients embrace intelligent audit, auditors will need intelligent systems to audit intelligent systems.
- The introduction of intelligent automation has greatly changed the risk characteristics. New and unprecedented risks are now part of every business. Flash-crash in financial markets, where markets lose significant value within minutes, has been attributed to autonomous and automated

trading. Auditors must scope out new risks and understand their impact on business.

■ A new, never-before-seen type of risk is taking shape due to intelligent systems. This is not an inherent risk, as it is not inherent in a business function or process, but it is induced and injected in the business intentionally by an adversary. Analogous to traditional cybersecurity risk where a malicious intentioned adversary attempts to harm the enterprise, this new risk also tries to do that. What makes it different from the cybersecurity risk is that it does not have to penetrate the firewall of a firm. I have termed it as the ex-asymmetric risk where "ex" signifies outside the firewall. In this attack, the adversary attacks the profit-generating or goal-achieving potential of a firm. Such attacks can be targeted to disseminate fear or concern about a company's products and services – which in turn leads to the going viral on social media. Intervention to dispel or quell the allegation, or to present the facts about the veracity of the claims, comes too late. This type of adversarial action can destroy significant value in a firm. It is often enabled by AI bots.

Based upon the above considerations, clearly, audit firms need to have far more serious and aggressive automation plans than the ones we have observed to date.

SOME OBVIOUS ETHICAL ISSUES

Our recent experiences show that there is a need to be concerned about AI technology. For example, AI systems have been shown to discriminate against minorities in legal, recruitment, and healthcare. In other areas, AI has been shown to be sexist and even racist. Some of the more obvious ethical issues from autonomous technology are as following:

■ **Risk of exploitation and manipulation:** Machines can process significant data about humans and hence feed selective information to humans. We observe that phenomenon when bots are used to create anger and conflict during elections or when fake news is used to arouse sentiments across populations.

- **Risk of overreliance on autonomous technology:** We can sometimes ignore the human instincts or outright signals of problems that our minds give us because of our overreliance on technology.
- **Risk of unemployment, wealth redistribution:** Automation can create risk of unemployment. It can make the rich richer, and the less fortunate poorer.
- **Risk of corruption:** It can corrupt, and equip criminals and fraudsters with even more dangerous technology.
- **Militarization risks:** Risks specific to military include the race to arm and irresponsible weaponization with AI.

GOVERNANCE OF AI: AN INTRODUCTION TO THE PROBLEM

Governance for artificial intelligence artifacts is a major consideration. What makes governance of AI hard is the fact that at the current state of the technology, we are unable to explain what goes on in the mind of a neural network and hence while we can see the inputs and impressive outputs, we don't really understand why the machine recommended what it did. In other words, if a judge in a court of law asks us to explain why the machine made a certain decision, we may not be able to explain that with full confidence. Scientists are working to create explainable AI (XAI), and based upon the published work, it is still in early stages.

The governance part of artificial intelligence is not only related to explaining the mental process of a machine, it also includes the behavioral aspects and social dynamics of machines. For example, what impact the actions of a machine create is an equally important question as what is the nature of the machine or what goes on in the mind of the machine. In other words, what a machine thinks is one question, whereas what a machine does is another question. Furthermore, the consequences of the thinking and the actions of the machine also require exploration.

Machines talk to other machines and interact with humans. They are now part of our social fabric. This means that machine-to-machine interaction and machine-to-human interaction also constitute important considerations. This also means that their processes, activities, and behaviors can have an impact on our social, economic, and political decisions, frameworks, and institutions.

A comprehensive model of governance must include such considerations.

 HUMANS AND AI

As we proceed to automate, we must consider the following human-related concerns:

- **Dignity:** When a human loses his or her job to a robot or when a person is interviewed by a robot and then not selected for a job, it is likely that the person's dignity and self-image may be impacted. As humans, when we interact with each other, we tend to understand how to express difficult messages without hurting human dignity. For instance, when a machine hangs up on you, it is usually very abrupt with a message, "Please try your call later." A human would explain the reason or at the very least apologize for why he or she was unable to help you. Even if a machine apologizes, you know that it is not coming from someone who might actually feel your pain.
- **Privacy:** The AI era is very intrusive and can lead to the invasion of privacy. Even today, our data – from healthcare or purchasing behaviors – is being used without our explicit permission.
- **Rights:** Firms and individuals with more resources can use AI to curb rights or gain unfair advantage and control over governments.
- **Safety:** Safety continues to be an important consideration as autonomous systems do not always perform in accordance with expectations. It is likely that the problems in recent Boeing 737 MAX crashes resulted from malfunction in autonomous control systems (Pasztor and Tangel, 2019).
- **Relationships:** AI has in the past, and will continue to, redefine how humans build, develop, and manage their relationships. For example, dating applications use algorithms to match people.
- **Rationality:** AI can be used to hijack human rationality by invoking targeted emotional responses from us via extremely personalized campaigns.
- **Values:** AI can be used to redefine values and create an alternative system of values that could be inconsistent with the generally shared and established values of human civilization. Perception engineering can fracture the bonds between social groups.
- **Institutions:** AI can be used to subvert the integrity of mission of institutions. It can be deployed to slowly diminish trust in strong institutions and

can lead to systematic structural weakening. For example, the rise of fake news can lead to people losing trust in media.

▪ **Cyber:** AI-based cybersecurity threats are increasing. With state actors also involved in such attacks, they pose a direct threat to companies and social/political institutions.

▪ **Power:** AI can give too much power to government agencies over individuals and companies.

 AIAI GOVERNANCE MODEL

AIAI's Artificial Intelligence Governance Model was developed in early 2016 and is presented below. AIAI defines governance as the actions and processes by which stable and safe AI artifacts develop and persist (Figure 18.1). This applies

ARTIFACT SAFETY & STABILITY MODEL

safe	processes and products to evaluate safety I know it is safe	processes and products to create safety-centric transparency I can show it is safe
stable	processes and products to evaluate stability I know it is stable	processes and products to create stability-centric transparency I can show it is stable
	accountability	**transparency**

—Stable means artifacts can only perform within the strict confinements of their goals

—Safe means the stated goals of the artifacts are legal and beneficial for humankind

—Accountabilty means establishing clear responsbility with users, designers and developers

—Transparency means being able to explain

FIGURE 18.1 The AIAI Governance Model

to both products and services. Notice this definition includes the role played by the users, designers, enablers, and developers of artificial intelligence.

The two elements of safety and stability are not afterthoughts, as they must be considered at the inception of AI system design. Safety and stability of autonomous systems is different than the non-intelligent systems because they are intelligent, autonomous, form a complex adaptive system, and can evolve.

The two dimensions of safety and stability interact with the two dimensions of accountability and transparency to give us four focus areas of being able to know and demonstrate safety and stability.

GOVERNANCE FRAMEWORK

The governance framework of AIAI is composed of three parts: the nature of the technology, the actions taken by the technology, and the impact or consequences of the technology (Figure 18.2). The nature of the technology is determined by data and algorithms. Its actions are determined by the interactions with the environment and other systems as well as from behavior and human–machine interaction. The wheel of impact provides a mechanism of determining the impact or the consequences of the technology on various human processes, including economics, politics, legal, society, business, and environment.

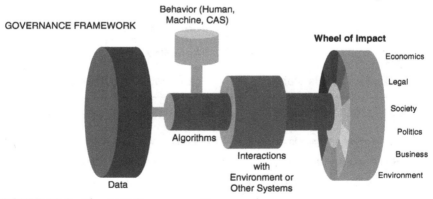

FIGURE 18.2 The AIAI Governance Framework

CAS in Figure 18.2 means Complex Adaptive System. A CAS is a system where if one understands the parts, that does not necessarily imply that he or she can understand the whole. These are nonlinear dynamical systems where complexity results from the dynamic network of interactions. They are adaptive, as they have self-organizing and emergent properties.

ETHICS CHARTER

Furthermore, as we become more intelligent and automated, we need to establish an ethics charter for our firms. The American Institute of Artificial Intelligence has created the following ethics charter:

- **Human Benefit:** I will strive to maintain the supremacy of humans over machines. I will ensure that technology and science benefit humankind. I will not use, design, or enable artificial intelligence technology in areas that will increase human suffering, diminish human dignity and privacy, or enhance human exploitation.
- **Human Protection:** I will protect humans and human institutions from the misuse of technology in social, political, and economic areas of human life.
- **Better World:** I will strive to maintain the supremacy of all natural lifeforms over machines. I will help create, and leave behind a better world. A better world ensures that natural lifeforms thrive, and both intelligent and less-intelligent natural lifeforms can coexist in a safe and healthy environment safe from artificial lifeforms.
- **Confidentiality:** I will protect and respect the confidentiality of the proprietary data and algorithms of my employer and my internal and external clients.
- **Law:** I will abide by the laws of my country and of all countries in which I do business.
- **Bias:** I will make my best efforts to ensure that the artifacts I design and work with will not be biased toward anyone, on the basis of religion, gender, ethnicity, color of skin, race, heritage, sexual preferences, economic status, and other such factors.
- **Learn:** I will constantly enhance my skills to become and stay relevant and valuable for my employer and clients.
- **Ethics:** I will maintain the highest professional standards and ethics.

Key Points

- AI is introducing new ethical challenges.
- Implementing AI without ethical and governance frameworks can be counterproductive and even dangerous.
- AIAI has pioneered the governance framework for AI. AIAI governance framework is based upon three areas: Nature of the artifact, Actions of the artifact, and Impact of the action.

 REFERENCE

Pasztor, A. and Tangel, A. (2019) Investigators believe Boeing 737 MAX stall-prevention feature activated in Ethiopian crash. *The Wall Street Journal*. 29 March. Available from: https://www.wsj.com/articles/investigators-believe-737-max-stall-prevention-feature-activated-in-ethiopian-crash-11553836204.

Index

Page numbers followed by *f* or *t* refer to figures or tables.